The Fantasy Sport Ir

Fantasy sport has become big business. Recent estimates suggest that there as many as 35 million fantasy sport participants in the US alone, spending billions of dollars annually, with many millions more around the world. This is the first in-depth study of fantasy sport as a cultural and social phenomenon and a significant and growing component of the contemporary sports economy.

This book presents an overview of the history of fantasy sport and its close connection to innovations in sports media. Drawing on extensive empirical research, it offers an analysis of the demographics of fantasy sport, the motivations of fantasy sport players and their significance as heavy consumers of sport media and as ultra-fans. It also draws cross-cultural comparisons between fantasy sport players in the US, UK, Europe and beyond.

The Fantasy Sport Industry examines the key commercial and media stakeholders in the production and development of fantasy sport, and points to new directions for the fantasy sport industry within modern sport business. It is therefore, fascinating reading for any student, scholar or professional with an interest in sports media, sports business, fandom, the relationship between sport and society, or cultural studies.

Andrew C. Billings is the Ronald Reagan Chair of Broadcasting and Director of the Alabama Program in Sports Communication in the Department of Telecommunication and Film at the University of Alabama. He is the author/editor of seven books including *Olympic Media: Inside the Biggest Show on Television* (Routledge, 2008).

Brody J. Ruihley is an Assistant Professor of Sport Administration in the School of Human Services at the University of Cincinnati. His primary research is in the areas of fantasy sport and public relations in sport.

Routledge Research in Sport, Culture and Society

The Fantasy
Sport Industry

Games within games

Andrew C. Billings and Brody J. Ruihley

Routledge
Taylor & Francis Group

LONDON AND NEW YORK

First published 2014
by Routledge
2 Park Square, Milton Park, Abingdon, Oxfordshire OX14 4RN

Simultaneously published in the USA and Canada
by Routledge
711 Third Avenue, New York, NY 10017

First issued in paperback 2014

*Routledge is an imprint of the Taylor & Francis Group, an informa
business*

British Library Cataloguing in Publication Data
A catalogue record for this book is available from the British Library

Library of Congress Cataloging in Publication Data
Billings, Andrew C.
The fantasy sport industry : games within games / Andrew C. Billings and
Brody J. Ruihley.
pages cm
Includes bibliographical references and index.
1. Fantasy sports. I. Title.
GV1202.F35B55 2014
793.93--dc23
2013006788

ISBN 978-0-415-52518-3 (hbk)
ISBN 978-1-138-89871-4 (pbk)
ISBN 978-0-203-11994-5 (ebk)

Typeset in Times
by Saxon Graphics Ltd, Derby

Contents

Figures

Tables

Acknowledgments

Two authors may be listed on this book cover, yet far more people were instrumental in making *The Fantasy Sport Industry: Games within Games* a reality. We would like to jointly thank our publisher, Routledge, and specifically Simon Whitmore for his support of this project and his willingness to provide timely, useful advice every step of the way. This project also would not be nearly as comprehensive and robust in detail and insight without the number of industry leaders within fantasy sport who embraced this book, often enduring follow-up emails and phone calls to ensure we got their stories "right." Specifically, the Fantasy Sport Trade Association has proved to be an invaluable resource; part of this book outlines seminal moments and key historical pivot points in the escalation of fantasy sport into mainstream culture and these FSTA leaders and members conscientiously offered insights to ensure that we are rendering stories with the highest possible degree of accuracy. We also have to jointly thank our families for supporting us in times when the hours became far longer than 9:00-5:00 and specifically our spouses for only registering mild skepticism when we said researching this book necessitated frequent trips to Las Vegas for events such as high stakes fantasy drafts and Fantasy Sport Trade Association meetings.

Specifically from Andrew Billings: I wish to thank the Department of Telecommunication and Film at the University of Alabama for providing the kind of inquisitive, creative environment that allows this type of book project to develop and, hopefully, flourish. I also want to acknowledge the University of Alabama Program in Sports Communication, for always being a tremendous resource and place for collegiality as well as the Ronald Reagan Chair of Broadcasting Endowment that helped to alleviate some of the costs associated with researching this project. I also must specifically thank my two research assistants, Natalie Brown and Young Ju Kim, who helped with everything from facilitating survey collection to transcribing interviews. Finally, I want to mention my sons, Nathan and Noah, who are just now discovering what fantasy sports are (and learning a bit of what dad writes about in the process) as well as my wife, Angela, whose constant support is honestly a Godsend. There are many critical decisions in one's life, but choosing the right partner has got to be right at the top of that list. Fortunately for me, I chose incredibly wisely.

Acknowledgments

Specifically from Brody Ruihley: I would initially like to thank my Lord and Savior for the many blessings of life. Beyond this, my personal acknowledgments have to begin with family. My wife, Monisa, has shown incredible patience and support in my career; specifically with after-hours work and writing; she is a true blessing from God. While my son, Liam, is too young to understand the inner workings of Dad's career and fantasy sport experiences, he is so much a part of my motivation to be a better man and father. His support comes in his excitement when I walk in the door after work each day. My parents, Bob and Carla, brother, Josh, and Grandpa Newcomb have also been instrumental in setting, reaching, and exceeding my goals. In addition, I am blessed to have in-laws that support the often-arduous lifestyle of a researching professor. On a final personal note, I would like to thank the members of the Chris Sabo's Goggles' Memorial for allowing me to share the fantasy sport experience with them for the past decade. I am very appreciative of people on a professional accord as well. I would like to thank my Ph.D. advisor, Dr. Rob Hardin, for his acknowledgement of the importance of fantasy sport and not looking at me funny when proposing fantasy sport as a worthy dissertation topic. I would also like to thank my colleagues at the University of Cincinnati; specifically, the leadership of Dr. Janet Graden and Professor Robert Brinkmeyer in the School of Human Services.

We hope everyone who reads this book finds information, insight, and enjoyment in equal measure. We have enjoyed this partnership and have learned from each other, believing the fusion of a sports media and sport management professor offers an eclectic, needed balance to the study of games within games.

1 Fantasy sport

The game changer

To stand out in the modern media landscape, it is not enough to win an Oscar, stage a splashy stock offering, or market a gadget that consumers demand. In virtually every media format, the ultimate goal is the game changer—the one development that promises to alter the way people consume media for the foreseeable future. In cinema, a "tent pole" film holds the potential to impact the box office revenues of virtually every other movie released that year. In smartphones and tablet technology, it's the "killer app" that suddenly is in such demand; people will upgrade a device or purchase a new platform just to get that alluring application.

All media are either profitably making use of such a game changer, or urgently in search of one. That includes sports media, which have pursued one potential Holy Grail after another. Aspirations have ranged from the overly broad ("The Internet will change everything") to the optimistically narrow ("Thanks to the 1999 Women's World Cup, North America will go mad for soccer").

Meanwhile, a true sports media game changer has emerged. It is fantasy sport, a phenomenon that is largely under the radar yet has participants in the millions and a financial impact in the billions. Though impressive, the numbers are not our primary concern here. Rather, we will explore how this game changer developed, how it is marketed, how fans become engrossed in it—and most of all, why.

Picture a typical American sports bar. Televisions are plastered on virtually every available inch of wall space. A mostly male clientele mingles while cognitively glued to a screen; beer is ever-present and ever-flowing. It is an autumn Sunday afternoon and National Football League (NFL) play is in full swing as eight early games escalate to their drama-packed conclusions.

Some odd scenarios are developing. A fan in a Minnesota Vikings' jersey suddenly screams with excitement at the bar—though the Minnesota game is at a commercial break. Another fan in a St. Louis Rams' cap is celebrating as well—but the St. Louis game has not yet started. At a nearby table, a fan appears to be cheering for *both* the New York Jets and New England Patriots. That's puzzling because those teams are fierce rivals. What is behind these counterintuitive reactions?

Decades ago, one could have posited some logical explanations. Perhaps the Vikings' fan is enthused about a hometown hero who is doing well for another team, and the Rams' fan might be happy because he just won a bet. But in this scenario, both fans happen to be fantasy football participants with Houston's Arian Foster as one of their prized players—so both are celebrating as Foster scores a second touchdown. As for the seemingly confused bar patron rooting for both the Jets and the Patriots, he's a fantasy football participant as well. He has both the Jets' Mark Sanchez and the Patriots' Aaron Hernandez on his team, so he cheers for both. (He will tell you his real favorite team, however, is the Cleveland Browns.)

This type of scenario unfolds daily in America—not just in sports bars and not just during football games. The reason: fantasy sport. And if the scenarios are complex, defining fantasy sport is even more so because it can take a multitude of forms. A somewhat cynical view of the phenomenon is exemplified by Vongsarath (2012), who labels fantasy sport as "a way for geeks and jocks alike to play out their lost dreams of playing actual sports" (para. 1). That view may have been typical as fantasy sport play emerged in the 1980s and early 1990s, but as it has gone mainstream, friendlier definitions have emerged. *Newsweek* author Starr (2005) offers a simple definition, saying that fantasy sport "uses real players and real stats to create faux teams in faux leagues" (Starr, 2005, para. 1).

As the game has evolved, game variations have proliferated, as has the statistical knowledge coveted by fantasy sport's keenest participants. For many, "fantasy football is not just a game. It's a game based on a game ... an oft-welcome and occasionally needed escape. A catharsis" (Pallister, 2011, p. 3). Virtually a lifestyle for some, fantasy sport for most participants might be defined somewhat facetiously by Gruss (2012), who states that it features people who "draft real players and pit them against each other in statistical battles through imaginary games, only to learn they know very little about sports" (p. E1). Yet, without question, it is essential to many modern sports fans. As the National Football league once tweeted: "Sundays without fantasy football are like a BBQ without burgers. Don't have a BBQ without burgers."

Operationalizing fantasy sport

An academic definition, the one we will employ throughout this book, comes from Ruihley and Hardin (2011b). They describe fantasy sport as "an interactive team management activity based on statistics accrued by athletes of real-life professional sport organizations and/or college athletics" (p. 233). Within this definition, however, it is important to understand where the line is drawn in terms of what does or does not constitute fantasy sport.

First, let us explore the activities that fit our definition. Representing the majority of play are fantasy leagues in which people pick players from professional sports associations and reconstitute teams that participants believe will be superior—at least statistically—to other teams amalgamated by other participants in the league. In the United States, the most popular of these leagues is, without question, fantasy football (Fantasy Sport Trade Association, 2012a). The far-reaching popularity of American football (23.8 million North American fans participating annually) dwarfs that of the next three most popular sports: baseball

(12.2 million), auto racing (8 million), and basketball (7 million), respectively (Dockterman, 2012). In European countries and most other parts of the developed world, fantasy sport is less evolved, but still a growing entity, with soccer being the primary league in which fantasy players participate. At the same time, many people outside of the United States still find participating in US-based fantasy leagues enjoyable (Montague, 2010).

As fantasy football, baseball and basketball gained popularity, many other forms of fantasy participation became available. These included sports such as golf, hockey, cricket, and auto racing, but also nonmainstream sports such as bass fishing, bowling, darts, and tennis. All of these sports have fantasy correlates involving the same key principles: (a) competing against a relatively limited group of others in the form of a league, (b) repurposing statistics to create some form of fantasy "score" to measure team performance, and (c) incorporating all or the majority of the actual season statistics from that professional association to create a fantasy season in which a winner will be determined at the end.

Meeting the criteria of the first two correlates but not the third are "daily leagues," which this book classifies as fantasy sport. The same parameters apply, with the exception that a player forms a new team each day; a winner results each night (for sports such as baseball and basketball) or each weekend (in the cases of football and NASCAR). Askeland (2012) notes the impressive growth of daily leagues such as FanDuel. It and other entries such as Daily Joust and 365 Fantasy Sports, cater to a highly involved player who enjoys the process of drafting players even more than watching the season unfold. For the purposes of this book, daily leagues match the established criteria because the leagues still involve the interactive management of a sports-based team using repurposed statistics from real-life athletes involved in major associations (professional or collegiate).

Still, it is worth noting that daily leagues offer less regression to the mean. From a gambling perspective, then, there is a larger percentage chance of luck in daily leagues than in season-long leagues. Such distinctions are being debated in courts, with lawsuits alleging that fantasy sport actually is gambling—an issue we will explore in great detail in this book. Some endorse the opinion expressed by Chad (2012) that "if fantasy sports isn't gambling, then *Penthouse* isn't pornographic. Fantasy football is as addicting, if not more so, than betting against the spread" (p. 5B). However, the majority of players and even outsiders regulating the activity parse differences between the two pastimes, especially when noting that stakes are small for the majority of fantasy players —approximately half of whom play for no money whatsoever. As such, the definition used in this book does not include a financial correlate; fantasy sport may involve the exchange of money from losers to winners, yet this does not appear to be a primary aim. As Starkey (2011) notes, "Are fantasy leaguers not gamblers? [No.] But you better believe they crave classified information. Lots of it" (n.p.).

This leads to some clarifications of what does *not* constitute fantasy sport, at least under the definition we use in this book. For instance, when one speaks of "games within games" in the United States, one celebrated example is "March Madness," when millions of people complete millions of brackets in an attempt to predict the performance of 68 teams in the NCAA Men's Basketball Tournament. This popular event does fit some parameters of fantasy sport. But in March Madness, statistics are not repurposed as much as final scores; team statistics are used to form predictions, but players are not reconstituted into new teams. Thus, while the tournament generates spirited involvement in many an office pool, it does not fit into the phenomenon we explore in this book: how and why fantasy players find immense enjoyment from consistent and long-term participation.

There are several other fantasy-based formats that certainly apply the same principles, yet do not meet the definition of fantasy *sport* as much as fantasy *games*. While we are only focusing our academic analysis on sport-based fantasy games, such ancillary games are worth noting—if only to establish the widespread proliferation of these games as they promote a sense of egalitarian "ownership" of various public entities and ideas. These related activities include:

- *Fantasy Congress:* Participants choose US representatives and senators to populate rosters. In this educational activity, participants are awarded points when legislators introduce bills, have bills passed out of committee, and have bills passed in each house of Congress ("Welcome," 2012).
- *Hollywood Stock Exchange*: Participants are handed millions in imaginary money to invest in upcoming film projects based on how they think they will perform at the box office.
- *Umpire Ejection Fantasy League*: The purpose of this league is to objectively track and analyze "umpire ejections and their corresponding calls with great regard for the rules and spirit of the game of baseball" ("Umpire," 2012, para. 1).
- *Celebrity Fantasy League*: Participants pick 25 celebrities with points awarded based on photos featured in magazines. Points also are given for births and marriages, but deducted for rehab stints and arrests (Dockterman, 2012).

Unfortunately, this notion of fantasy gaming also includes some potentially disturbing associations, including:

- *Fantasy Death League/Dead Pool.* Participants draft a team of celebrities and/or public figures with a focus on who might die within a given time period. Points are scored when their picks pass away.
- *Fantasy Reality Shows:* Participants choose contestants on popular American reality shows such as *American Idol, The Voice, The Bachelor/Bachelorette, Big Brother*, and *Survivor*. There is even a fantasy game revolving around events on multiple reality shows, with points awarded based on colorful categories such as intoxication, fighting, hot tubs, nudity, and crying. ("Grantland's Reality," 2011).

From the benign to the bizarre, the intriguing to the troubling, it is clear that these and many other types of games trace their roots to the origins of fantasy sport. Indeed, fantasy sport has resulted in new ways to consume media, understand public culture, and interact with others in society. The communication surrounding these types of activities is of particular import, as these fantasy activities involve the owning of something that was not previously regarded as property, typically a person (in this case, an athlete), who is now commodified and, arguably, dehumanized in the process. As Kellam (2012) argues about the rhetoric imbued within fantasy football:

> Fantasy football discourse does more than just describe players or detail their achievements within statistical language. Instead, this language performs a colonial function of othering NFL players, maintaining a discourse that positions them as a commodity to be owned, monitored, and consumed by fantasy football participants. (p. 52–53)

Thus, the communicative imperative in understanding the motivations embedding this activity is underscored, with ascertaining the factors that collectively make the fantasy experience compelling (and often addicting) being critical for exploration.

Enduring popularity

Fantasy sport is now mainstream and worldwide, representing a game-changing development in how people watch and consume real-time sporting events. The Fantasy Sport Trade Association (FSTA) reports that as of 2012, 35 million Americans participate in fantasy sport each year. Moreover, they are avid sports fans. ESPN Integrated Media Research (2010) indicates that while the average sports fan consumes approximately seven hours of ESPN media each week, the average *fantasy* sport fan consumes more than *three times* that amount (22 hours and 40 minutes).

For a better understanding of the permeation and impact of fantasy sport, let us consider these two statistics separately. First, 35 million people play fantasy sport in America and Canada. Consider how that number compares to other phenomenon receiving substantial coverage in news and popular culture. For instance, the number of Americans who check their Twitter accounts daily is approximately 14 million (Sonderman, 2012). Almost 25 million Americans own a Nintendo Wii (VGchartz, 2011). Slightly more than 20 million Americans watched the final performances of *American Idol* (Seidman, 2011). As of 2012, 18 million Americans owned an iPhone (Gustin, 2012). Fantasy sport trumps all of these things—and these are just American comparisons. Take into account the millions of people participating in fantasy sport in Europe, Asia, and other parts of the world (discussed more in Chapter 7) and it is clear that this game within games is far from a niche activity played only by statisticians with time on their hands.

Now consider that second statistic: ESPN reported that sports media consumption more than triples if a person participates in fantasy sport. To be clear, we cannot draw conclusions about cause and effect—people do not consume an extra 15 hours of ESPN media each week solely because of their involvement in fantasy sport. However, we can draw conclusions about linkages: if you want to find the greatest sports media enthusiasts, fantasy sport play is the perfect place to look. Sports teams, organizations, and media outlets devote a considerable amount of time and effort finding ways to cause even slight upticks in ratings, interest, and advertising/promotional dollars. Yet fantasy sport, often covertly and with little fanfare, has managed to trump many social media functions, iPad applications, and technological advancements as *the* way to secure sports fans for a multitude of offerings. As Jonsson (2012) notes, "fantasy players have real clout" (n.p.).

The logical counterpoint to this clout is to question the statistics: "If fantasy sport is so popular, why don't I hear more about it?" The simplest response is that this is an activity whose popularity is matched by its insularity. While the games are incredibly meaningful to participants within a given league, the rest of the world is so clueless about them that fantasy sport is not much of a conversation starter, at least within the most basic level of play. As Gruss explains, "Just as you would not share your adventures in the grocery store or from a pickup basketball game with someone who wasn't there, there is no reason to talk about fantasy sports" (Gruss, 2012, p. E1). Even with 35 million players in North America, that leaves more than 400 million people who are uninitiated to the nuances of fantasy play. Moreover, to the casual observer, fantasy sport seems to have a steep learning curve (although fantasy sport industry leaders believe the complexity of participation is overstated). Hearing chatter about fantasy sport, many respond like Robinson (2010), who writes: "Fantasy football fans hear me now: I have no idea what you are talking about. Bleep, blurp, dun-dun is all I hear when you gather and yammer about something Peyton Manning did" (p. D4).

As a result of all these factors, fantasy sport represents a greatly underreported phenomenon; it is mainstream to some and hopelessly esoteric to others. Yet the numbers do not lie and neither does the bottom line: fantasy sport has a financial impact registering in the billions (Wang, 2010). Even popular athletes take it quite seriously. British tennis star Andy Murray keeps his fantasy soccer trophy in front of all his other tennis trophies (Newman, 2012). While US fans continue to flock to the aforementioned mainstream offerings—fantasy football, baseball, and basketball—millions of Americans spend a great deal of time playing games such as fantasy golf, and auto racing. Fantasy participants in European nations find they have clout in the large, mediated world of football/soccer, while continually finding new avenues for growth, such as fantasy cricket and rugby, which now hold their appeal in these nations and beyond. The sports media world has found its literal and figurative game changer.

Processes of play: from draft day to championship games

The basics are the same in all forms of fantasy leagues: take already-occurring sporting events within society and find a way to reconstruct the people acting in the event to predict and perform new assimilated meanings to the existing actions. Leagues are formed in all sizes and formats, but can be subdivided into face-to-face and online leagues. Either type typically requires the participation of 10–12 people (although this can vary), but whether they participate in person or online alters the interaction and overarching structures substantially. Many face-to-face leagues involve family, friends, or coworkers—people who already live in a fairly close proximity to one another. Conversation can easily take place at work, around the dinner table, or at other social events. Online leagues can include the same close friends and family, but also can involve perfect strangers or "friends of friends" sharing the love of fantasy sport. The interesting aspect of the latter scenario is that the acquaintance may only be built on fantasy activities. Being friends of friends or even strangers, participants really have only one common topic. Whether embarked on with friends or strangers, the fantasy sport experience is typically filled with jovial trash-talking among rivals, fluctuating competitive fates, elaborate information searches, and massive media consumption to see fantasy players perform—not to mention conflicted loyalties when the fates of one's favorite "real" team and one's fantasy team are at odds. A typical experience is likely to include (a) drafting of players, (b) lineup generation, (c) searches for information, and (d) enacted competition. Each will be explained in greater detail.

Draft

Drafting is one of the most exciting parts of the fantasy sport experience for most participants because it is where one's team takes shape (Criblez, 2012). Whether in person or online, the draft is often filled with excitement, socializing, and strategy. In-person drafts occur when all members of a league meet in one location to choose their teams. Some in-person drafts use computers to assist with selection of players, while other in-person drafts are done with pen and paper or on a draft board. Figure 1.1 offers a glimpse of an in-person draft.

Figure 1.1 In-person draft

Online drafts can be completed in a live format with all owners drafting in one draft room, or automated, with the fantasy program quickly selecting players to rosters based on draft style and prerankings set by each team owner. Figure 1.2 features a screen capture of an ESPN online draft room as an example of the online draft experience.

Prior to a draft, league participants have the option to read draft magazines (such as *Fantasy Football Index*), seek out expert opinions, complete mock drafts, and pre-rank players. Many participants will have targeted players they want to draft and will try to acquire those players within the draft, creating complex strategies and multifaceted plans, sometimes weeks or months in advance.

Choosing players to become members of a fantasy team is conventionally accomplished by draft format, with participants selecting athletes in a "snake" draft with predetermined turns. Or teams can be formed through an auction-style format, where participants bid against other league participants to build their teams. A snake format involves drafting players in a predetermined order and reversing the order in the subsequent rounds; thus, in a 10-player league, the person who has the 1st pick would have the 20th pick; the person who has the 10th pick would also receive the 11th pick, and so on. Each participant selects a player when it is his or her turn to draft. While preparation is a key correlate to success, there is still a great deal of luck involved in the process as a participant auto-drafting (i.e. auto-pilot) or selecting based on expert rankings, can still draft high quality players.

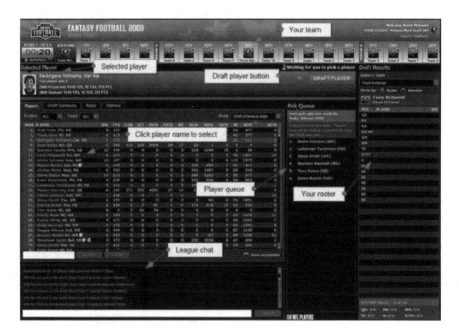

Figure 1.2 ESPN online draft room

The second primary draft style, employed considerably less frequently than the previous one, involves an auction format. Within this format, participants are each given a set amount of imaginary dollars. Each team takes turns nominating/selecting players to be bid upon. Once a player is nominated, teams make bids (using imaginary dollars) on the player. The highest bid wins and the player is added to the roster. The concept of this type of draft is that participants have to budget carefully when bidding and developing their teams. A team could be built around a handful of star players with little talent surrounding them, or could be devoid of star players with consistently performing average talent throughout the roster (much the same as modern professional sports league management). Research and analysis must influence one's preparation in this setting. Making the case for auction-style drafting, ESPN.com writer Cockcroft (2012), also defines this form appropriately:

> Gone are the frustrations of knowing that only one person in the room, one purely lucky individual, will even have a crack at Arian Foster [NFL running back]. Gone is the internal struggle over how early you should select your quarterback, or your tight end. Gone is the annoyance that is losing the player that you *oh-so-wanted*, vultured by the very team with the pick right in front of you. In an auction, it's no-holds-barred. If Foster is your object, you've got a can't-miss way to get him: just open up your wallet and pay the extra buck. Want three first-round draft talents at the expense of having to fill the cracks with late-round, sleeper-caliber material? You can do that too. Have you always wanted to spread your risk, sacrificing top-shelf talent for the effective equivalent of populating your roster with every fifth-rounder in a draft? Again, that's a can-do. (p. 7)

Fantasy host sites, utilizing snake or auction drafting, assign dollar amounts, points or other rankings to individual players prior to a draft and during the season. For snake-style drafts, assigning value may be a rank-order list of the Top 200 fantasy basketball players based on their projected point totals. Similarly, this ranked list can be sorted by each position, ranking the top guards or centers. Auction-style drafts offer similar rankings but also include a projected dollar amount one would spend in an auction. Figure 1.3 offers a snapshot of ESPN's Top 200 fantasy basketball players for the 2012–2013 season.

The best fantasy participant takes all information, analyzes team needs, synthesizes player projections, and selects a group of players that, statistically speaking, will perform better than his or her peers in the league.

Once the draft begins, decisions must be made in an ever-changing landscape. Another participant drafts-targeted athletes, athletes of high acclaim fall in the draft, different positions are depleted quickly, and intuition-based hypotheses about player outcomes are employed. With every pick, the scenarios change. Players must adjust their decision-making accordingly to form the most competitive teams possible. For an extended and true snapshot of the preparation and sheer amount of information that can go into drafting a team, look no further than Sam Walker's *Fantasyland*. In this text, Walker (2006) examines how to best

Fantasy basketball: Top 200

By **Fantasy staff** I ESPN.com   Updated: October 30, 2012, 3:41 PM ET

2010-2011 Fantasy Basketball Top 200			
ESPN Rankings: Top 200 **Sort By Position:** PG	SG	SF	PF	C **More Ranks:** Brian McKitish's Top 150			
Rank	Player	Pos Ranks	Auction
1	Kevin Durant, SF, OKC	SF1	$70
2	LeBron James, SF, MIA	SF2	$70
3	Chris Paul, PG, LAC	PG1	$66
4	Dwyane Wade, SG, MIA	SG1	$65
5	Deron Williams, PG, BKN	PG2	$62
6	Russell Westbrook, PG, OKC	PG3	$59
7	Josh Smith, PF/SF, ATL	PF1	SF3	$57
8	Andrew Bynum, C, PHI	C1	$55
9	Kobe Bryant, SG, LAL	SG2	$53
10	Al Jefferson, C/PF, UTAH	C2	PF2	$50
11	Kyrie Irving, PG, CLE	PG4	$49
12	LaMarcus Aldridge, PF/C, POR	PF3	C3	$48

Figure 1.3 ESPN's Top 200 fantasy basketball players for the 2012-2013 season

prepare for an all-expert fantasy league. Hiring a small team of qualitative and quantitative personnel, Walker explores all options prior to the ever-crucial draft.

Lineup generation

Once the draft is complete and the season begins, teams compete using statistics generated by real athletes in real games as points to a fantasy team. More specifically, "the basic statistics of those players are then aggregated after each real-world game to determine how well the team is doing" (Pew Internet and American Life Project, 2005, para. 3). The actions and decisions made by a fantasy participant are similar to those made by real-life general managers, coaches, or sport management professionals (Davis and Duncan, 2006; Roy and Goss, 2007). General manager responsibilities granted to fantasy participants include the actions of starting or reserving talent on their teams, trading players with other teams in their leagues, dropping players from their rosters, or adding players found on a list of available players not already chosen by a team.

The action of starting or reserving players involves selecting which players on the team will "start" and accumulate fantasy points in the scoring time period and which ones will remain on the team but not contribute any points. Figure 1.4 provides a standard view of a fantasy football owner's roster.

In this particular snapshot, the league allows eight starting players and eight reserves. A lot of effort can go into determining which players will start (meaning

Figure 1.4 A fantasy football owner's roster

their accrued points will count) and which will remain on the bench (meaning their accrued points will not count). Projections, trends, matchups, weather, and myriad other factors can alter an owner's decision. Before competition, owners often scour the vast sports media landscape for any minutiae that can help their teams. Through resources ranging from fantasy magazines and columns to Internet-based websites and podcasts, fantasy sport participants can find information about their teams just about anywhere. Allowing the fantasy sport consumer easy single-click portals, fantasy host websites (e.g. Yahoo! and CBS Sports) have their own analysts and commentary, keeping consumers on their sites. Other information options include viewing analysts on television networks (e.g. ESPN and Fox Sports), organization websites (e.g. NFL, MLB, NBA, and NASCAR), and fantasy-specific radio shows (i.e. ESPN Radio, Fox Sports Radio, and Sirius XM Fantasy Sports). There are also entire organizations devoted to providing fantasy sport information (e.g. Rotoworld.com and Rotowire.com). All of these resources will be discussed in detail throughout this book.

During competition

During competition, fantasy sport participants seek out further information based on athlete performance, but the main activity involves following the players on their teams (either watching the actual games unfold or checking statistics at various time periods) to witness how they perform. As shown in Figure 1.5, many fantasy scoreboards provide live updates on player performances that impact fantasy competition.

Many owners will use the scoreboard as a gathering spot during competition. The primary way to follow a player's performance is by watching a visual feed on television, phone, or computer. Participants also can keep up with their teams by listening to a game on radio or following a play-by-play report on the Internet.

The history and evolution of fantasy sport

Fantasy sport has existed for more than half a century, with several notable advancements that have transformed the games from the province of statistics-oriented sports insiders into a viable form of entertainment for the masses. Harvard professor William Gamson is credited with creating the first form of fantasy sport (although he did not call it that) using professional baseball in 1960 (Schwartz, 2005). Several of his professor colleagues joined him in a fairly informal game in which each would score points based on how selected players performed in areas ranging from batting average to home runs to earned run average. Utilizing an auction-style draft of Major League Baseball (MLB) players, teams in Gamson's Baseball Seminar were formed in a similar fashion to how real owners and general managers fill a team. To recreate this process even further, Gamson and colleagues would buy in with $10, translating into an imaginary budget of $100,000 to bid on players to form their teams (Walker, 2006). Once teams were formed, the game began. In a much simpler technological time, a byproduct of participation was the fact that "the simple act of reading the box scores had become a daily thrill ride" (p. 62).

OVERVIEW STATS NEWS PROJECTIONS SCHEDULE RANKS RECOMMEND

STARTERS		WK 10		2012 SEASON				WEEK 10				
SLOT	PLAYER, TEAM POS	OPP	STATUS ET	PRK	PTS	AVG	LAST	PROJ	OPRK	%ST	%OWN	+/-
QB	Drew Brees, NO QB	Atl	Sun 1:00	3	174	21.8	15	18	18th	93.6	100.0	+0
RB	LeSean McCoy, Phi RB	Dal	Sun 4:25	10	96	12.0	12	14	16th	96.7	100.0	+0
RB	Alfred Morris, Wsh RB		** BYE **	7	105	11.7	7	--	--	80.8	100.0	+0
WR	Dwayne Bowe, KC WR	@Pit	Mon 8:30	25	69	6.6	5	11	9th	70.4	100.0	+0
WR	Marques Colston, NO WR	Atl	Sun 1:00	9	94	11.8	10	15	6th	92.4	100.0	+0
TE	Tony Gonzalez, Atl TE	@NO	Sun 1:00	4	71	8.9	3	12	5th	91.3	100.0	+0
FLEX	Eric Decker, Den WR	@Car	Sun 1:00	6	96	12.0	21	13	3rd	58.3	100.0	+0
D/ST	Packers D/ST D/ST		** BYE **	11	63	7.0	7	--	--	80.9	96.9	+4.2
K	Shaun Suisham, Pit K	KC	Mon 8:30	9	76	9.5	6	10	27th	21.9	24.3	+9
BENCH		WK 10		2012 SEASON				WEEK 10				
SLOT	PLAYER, TEAM POS	OPP	STATUS ET	PRK	PTS	AVG	LAST	PROJ	OPRK	%ST	%OWN	+/-
Bench	BenJarvus Green-Ellis, Cin RB	NYG	Sun 1:00	24	63	7.9	11	13	9th	62.3	100.0	+0.1
Bench	Jordy Nelson, GB WR		** BYE **	14	82	9.1	0	--	--	65.0	100.0	+0
Bench	Matt Ryan, Atl QB	@NO	Sun 1:00	6	154	19.3	13	26	32nd	71.7	100.0	+0
Bench	Torrey Smith, Bal WR	Oak	Sun 1:00	22	79	9.4	10	14	15th	45.9	100.0	+0
Bench	Aaron Hernandez, NE TE	Buf	Sun 1:00	37	28	3.1	--	3	26th	27.1	94.4	-1.9
Bench	Rashad Jennings, Jac RB	Ind	Thu 8:20	49	33	4.1	6	14	27th	49.7	81.4	+17.4

Figure 1.5 A fantasy scoreboards providing live updates on player performances

The first documented form of fantasy (US) football arose three years later, when four people connected to the Oakland Raiders organization developed a fantasy league called The Greater Oakland Professional Pigskin Prognosticators League (St. Amant, 2005). Based on the same concept as the Baseball Seminar (selecting players from different professional teams and assigning points to them based on their performance) the league developed gradually, although it was never patented or sold to the public.

A major turning point in the evolution of fantasy sport occurred in 1979, when a group of New Yorkers, led by writer Daniel Okrent, developed a more sophisticated form of fantasy baseball called *rotisserie.* (The name stemmed from the location where the group often met to eat, New York restaurant La Rotisserie Francaise.) Okrent's brainstorm was intertwined with those of other early fantasy enthusiasts. In 1962, Gamson's career took him to the University of Michigan; his Baseball Seminar followed and expanded to 25 teams. Robert Sklar, an assistant professor of history, owned one of those teams. One of Sklar's advisees was Okrent. In subsequent conversations following graduation, Sklar introduced Okrent to the Baseball Seminar. Then Okrent created his version of fantasy sport in 1979. This is where La Rotisserie Francaise enters the picture, as the group of friends met and formed the "Phillies Appreciation Society" (Walker, 2006, p. 66). Okrent and colleagues discussed and created their version of rotisserie baseball.

Ironically, it was the stoppage of Major League Baseball during the long strike of 1981 that hastened the growth of rotisserie baseball. With no games to cover, journalists turned their attention to the fantasy alternative as the strike dragged on. Baseball enthusiasts became more familiar with Rotisserie Baseball because of an article written for *Inside Sports* called "The Year George Foster Wasn't Worth $36." The author was Daniel Okrent, and the story included the rules for the fantasy game. As noted by Vichot (2009) and Walker (2006), this one article in a baseball-strike year prompted many sportswriters to form their own fantasy leagues. Contributing to the popularity of fantasy sport in the early 1980s was the inaugural edition of *Rotisserie League Baseball,* first published in 1984 (Vichot). Again, Okrent was involved: he was the editor of this publication.

Participating in fantasy sport in the 1980s was a burdensome undertaking. Drafts were completed in person. Surveying the sports landscape involved reading box scores, listening to the radio, or catching the few televised games. Statistics and standings were computed by hand, and trading or making roster moves required communication tactics that seem onerous in today's technology-friendly environment. One of the first appraisals of fantasy sport consumption took place in 1990 when *USA Today* estimated the industry at 500,000 participants (Vichot, 2009). Years later, with assistance from the advent of the Internet, the needle moved and the industry grew to an estimated 3 million ("Fantasy Sports," 2008). The Internet and the World Wide Web, as with almost everything, provided a new model for an activity that formerly took place with paper and pencils (Vichot, 2009, p. 16). Suddenly, many people who loved sports, but did not previously participate in fantasy sport because of the legwork required, opted to join online fantasy leagues. Acquiring statistics was easier and so was league upkeep: the Internet provided the needed platform. In addition, baseball in particular spurred the growth of fantasy sport, in part because it involves a plethora of statistics. Many statistics experts came to the forefront of the sports world during this time (Vichot, 2009).

With better technology, more options, and more attention, the fantasy sport industry continued its growth and in 2003, the FSTA estimated participation at nearly 15 million participants ("Fantasy Sports"; Farquhar and Meeds, 2007; Hu, 2003). Fast-forwarding nine years to 2012, the FSTA estimates 35 million Americans and Canadians participating in fantasy sport (Fantasy Sport Trade Association, 2012a). Even with incredible growth in one decade, fantasy sport industry professionals do not anticipate the overall growth trend to diminish in the near future (Billings and Ruihley, 2012).

Book overview

What are the ramifications when tens of millions of people (possibly hundreds of millions worldwide) are playing this game within a game? There are implications not only for overall consumption of sports media, but for fandom as a whole— particularly in cases such as our opening scenario in the sports bar, where traditional team allegiances intermingle and sometimes clash with fans' desires for their fantasy teams. The number of people playing continues to escalate (Fantasy Sport Trade Association, 2012a), but this book aims to go beyond the numbers.

Instead, we ask *why*. *Why* do people participate? *Why* does a fantasy sport participant devote an extra 15 waking hours each week to sporting events and sports information resources? *Why* do sports fans become uber fans when playing fantasy sport? *Why* do they prioritize these games, sometimes above family, friends, work, or religion? And *why* do some of them ultimately quit playing while others appear to be lifelong players (or even addicts) of fantasy sport?

To answer these questions, **Chapter 2** will use survey techniques to outline and uncover the primary motivations for fantasy play, ranging from the desire to interact with others to the desire to win money to the desire to be the "smartest person in the room." **Chapter 3** will delineate how these motivations can vary depending on demographic issues such as gender, race, and marital status, among many others. **Chapter 4** will focus on what has grown to be a robust billion-dollar industry, interviewing integral people within the Fantasy Sport Trade Association and Fantasy Sport Writer's Association. **Chapter 5** will delve into the question of whether motivations for play change substantially when the amount of money at stake in a league changes from none to a little to a large amount. **Chapter 6** will look at the question of *why* people play by exploring a group of people who have decided *not* to play, querying former fantasy sport participants as to why they opted out of the activity. Finally, **Chapter 7** will hypothesize on the future of fantasy sport games as well as expand notions of fantasy play beyond North America, offering insights about the potential global impact of fantasy sport play.

Through this series of diverse data-gathering methods, we explore the phenomenon of fantasy sport in what we hope is an evenhanded manner. We don't malign fantasy sport participants as geeks who need to get a life, and we also don't subscribe to the notion that fantasy sport is a reality-defining metaphor for twenty-first century existence. We survey people from the United States, Canada, Europe, and China, analyzing their motivations for play and for overall sports media consumption. We interview insiders in the fantasy sport industry, many of whom have become celebrities as the industry has grown. We speak with participants of the games at the highest level—those who spend major portions of their annual salaries to compete in high-stakes leagues—in an attempt to determine what makes them do what they do. We even assess the "burnouts" that once played fantasy sport but decided the benefits ultimately did not outweigh the drawbacks.

Through it all, we have received input from thousands of people, young and old, male and female, from diverse ethnic and socio-economic backgrounds. Our goal is not to promote their pastime or to denigrate it, but to be comprehensive—to employ multiple methods to shed light on the multiple constituencies related to fantasy sport. Sometimes our analyses ended up confirming our initial hypotheses; other times the results challenged foundational assumptions about fantasy sport. Through it all, we found fantasy sport to be a compelling glimpse of the complex roles of sports, gaming, and media in our culture.

2 More than just an excuse to watch sports all day

Why people participate in fantasy sport

Charland (1987) once noted that for an entity to constitute itself as a separate and unique culture, three rhetorical tenets should be present. Fantasy sport arguably encapsulates all three of Charland's postulates. First, an entity must establish its own language. While this traditionally involves full linguistic differences (e.g. English vs French in eastern Canada), groups such as fantasy sport participants certainly incorporate lingo and other forms of vocabulary that are seemingly foreign to non-players. (Even an avid sports fan may be baffled when told a fantasy football league is a "PPR league," which in fantasy lingo means "points per reception.") Second, according to Charland, the entity must explicitly declare itself a formal culture. The formation of groups such as the Fantasy Sport Trade Association (to be discussed in detail in Chapter 4), coupled with many online and traditional media outlets specifically dedicated to not just playing but discussing fantasy sport, fulfills this tenet. Finally, for an entity to be constituted as a culture, there must be both an in-group and an out-group (see social identity theory; Tajfel and Turner, 1986). In essence, to define itself as *something*, an entity also must define what it is *not*. Subcultures often are defined not just by their avid members, but also by the fact that not everyone "gets" them. Pro-gun cultures are an exemplar of such a divide: they believe the right to bear arms is a critical part of modern existence, while others, members of an out-group, fail to comprehend the seeming obsession with firearms. The same is true for aficionados of everything from vampire literature to model trains. It also is true for fantasy sport, as the motivation for play is self-evident for some and inexplicable for others who do not understand the broad-range appeal. This chapter is intended for both the in-groups and out-groups of fantasy sport. We will delve deeply into general conceptions of why people play, offering explanations for non-fantasy players. We also will explore specific emotional responses and desires generated by fantasy sport, for those who feel the compulsion to play more frequently in more immersed manners without fully understanding why.

Why do people participate in fantasy sport? Do fantasy sport participants consume sports media differently? What attributes validate fantasy sport as an activity worthy of participation? Why and how does it attract and maintain our attention? The answers to these questions greatly impact our understanding of modern culture—touching on sociological trends, business tactics for recruiting and retaining participants, and even how players navigate their (mostly online) experience. For fantasy sport professionals, many strategies are involved, including: marketing efforts, pay vs free participation models, writing styles, and types of leagues or games offered. Much can be learned from understanding the *why*. With an estimated 20 million (ESPN Sports Poll, 2011b) to 35 million (Fantasy Sport Trade Association, 2012a) people playing in North America alone, many comprehend why fantasy sport is worthy of investigation from a sheer magnitude/penetration rate standpoint (Billings and Ruihley, 2012; Davis and Duncan, 2006; Farquhar and Meeds, 2007; Roy and Goss, 2007; Ruihley and Hardin, 2011a). Yet numbers do not necessarily provide instant legitimacy to the masses. Many people—outsiders who know it has become a major part of sports media culture—do not "get it." Thus, consumer behavior—a very important factor in any business strategy—becomes a central focus as we establish broader conceptions about the who, what, where, when, and especially *why* of fantasy sport participation.

The major literature relevant to contemporary motivation and consumption research is limited in number of pieces, but significant in-depth of insight. For instance, in one of the initial investigations of the activity, Davis and Duncan (2006) examined masculine privilege as an outcome of fantasy sport participation. The authors identified a typical fantasy sports player as a young, White, educated male, with substantial time for leisure activities, proficient computer skills, and access to the Internet. Their analysis indicates male fantasy sport participants emphasize the importance of sharing their sports knowledge, as they dedicated a considerable amount of time to searching the Internet for statistics and injury reports. Davis and Duncan (2006) also found male fantasy sport participants to be highly competitive, often using message boards to form alliances with other players. The authors underscored the primary issues of male bonding, control, and competition arising through participation in fantasy sport.

Early consumption-based and motivation literature (Farquhar and Meeds, 2007; Roy and Goss, 2007; Spinda and Haridakis, 2008) assisted in paving the way for this and other examinations of the topic. Farquhar and Meeds (2007) are responsible for one of the first examinations of fantasy sport participation motives. Utilizing Q-methodology, their analysis revealed five types of fantasy sport users (or FSUs) including (a) casual participants, (b) players, (c) isolationist thrill-seekers, (d) trash-talkers, and (e) formatives. In addition, their exploration highlighted two primary motivations consisting of arousal (i.e., positive stress or eustress) and surveillance (i.e., the gathering of sport information utilizing the sport media). Roy and Goss (2007) examined FSUs by exploring certain influences of fantasy sport consumption. Results outlined three major areas of psychological, social, and marketer-controlled influences. The variables contain some of the major motivational factors, including: psychological areas of achievement, control, and escape; social areas of community and socialization; and market-controlled aspects surrounding the product, price, and promotion. Using a mixed-methods approach, Spinda and Haridakis (2008) outlined six main motives for fantasy football participation: ownership, achievement/self-esteem, escape/pass time, socialization, bragging rights, and amusement.

In more recent research, Dwyer and Drayer (2010) segmented fantasy football users based on differing product and media consumption. Their findings produced four sport consumption modes consisting of: (a) light consumption, (b) fantasy dominant, (c) favorite team dominant, and (d) heavy consumption. Ruihley and Hardin (2011a) updated factors measuring social aspects of participation while introducing a competition factor and simultaneously validating several preexisting motivations. In addition, their work augmented and/or clarified several more motivations including achievement/self-esteem, arousal, escape, fan expression, fanship, ownership, pass time, and surveillance. Billings and Ruihley (2013) compared motivation and consumption of traditional sport fans to fantasy sport users, classifying fantasy sport participants to be "enhanced" sport fans (p. 21).

Thus, established research focusing on fantasy sport has provided the groundwork for a more comprehensive glimpse of motivations, including a plethora of motivational and consumption factors to consider. Taking into account these various academic investigations, this text will focus on these factors: arousal, camaraderie, competition, control, enjoyment, escape, fanship, ownership, pass time, self-esteem, social sport, and surveillance. We will define each of these motivational areas in much detail in the pages that follow, but one commonality is that each carries four specific key points of relevance: (a) emotion, (b) meaning, (c) story, and (d) experience for the fantasy sport user. To continue the exploration of this activity and its participants, each motivational factor was included in exclusive data collection and analysis for this book—a process involving the surveying of 1,201 North American participants about their tendencies and aspirations within the realm of fantasy sport play. The data collection also included open-ended responses to questions about participation as players answered questions detailing their fantasy sport experience. Before we discuss the survey research and analysis of these motivations, it is critical to provide a detailed discussion of how each concept is operationally unpacked, relating each to fantasy sport play. Some of the open-ended comments will be provided in the descriptions to allow further clarity.

Description of motivations

It is important to note that all of the proceeding explanations of fantasy sport motivations are extrapolations upon a composite of prior work in the field (Farquhar and Meeds, 2007; Hur, Ko, and Valacich, 2007; Lewis, 2012; Roy and Goss, 2007; Ruihley and Hardin, 2011a; Seo and Green, 2008; Spinda and Haridakis, 2008; Wann, 1995). The primary purpose of this chapter is not to redefine and reformulate them, but to test them as a holistic composite on a larger scale (in the current chapter) and then deconstruct the findings among key demographic groups (in Chapter 3). In other words, the delineated list of motivations is fairly established, yet the magnitude of each in comparison with the others is still ripe for investigation in this chapter. However, before formally extrapolating upon each motivation, one must first comprehend the role of one critical factor that significantly influences all of the following motivations: the concept of fanship.

Fanship

In the context of online sport consumption, Seo and Green (2008) measured and defined fanship as the "reason that one considers oneself a huge fan of particular sports and teams" (p. 86). This concept is a useful tool in participant-based research, gauging the level of fandom of a particular sample or subset groups within the sample. Fanship is measured in fantasy sport research to determine if being a fan—of a particular basketball team or league as a whole, for instance—plays a role in participating in an activity recognizing individual accomplishments above the team or league. With that in mind, fantasy sport can be seen as an activity of dual purpose, as players may wish to root for their favorite teams, but still have a vested interest in the outcomes and results of the players on their fantasy teams. As Maguire, Armfield, and Boone (2012) explain:

> Participation in fantasy sports leagues supersedes the traditional ideas of fanship. No affiliation with the fantasy team existed before the individual's creation of the team. Whereas fanship of real football teams can be a lifetime affair, the fantasy sports owner will build up and tear down rosters one year from the next. (p. 287)

Sandomir (2002) argues that this creates a fan who will "root, root, root for no team (Para. 1)." Lee, Ruihley, Brown, and Billings (2013) found that 41.4% of fantasy players reported that they seek a win from their fantasy team more than from the team they support within traditional sport. As such, fanship becomes a measure of these two interlocking circles. It is clear there is a relationship between traditional sports fandom and fantasy sport play, yet the degree of impact between the two is not fully established.

One key manner in which to establish relationships involves exploring the rest of the motivations for fantasy play, noting that many of these could also be cited as reasons for being a traditional sports fan as well. Listed alphabetically, these motivations are:

Arousal

The first motivation of arousal assists in explaining the daily, inconsistent, and emotional nature of a sports fan. Wann (1995) and others (James and Ridinger, 2002; Trail and James, 2001; Wann, Schrader, and Wilson, 1999) explored this concept under the title of "eustress" in several investigations of sports fan consumption and motivations. Wann (1995) operationalized the term eustress, stating that for "certain fans, sports are enjoyable because they arouse their senses and provide them with the [positive forms of] stress they seek" (p. 377). In some of the variables used to measure eustress, Wann (1995) incorporated words and phrases such as "pumped up," "psychologically aroused," and "stimulation" to help describe this factor (p. 382–383). While "aroused" and "stimulation" connote different meanings in different contexts, in the case of sports consumption, the terms embody the emotional rollercoaster a fan chooses to ride when cheering for any given team or individual athlete. The emotional highs of a basketball game-winning three-point basket, a last-minute touchdown pass in football, or a penalty kick in the closing minutes of a soccer match are a few of the many situations that can emotionally arouse a fan during a competition. Depalma and Raney (2003) found that unscripted sports (such as boxing) yielded higher levels of this type of motivation than scripted (professional wrestling). Moreover, Bryant, Brown, Comisky, and Zillmann (1982) noted that arousal (and enjoyment) were higher when watching matches pitting rivals or enemies. Thus, the "highs" are higher when the outcome is unknown and/or unpredictable as well as when the stakes are elevated. The same type of stimulation can be applied to fans enduring the negative aspects of those miraculous performances. Many fans can relate to jumping up and down in joy over a victory and hanging their heads in disappointment after a crushing defeat. Consequently, eustress encompasses sports fandom at its most intense, most passionate, and most emotional moments and it is this kind of emotional stimulation that excites, keeps interest, and boosts sport fandom.

In a similar vein, fantasy sport participants feel many of these feelings of arousal, but in starkly different formats. Fantasy sport participation is closely connected to overall sports fandom, in that arousal is still concerned with conceptions of team and outcomes of matches, yet it is different because a roster comprises many players from different "real" teams. Within sports consumption, there is similar temporal ebb and flow of the game (see Halone and Billings, 2010), but fantasy sport contrasts with traditional sport formats in that the ebb and flow of the game actually take place over many different dates, games, and time periods. Fantasy sport arousal can come in many different forms: cheering on a player on one's own roster, cheering against a player on the opposing roster, or cheering for a completely different outcome that has implications in the league's standings. A single basket in the middle of a game could have considerable ramifications for multiple teams in a league. Complex matrices and permeations of fantasy sport are typically enacted, particularly for the heavy player. The amount a fantasy sport player understands about the game at hand, combined with the amount of time and energy invested in the outcome, impacts the amount of arousal ultimately featured within what most would regard as a generally benign play (e.g., a ground ball to first base, or the success of a relatively easy 25-yard field goal).

Camaraderie

The motivational area of camaraderie focuses on relationships with other people. In a generalized sporting sense, camaraderie may be the initial reason many people become fans in the first place. Perhaps it involves playing catch with a family member. Perhaps it involves attending a Manchester United game with your friends from school. Perhaps watching the British Open golf championship provides a window into the psyche of an otherwise stoic grandparent. In small towns, attending a local high school basketball game might be how almost everyone spends a Friday evening and could be the primary topic of discussion the following day. From families (see Gantz and Wenner, 1991) to friends (see Smith, 2008) to total strangers at a restaurant or sports bar (see Eastman and Land, 1997), people experience the desire for connection as crucial to the sports media experience. Melnick (1993) notes the concept of the "sports encounter" (p. 49), which is similar to other shared experiences, such as airline travel or watching a film in a theater. People wish to be a part of something with a group, and camaraderie is the motivation that matches these aims.

In fantasy sport, camaraderie is a close sibling to traditional sports fandom, but differs in that physically going to a game or participating in a sport is not a primary prerequisite. Players find other ways to jointly experience sport, typically online. This concept was examined with fantasy sport under the umbrella term of "socialization" in prior work (e.g. Seo and Green, 2008; Spinda and Haridakis, 2008). It was not until the work of Ruihley and Hardin (2011a), with the use of an exploratory factor analysis (EFA), that the specific camaraderie factor was measured in isolation from other social aspects of fantasy sport play. Measuring the social motivations of fantasy sport play and utilizing constructs developed in Seo and Green (2008) and Spinda and Haridakis (2008), an EFA produced two separate factors: camaraderie and social sport. For most, it may involve an electronic relationship replete with phone calls, text messages, message board posts, and trash talking. It should be noted that a key word in the previous sentence is "relationship." As tested in research by Ruihley and Hardin (2011a), camaraderie in fantasy sport involves several types of relationships and focuses on getting along with others and staying in touch with people. Often, this camaraderie may involve staying in touch with friends from college/university or may be used to create a common bond with coworkers. When many individuals struggle to find topics on which to converse with people they still genuinely care about, fantasy sport fills the void—providing a systematic mechanism for at least having some interaction among people for months at a time when a sport is in season. In one instance mentioned in Ruihley and Hardin (2011a), family was the focus, as it provided an outlet for a father to "have fun with the boys now that they were older" (p. 241). In another case, it was a boss seeking to have something in common with his employees.

Competition

The spirit of competition is what drives many to the sport landscape. From enacting to watching sport, competition is at the core of sport. Bryant and Raney's (2000) disposition theory of sports spectatorship essentializes how competition relates—often quite directly—to enjoyment. Zillmann and Paulus (1993) offer a relatively common sense formula in which competition is of ultimate enjoyment when a loved team defeats a hated team. In fantasy sport, competition follows similar patterns. Most other motivations represent indirect desires such as the previously mentioned camaraderie, but competition represents the objective of the directly enacted activity: one plays to win the game, and all other motivations arise from the success or futility experienced by each player. Competition has not been frequently measured in fantasy sport focused research, but in their mixed-methods examination of fantasy sport motivations (e.g. qualitative online focus groups and a quantitative online survey), Ruihley and Hardin (2011a) brought competition to the forefront of fantasy sport motivation research. They did so based on qualitative focus group descriptions from fantasy sport participants. The factor of competition was then developed, tested, and validated though quantitative survey methods. When testing the relationship of fantasy sport motives to overall satisfaction and intentions to return to the activity in the future, competition was heavily present in both instances. While some could characterize competition to include a variety of factors, most notably arousal, competition was defined as related, yet operationally different—a joint understanding of the desire to both succeed and dominate. It was such a primal factor in the analysis from Ruihley and Hardin (2011a) that competition was ranked second highest among the motives measured behind overall sport fanship.

Control and ownership

Premier athletes such as Lionel Messi or Kobe Bryant possess skills so transcendent as to seem foreign to the common fan. Few fans would argue they could duplicate these performances if only granted the opportunity. However, coaching and administration are different: those skills seem much easier to duplicate (even if this is far removed from the reality). Second-guessing decision makers is seen as essential to the fun of being a fan, as many wonder, "What is the coach thinking?" or "Why don't they trade Player A to get Players B and C?" Fans typically question the conduct of their favorite team's administration, convinced that they could do a better job of managing a team and roster. Such desires, long manifested within sports fandom, essentialize what fantasy sport brings to the table: an opportunity to manage and control your own players. Not only are participants allowed to control their own rosters, but they also have a chance to prove their managing superiority as they compete with other fantasy sport owners.

For those wishing to test their roster management and ownership skills in the areas of drafting, trading, adding, or dropping players, and controlling a myriad of other player-personnel decisions, fantasy sport is a perfect conduit to fulfill these desires. Fantasy sport features some of the activities a real general manager or owner would be faced with daily. In one of the earliest explorations of fantasy sport motives, Spinda and Haridakis (2008) introduced factor scale items discussing the ownership opportunities available through fantasy sport. They measured this concept by providing statements to participants related to feeling like a general manager or a coach of the team, having a team to control, managing the lineup, and enjoying the feeling of ownership. Spinda and Haridakis (2008) found ownership to be a foundational motive, trumping other factors of self-esteem, escape/pass time, socialization, bragging rights, and amusement.

While certainly related, ownership and control now are justified as being measured as separate constructs within the study about to be reported upon in this chapter, as the former focuses on the emotion of owning or managing a team and the latter revolves around the actions of controlling and manipulating players and a fantasy team, a distinction first offered by Billings and Ruihley (2013).

Escape

The motivating factor of escape involves disengaging from daily issues and temporarily forgetting about or disengaging from life's worries (e.g. work, relationships, health, etc.). Similar to mental diversions offered by watching movies or television shows, listening to music, reading a book, or exploring the Internet, sports media consumption remains the most utilized diversion (Gantz and Wenner, 1995). For sports fans, this may include watching a baseball game, going to a soccer match, viewing a round or two of a golf tournament, or watching 11 hours of football coverage on Sundays (Krohn, Clarke, Preston, McDonald, and Preston, 1998). In an exploration of online sport consumption, Hur, Ko, and Valacich (2007) describe the factor of escape as breaking away from the "daily routine" (p. 530) while Seo and Green (2008) explain it as a way to "escape from reality" and "forget about work" specifically (p. 103). This type of escape and diversion is employed to relax and divert minds from stressful matters and concerns. This motive also is a measurement for fantasy sport participants. If sports deviate from the "real world," fantasy sport may offer yet another level of deviation, as many would argue that it offers the opportunity to escape from the traditional sports media world—reshuffling the competitive deck to potentially produce a more desirable outcome for the fan/participant.

Pass time

Passing time has been a part of motivation research for many types of mass communication media including radio (Rubin and Step, 2000), television (Gantz, 1981; Palmgreen and Rayburn, 1979; Rubin, 1983, 1984), and Internet (Flanagin and Metzger, 2001, Kaye, 1998; LaRose and Eastin, 2004). The Internet, particularly its social networking sites, has provided a perfect stage for many to decipher the manner in which one manages to pass time. While escape involves mentally avoiding or forgetting about an occurrence or issue, passing time purposely allows the clock to tick and time to pass, with the goal for nothing major to occur, seemingly to a relaxing or mind-clearing effect. Seo and Green (2008) examined passing time by those using professional sport teams' websites. Their measurements focused on the free time one may have and how one solves the problem of boredom. With all the options available and information to gather in fantasy sport play, this activity allows participants to pass time in several different ways. In most leagues, studious owners have an abundance of statistics to survey, matchups to examine, and free agent players waiting to be analyzed. Such information is readily available for dissection by an engaged participant, so a quick lunch-hour check of game scores or the setting of a lineup can easily turn into hours of closer examination. With traditional sport, one studies teams, as they exist, paying less attention to the infinite but hypothetical possibilities of trades, injuries and lineup decisions. Conversely, fantasy sport gives players the opportunity to think endlessly about these changes in realistic terms: fantasy sport team owners can put such strategies in action because of the control they exert. Significant amounts of time may pass as they engage in all this cognitive activity, which appears to be desirable based on previous research on the subject (Seo and Green, 2008).

Self-esteem

In sports, some live and die with their teams (hence the term "die-hard sports fan"). Some feel good when their team wins and feel bad when their team loses. Others do not care at all; to them, sports are for entertainment purposes only. Wann, Schrader, and Wilson (1999) argue that sports fanship (or the level to which people self-identify as sport fans) assists in the way individuals "create and maintain a positive self-concept" (p. 115). The authors state that when a "fan's team is successful, he or she gains a feeling of achievement and accomplishment" (p. 115). Subsequent studies reveal that sports not only affect mood, but also affect self-esteem that ultimately constructs self-fulfilling prophecies (see Hirt, Zillmann, Erickson, and Kennedy, 1992; Madrigal, 1995). Having one's team win an important game or championship can make the fan feel both smarter (for choosing the "right" team) and justified (in devoting considerable portions of his or her life to rooting for said "right" team). Put simply, there is a payoff for participation, resulting in a spiral as people dedicate more money, energy, and time to following and cheering for a favorite sport team. Fans talk, debate, argue, and even fight about their teams because of the linkage with overall self-concept. It logically follows that self-esteem fluctuates with the ups and downs of team performance.

When focusing on fantasy sport, research has measured achievement and self-esteem together (Maguire, Armfield, and Boone, 2012). These concepts are important areas to consider within fantasy sport because of its inherent competitive nature, the type of game format fantasy offers, and the desired ability to manage a team more astutely than one's opponent. In describing achievement, Roy and Goss (2007) highlight the competitive nature of fantasy sport and state that the "need to achieve success and outperform" is the reason participants invest time and money in such an activity (p. 101). Similarly, Spinda and Haridakis (2008) measure and describe this factor as a situation in which one feels better about one's self when one's fantasy team wins. Thus, the more personal nature of fantasy sport (getting to choose one's own players) results in greater potential fluctuations in self-esteem. If your favorite team performs poorly, you can always blame poor management for not assembling the team properly; when your fantasy team performs poorly, you bear the onus of blame as the assembler of the team.

Social sport

The motivation of social sport has been classified under the terms "socializing" or "social interaction" in past research (Farquhar and Meeds, 2007; Roy and Goss, 2007; Spinda and Haridakis, 2008). However, further classification was warranted with Ruihley and Hardin (2011a) bifurcating a general socialization category into the two areas of camaraderie and social sport. The former was defined as more relationship-oriented and the latter focused on discussions surrounding the sporting activity itself. In Ruihley and Hardin's (2011a) investigation, online focus groups revealed a great deal of insight regarding the socialization factor. In open-ended comments, participants revealed that they used fantasy sport activities not only to be with people, associate with a group, or have something in common with friends and family, but also to talk specifically about sports with a multitude of societal constituencies. This notion was then supported with the quantitative analysis split of factor, refining social sport in the fantasy sport context to the actual act of talking with someone about sport, including sharing opinions about leagues, teams, and players and debating sport-related issues and events (Hur *et al.*, 2007; Ruihley and Hardin, 2011a).

Surveillance

Finally, the motivation of surveillance can also be equated to information gathering. Using the construct entitled "information" to describe the motivation to gather a "large volume of sport information and to learn about things happening in the sport world" (p. 86), Seo and Green (2008) discuss this type of motivation as it relates to online sports consumption. In addition, Hur, Ko, and Valacich (2008) also use the term information when describing online sports consumption. Their research highlights the idea that sport consumers have a need to "gain up-to-date information regarding sport teams, players, products, and current trends of sport business" (p. 525).

For traditional sports fans, actions of surveillance may revolve around a single athlete, hometown team, division/conference, or league as a whole. A fan may know a large amount of information about a particular university baseball team, including numerous facts about the team's history, schedule, player backgrounds, coach profiles and team/player statistics. Being this heavily invested may cause fans to seek out seemingly benign information about the weather, competitors, injury updates, and post-season scenarios, as they desire any information that could be deemed both related and new to the team they avidly follow. Such examples constitute "surveying the landscape" to become a better-informed fan.

Fantasy sport participants frequently act in the same manner, albeit sometimes in more byzantine ways. Whereas a traditional fan may survey the landscape as it relates to one team or conference, fantasy sport owners could survey the landscape for their own teams, focusing on as many as 20–30 players (depending on the sport), as well as a range of free agents available to add to their current teams. Studying this many players creates an interconnected and knowledgeable consumer.

Therefore, fantasy sport surveillance is measured utilizing items from past research (Hur, Ko, and Valacich, 2007; Ruihley and Hardin, 2011a; Seo and Green, 2008), including items concentrated on easy access to large amounts of sports information, obtaining information about players and teams, being up to date with sports information, and having an increased awareness as it relates to sports.

Analysis of motivations

To analyze the motivations of fantasy sport participants, an online questionnaire was created specifically for this text and completed by 1,201 participants from the United States and Canada. The questionnaire was designed to glean more information about the fantasy sport experience and the motivation for play and is offered in Table 2.1.

Leaning on industry insight, sport consumption research, and fantasy sport research (Billings and Ruihley, 2013; Hur *et al.*, 2007; Farquhar and Meeds, 2007; Ruihley and Hardin, 2011a; Ruihley and Hardin, 2011b; Seo and Green, 2008; Spinda and Haridakis, 2008; Wann, Schrader and Wilson, 1999), the questionnaire specifically addressed demographic representation, sports media consumption, and motivation for participation. Qualitative (i.e. open-ended questions) and quantitative (i.e. Likert scales) items were utilized. For the purposes of this chapter on why people participate, we will offer results on two levels. First, multiple quantitative views of the motivations are addressed to determine the most important fantasy sport motivations, including (a) rank order of the motivational averages, (b) linear relationship to enjoyment, and (c) linear relationship to overall satisfaction in the activity. Second, qualitative responses to the open-ended questions are provided to support the definitions and findings for each motivational area.

Motivations of North American fantasy sport users

In rank order, the aforementioned motivation factors are organized by their mean factor score (anchored by 1 [strongly disagree] to 7 [strongly agree]) as to why the respondents (n= 1,201) reported participating in fantasy sport. The top three motivating factors are self-esteem (μ= 6.0), social sport (μ= 5.8), and control (μ= 5.8). The bottom three motivating factors are pass time (μ= 5.0), Ownership (μ= 4.4), and escape (μ= 4.0). For a complete list please see Table 2.2.

While the top factors are most noteworthy, it is also significant that all factors reached the median level of 4.0 [mid-range between strongly disagree and strongly agree]. While escape could be seen as featuring scores equally between the two poles, every other factor should be interpreted as being either moderately or substantially agreed upon in regard to motivations for the play of these 1,201 respondents.

Motivation and enjoyment of North American participants

Every organization aims to produce enjoyment in a product, service, or business relationship. Consumer enjoyment of a product is likely to enhance the chances of

Table 2.1 Motivation and scale items used

Motivation	Author
Arousal	
Because I get pumped up when I am watching my team	Wann, 1995
I like the stimulation I get from participating in fantasy sport	Wann, 1995
I enjoy being emotionally aroused by the competition	Wann, 1995
Camaraderie	
It allows me to get along with others	Seo & Green, 2008
I enjoy the camaraderie of other participants	Spinda & Haridakis, 2008
It helps me stay in touch with people	Ruihley & Hardin, 2011a
Competition	
I enjoy winning	Ruihley & Hardin, 2011a
Winning the league prize (recognition, trophy, money, etc.) is important to me	Ruihley & Hardin, 2011a
Being better than my opponent is important	Ruihley & Hardin, 2011a
I enjoy competing against other team owners/managers	Ruihley & Hardin, 2011a
Control and ownership	
I feel like a general manger of an actual sports team	Spinda & Haridakis, 2008
I feel like a coach of a team	Spinda & Haridakis, 2008
It's like having a team in my control	Spinda & Haridakis, 2008
I enjoy controlling the lineup	Spinda & Haridakis, 2008
I enjoy drafting my own players	Ruihley & Hardin, 2011a
I love the feeling of ownership	Spinda & Haridakis, 2008
Escape	
I can escape from reality	Seo & Green, 2008
I can forget about work	Seo & Green, 2008
It allows me to escape from my daily routine	Hur, Ko, & Valacich, 2007
Fanship	
I consider myself a fan of sport	Seo & Green, 2008
I am a huge fan of sport in general	Seo & Green, 2008
I am a big fan of my favorite team	Seo & Green, 2008
Pass time	
It gives me something to do to occupy my time	Seo & Green, 2008
It passes the time away, particularly when I'm bored	Seo & Green, 2008
It is something to do in my free time	Seo & Green, 2008
Self-esteem	
I feel a personal sense of achievement when my fantasy team does well	Spinda & Haridakis, 2008
I feel like I have won when my fantasy team wins	Spinda & Haridakis, 2008
Winning at fantasy sport improves my self-esteem	Spinda & Haridakis, 2008
Social sport	
I like to chat with people about sports	Hur, Ko, & Valacich, 2007
I like to share my opinions about sport teams and players	Hur, Ko, & Valacich, 2007
I enjoy debating sport-related issues	Hur, Ko, & Valacich, 2007
Surveillance	
It provides me with quick and easy access to large volumes of sport information	Seo & Green, 2008
I am able to obtain a wide range of sport information	Seo & Green, 2008
I can learn about things happening in the sport world	Hur, Ko, & Valacich, 2007
It provides me with more information about real players and teams	Ruihley & Hardin, 2011a
The fantasy sport related information obtained from my participation is useful	Hur, Ko, & Valacich, 2007
I feel more up-to-date with sport information	Ruihley & Hardin, 2011a
It provides me with an increased awareness of the athletes and teams	Ruihley & Hardin, 2011a

Table 2.2 Mean rank of motivating factors

Variable	Mean[a]
Self-esteem	6.0 (SD=0.9)
Social sport	5.8 (SD=1.1)
Control	5.8 (SD=1.1)
Competition	5.7 (SD=1.0)
Camaraderie	5.7 (SD=1.2)
Arousal	5.6 (SD=1.1)
Surveillance	5.5 (SD=1.3)
Pass time	5.0 (SD=1.5)
Ownership	4.4 (SD=1.6)
Escape	4.0 (SD=1.6)

[a]Measured on a 1 to 7 Likert-type scale.

repeat purchase, viewing, or amplified consumption. Utilizing the copious work conducted on the topic of media enjoyment, (Oliver, 1993; Raney, 2003; Zillmann, 1988; Zillmann and Bryant, 1994), Nabi and Kremar (2004) define media enjoyment as a "general positive disposition toward and liking of media content" (p. 290), arguing that one develops beliefs about an attitude object "through direct or indirect experience with it" and that those beliefs will have "favorable or unfavorable" implications on the attitude (p. 292). In turn, these experiences with an attitude object will have a major impact on the underlying structure of the attitude, influencing cognitive, affective, and behavioral responses (Eagly and Chaiken, 1993; Nabi and Kremar, 2004).

As part of the data collection for this study, enjoyment was measured and subjects asked to what extent fantasy sport is fun, enjoyable, and a hobby (Billings and Ruihley, 2013). A stepwise regression was conducted to determine what motivational factors significantly weigh on enjoyment. The results of the regression indicated four variables weighing the heaviest on enjoyment: self-esteem, arousal, social sport, and pass time. These factors accounted for 29.3% of total variance (r =.543, r^2 =.295, Adjusted r^2 =.293), meaning that even when combined, the four factors still did not comprise one third of the total contribution to overall enjoyment, leading to the conclusion that fantasy sport participation is a very hybrid and complex mechanism for understanding. Nonetheless, standardized coefficient data show four factors with significant beta weights. Self-Esteem was the heaviest factor, possessing a higher beta weight (β=.233, p=.000) than arousal (β=.221, p=.000), social sport (β=.176, p=.000), and pass time (β= .140, p=.000).

Motivation and overall satisfaction of North American participants

Satisfaction is just as crucial as enjoyment as a factor for understanding overall motivation. Satisfaction was measured with constructs forcing participants to reminisce about their experiences within fantasy sport to determine whether they were glad they chose to participate (Ruihley and Hardin, 2011a). A stepwise regression was conducted, producing four variables significantly influencing overall satisfaction: self-esteem, social sport, arousal, and surveillance. Those four variables accounted for 20.0% of total variance $(r=.450, r^2=.202$, Adjusted $r^2=.200)$. Standardized coefficient data show four factors with significant beta weights. Self-esteem again was the heaviest factor (as it was for enjoyment), having a higher beta weight $(\beta=.230, p=.000)$ than social sport $(\beta=.171, p=.000)$, arousal $(\beta=.142, p=.000)$, and surveillance $(\beta=.076, p=.011)$.

Top-ranked motivation scores

Since Table 2.2 reports overall mean scores, it was also valuable to determine the strength of each of these scores. Such strengths can be measured in simple standard deviations, but an ancillary analysis was conducted to provide more meaningful results. The scores were reconstituted in a binary notion of "top" motivation (the highest score each participant rendered among all motivational scores) and "other" motivations (any score that was not the top score among all motivations). Table 2.3 reports how these "top" motivations ultimately change rankings of why people play fantasy sport:

Note that the percentages offered in this table add up to more than 100% because some people had more than one "top" motivation (e.g., scoring three different variables as a "7"). In this case, all three of those were entered into this analysis as "top" motivations. As delineated in Table 2.3, the top two motivations stay the same in this new formulation of the data compared to the results featured in Table 2.2, with self-esteem and social sport again scoring higher than all other motivations. However, the order of the next three factors does change, with camaraderie now trumping both control and competition when solely considering the primary motivation for play above all others. It appears that the desire for belonging and bonding with friends and family is more central to many experiences than is the desire to control one's own team or to compete on a regular basis.

Table 2.3 Comparison of motive means and number of occurrences motive is top of participants' motive set

Mean factor average[a]	Motive	Motive	Top motive for participants[b]
6.0 (SD=0.9)	Self-esteem	Self-esteem	459, 38.2%
5.8 (SD=1.1)	Social sport	Social sport	417, 34.7%
5.8 (SD=1.1)	Control	Camaraderie	340, 28.3%
5.7 (SD=1.0)	Competition	Control	296, 24.6%
5.7 (SD=1.2)	Camaraderie	Competition	230, 19.2%
5.6 (SD=1.1)	Arousal	Arousal	226, 18.8%
5.5 (SD=1.3)	Surveillance	Surveillance	222, 18.5%
5.0 (SD=1.5)	Pass time	Pass time	195, 16.2%
4.4 (SD=1.6)	Ownership	Ownership	98, 8.2%
4.0 (SD=1.6)	Escape	Escape	72, 6.0%

[a]Motivations measured on Likert-type scale (Anchored by 1=Strongly Disagree to 7= Strongly Agree).
[b]Occurrences of multiple-tied top motives included in count.

Qualitative definition support

Of course, numbers frequently fail to tell the whole story. Examining the words of the participants and the descriptions of their experience is important in seeing the entire picture of fantasy sport play; much can be learned from the open-ended responses of the participants. For example, when asked why they participate in fantasy sport, 394 comments (37.3% of 1056 comments) had some form of the word "friend" in it and 389 comments (36.8% of 1056 comments) specifically mentioned some form of the word "compete/competition." For the purposes of this chapter, the open-ended comments are used to provide additional background on each of the analyzed motivations defined earlier in this chapter. A word cloud combining the collective responses of all respondents is offered in Figure 2.1.

The following paragraphs include direct quotes from fantasy sport participants to support each motivation.

- **Arousal** was best described when a fantasy sport participant stated that participating in fantasy sport is the favorite time of year because the "highs and lows one goes through and the excitement of winning is an awesome feeling."
- In support of the **camaraderie** motivation, one participant stated, "I enjoy the camaraderie and how having a league with old acquaintances allows those relationships to stay strong even with people moving away and losing touch other times of the year. With coworkers, it allows me to meet and get to know [them] better during the draft or during the season."
- Many of the participants spoke of their "competitive nature" or drive to be the best. Some comments about **competition** mentioned fantasy sport as a competitive outlet for their own fading athletic abilities, while others spoke of a lack of personal athletic skills—fantasy sport was a replacement for athletic activity. To that point, one participant stated that fantasy sport is another way to compete since he/she "wasn't good enough to continue playing after high school, and it's a way to stay involved in a sense." Another simply enjoyed the competition, indicating that part of the enjoyment came from matching "wits against the world."
- A quote embodying **control** and **ownership** came from a participant describing the fantasy sport experience. The participant described fantasy sport as an activity allowing him or her "to feel and act like a GM [General Manager] of [a] team. Getting to control everything from the draft, weekly adds/drops, trades, lineups, and keepers keeps it exciting every week." Another participant added, "I am not a professional athlete and I never will be. I will never coach a real sports team, so fantasy sports is my closest bet."
- To describe the use of fantasy sport as a way to **escape**, one participant explained that the activity "allow[s] the participant to become more actively engaged in the detailed-nature of the sports world, ultimately, as an escape from the doldrums of modern life." Another participant said fantasy sport "keeps me entertained for five months at a minimal cost. [I] enjoy the distraction when not working otherwise I used to bring a lot of my work home."

Figure 2.1 Word cloud of open-ended responses of participants

- **Fanship** is measured to gauge the magnitude to which someone is a fan of a particular sport or league. Fantasy sport supports fanship in many ways. One participant stated that being a fantasy sport participant has provided "extra rooting interest in games in which I am not a fan." Another participant said, "Fantasy football allows me to get more interested in the NFL and find any game intriguing." To help describe this motivation and validate fantasy sport participation as an additional level of sport fandom (Billings and Ruihley, 2013), one participant commented, "Fantasy sport is just an extension of my passion for sports. I enjoy watching/participating in sport and fantasy [sport] just enhances this experience."

- The motivation of **social sport** encompasses talking about sports and fantasy sport-related content. Participation offers ample opportunities for these conversations, and several statements validate this as a key motivational factor. One participant offered, "I feel more knowledgeable about so many players on so many different teams that I can hold intelligent conversations with die-hard fans of these teams regarding their outlook for the upcoming season." Another participant said, "I ... enjoy friendly trash talking and trading with fellow fantasy players." Said another: "I ... enjoy talking with the other owners in the leagues. Talking stats, whose player is better, whose team is better, [and] who drafted better."

- In describing the motivation of **surveillance**, one fantasy participant described fantasy sport as an "interesting way" to keep involved in sport. The participant added, "It ... helps me to be more in-depth with analysis and statistics and helps me keep up to date with news." Another participant commented that "fantasy sport gives me a chance to sort through data on players and teams, trying to best my friends in discerning the market—who's going to break out, who's going to slump, where can I find value in this group of players over what I have now? I also love following sport; I enjoy being seen as a source of information, and fantasy leagues take the knowledge depth to the next level. The allure of fantasy sport is the potential for being seen as more knowledgeable than others."

- Similar to the escape motivation is **passing time**. One participant stated that fantasy sport is a good way to pass time and that it is "enjoyable to talk about over beers." Another participant mentioned that fantasy football can assist in passing time now that he or she is "able to watch football games, outside of my own team's games, and pay more attention to individual players."

Importance of knowledge

In addition to all of the motivational factors that relate to fantasy sport participation, prior scholarship underscores the role of knowledge—both the acquisition and rending of it—as essential to many fantasy sport players. After all, the stereotype of the "sports geek," who plays fantasy games in their mother's basement, only takes hold if there is some basis for that assumption, with some studies indeed uncovering a high degree of interest in what is constituted here as mavenism and Schwabism.

First, one must understand the background and justification for both of these concepts. Consumer market research is vital to organizations because of the potential impact results have on advertising campaigns, product integration, and/ or overall attitudes about a service. Organizations often attempt to learn more about consumers, locating the people who are willing to share their thoughts about a product or service with those who are close to them—opinion leaders. Referencing seminal work of Lazarsfeld, Berelson, and Gaudet (1948), Feick and Price (1987) define opinion leaders as "individuals who acted as information brokers intervening between mass media sources and the opinions and choices of the population" (p. 84). Opinion leadership, then, is characterized as an occurrence "when individuals try to influence the purchasing behavior of other consumers in specific product fields" (Flynn, Goldsmith, and Eastman, 1996, p. 138). These types of consumers are important because of the influence they can have over other consumers. This type of interpersonal communication is influential and persuasive when it comes to purchasing behaviors and intentions. These types of leaders are often seen as being an "expert within a specific product category [that] both spreads and is consulted for information about that specific product category" (Stokburger-Sauer and Hoyer, 2009, p. 101; King and Summers, 1970).

Feick and Price (1987) introduced a different type of influential ally in marketplace research: "market mavens" who are defined as "individuals who have information about many kinds of products, places to shop, and other facets of markets, and initiate discussions with consumers and respond to request from consumers for market information" (p. 85). Mavens are considered different from opinion leaders because they are not product specific experts; rather they possess general knowledge of the marketplace. Mavens are not required to be early adopters of the product and are not required to be users of the product in which they have information; they are typically people of knowledge, even if they lack the motivation or capacity to act upon that knowledge. Goldsmith, Clark, and Goldsmith (2006) state that mavens are "exposed to a variety of media where they seek out and acquire information about products, services, stores, and shopping and buying in general" (p. 412).

Market mavens have been described as highly attentive, involved, and interested consumers within a marketplace (Chelminski and Coulter, 2007; Clark, Goldsmith, and Goldsmith, 2008; Feick and Price, 1987), qualities that could just as easily be ascribed to fantasy sport participants. These are also consumers that enjoy sharing their information, knowledge, expertise, and experience with others (Higie, Feick, and Price, 1987; Stokburger-Sauer and Hoyer, 2009). Market mavens are important not only for their loyalty to marketplace knowledge and information-seeking attitude but also because of their willingness to inform others. With the word-of-mouth potential, the market maven is an influential consumer, also representing a possible ally or enemy to an organization. This concept is included in this text because of the potential connection between sport, fantasy sport, and mavenism. Fantasy sport participants could be knowledgeable about sport in general or about a specific sport league or team. Many participants enjoy and may even be considered experts in sport statistics.

Additionally, Ruihley and Runyan (2010) introduce a concept for these types of experts, the sport fan believing he/she is an expert in sport statistics and information. This know-it-all is actively engaging in "Schwabism." This term is based on the ESPN trivia show *Stump the Schwab;* a now-defunct program pitting know-it-all sport fans—who thought they knew everything there was to know about sport—against ESPN master statistician (and self-proclaimed sport trivia maven), Howie Schwab. The overall aim of the show was to prove that many avid sport fans, in fact, do *not* know it all.

Using scale items tested in prior research (Billings and Ruihley, 2013; Ruihley, 2010), participants in this research were tested on factors of mavenism and Schwabism. Measured on a seven-point scale (1 = least associated to 7 = most associated), participants identified with mavenism with a score of 6.0/7.0 and 87.3% of the sample scoring a 5.0 or higher. Participants identified Schwabism with a score of 5.0/7.0 and 52.2% of the sample scoring a 5.0 or higher. These figures prove that this group of 1,201 fantasy sport participants are highly attentive, in tune with products, and regularly share information with others—sometimes compulsively. In addition, one of every two fantasy participants feels they "know it all" in regard to fantasy sport play. Given that most leagues feature 10–12 teams, the presence of an average of 5–6 know-it-alls per league likely results in interesting competition and conversation between participants. Additionally, knowing that 50% of participants feel that they have the right answers is appropriate once one considers that activity is based on trying to out-manage other competitors. It would be unsurprising to find similar levels of sports teams who feel they have the ingredients to win a championship.

Applying the *Why*

Understanding *why* people consume and participate in fantasy sport is important for many reasons. Three of the most crucial areas of application are segmentation, content, and promotion, as these three aspects assist in identifying and recruiting consumers, providing them with a product they desire, and retaining their consumption from season to season.

Market segmentation is defined as identifying pockets of consumers based on their common or homogeneous needs (Doyle and Saunders, 1985; Shank, 2009) and as recognizing that people are different and have unique backgrounds and purchase frequencies (Mullin, Hardy, and Sutton, 1993; 2007). In early research, Smith (1956) states that segmentation is "based upon developments on the demand side of the market and represents a rational and more precise adjustment of product and marketing effort to consumer or user requirements" (p. 5). Segmenting the consumer is important so that organizations do not overgeneralize the market (Smith, 1956). The research presented in this book assists in determining different types of motivations and their influence on aspects and factors associated with fantasy sport participation.

Segmentation is a key aspect because not all sport fans are created equal; therefore, the fantasy sport participant should not be considered just another sports fan. In a comparison of traditional sport fans and fantasy sport participants, Billings and Ruihley (2013) found fantasy sport participants to be to be amplified fans, while starkly different from traditional sport consumers. Their findings favor this claim in reporting a near doubling factor in rate of media consumption, a higher fanship factor score, higher scores on the majority of all factor scores, and major differences in how people in each group perceive their sports knowledge. Knowing there are differences and understanding more about a specific set of consumers is vital for organizations to effectively and efficiently use their marketing resources—bringing segmentation to the fore. Pedersen, Miloch, and Laucella (2007) state that without market segmentation, an organization may not be able to "effectively communicate its core messages to consumers" (p. 245). Segmentation offers the unique ability to shape marketing and advertising strategies to a specific set of homogeneous consumers.

Content is a second major practical implication of this form of motivational and consumption research. Discerning the factors leading to higher enjoyment (self-esteem, arousal, social sport, and pass time) and overall satisfaction (self-esteem, social sport, arousal, and surveillance) can assist with decisions about the type of content placed on fantasy sport host sites and related sites. With the noted motivational results, content may be altered to meet the participants' desire to gather statistics, survey a team or athlete's performance, or socialize with others about the activity. Many fantasy sport host websites grant access to an enormous amount of information immediately on the site. Prolonging the stay on the host site allows for more page views and in turn, more eyeballs on advertisements. Offering quick and easy access to message boards or other social networking applications gives participants a platform for sharing their thoughts, opinions, trash talk, or overall experience with others. In many instances, message boards are embedded into the host site of the fantasy sport league or even on the scoreboard page. The scoreboard can easily become the proverbial water cooler for league members to share and have discussions. In one particular design, CBS Sports' fantasy sites have a permanently embedded league message board at the bottom of the scoreboard. The message board is continually present regardless of what matchup a participant may be following. This is unique because it encompasses all the games and all league participants can be gathered in the same place with one topic in mind—their fantasy sport team, results, and overall experience.

Promotion is the third and final major marketing implication in applying the *why*. Shank (2009) simply defines promotion as "all forms of communication to consumers" (p. 443). When developing a marketing or promotional campaign targeting fantasy sport, it is useful to understand the consumer habits of fantasy sport participants, motivations of participation, media consumption, and influences on enjoyment and satisfaction. Communicating the excitement, competitive nature, social benefits, and surveillance features of this activity would be important after the results indicated the importance of each aspect. Also, promoting the use of message boards as part of the fantasy sport experience would encourage participants to consider using this feature and, in turn, become more social.

Conclusion

The goal of this chapter is to inform the reader of the type of person consuming fantasy sport. Definitions were provided and supported by qualitative responses to open-ended questions. We used quantitative data to determine the most compelling motivations in rank order and as they relate to enjoyment and overall satisfaction. In addition, two types of sport knowledge, mavenism and Schwabism, were discussed. As the discussion reveals, knowing more about the consumer is important for many reasons. Researchers and practitioners alike are able to expand their knowledge and expectations of the industry with this kind of specific information. Boundaries of research, marketing, content, and advertising can also be magnified as a result of this information. The next chapter will use this data to break down the information further to provide more insights on the immense group of people known as fantasy sport users, detailing how people of different backgrounds, identities, and fanship levels love the games within fantasy sport— yet sometimes for divergent reasons.

3 Different sports, different identities

Player's heterogeneity and fantasy sport play

Sports fans share common bonds and speak common languages, yet are quite different in virtually all aspects of their fandom—varying in their fervor, their dress, their game-day rituals, and the degree of their loyalties (Earnheardt, Haridakis, and Hugenberg, 2012). Fantasy sport participants have many presumed similarities, such as the correlation between fantasy sport participation and some degree of overall fandom. But while fantasy sport participants have typically been labeled as monolithic, this is far from the case. As Billings and Ruihley (2013) argue:

> The easy conclusion that 'fantasy sport participants are just like sports fans but with higher motivations and more investment' is, indeed, too simple a summary. The modern sports fan is anything from homogenous in terms of their economic and cultural backgrounds just as any multimillion-person collective would be. (p. 21)

Based on the findings of Chapter 2, one could easily make the same mistake, labeling fantasy participants as a version of "sports fandom on steroids" while creating a prototype that could be viewed as the Sports Fan 2.0. Given that all of the motivations for play were found to be moderately to extremely high, with the lone exception of escapism, and the finding that these motivations are significantly higher than for traditional sports fandom (Billings and Ruihley, 2013), one could conclude that in terms of motivation, fantasy sport is like the proverbial rising tide that lifts all boats. Such a simplistic conclusion would be in error—and would render this current chapter unnecessary.

As the first two chapters demonstrated, there are broad truisms that characterize fantasy sport participants: they consume substantially more media than do traditional sports fans, for example, and self-esteem is the highest motivating factor for play. These conclusions are indeed supported and thus have a great deal of heuristic value. In this chapter, however, we will build on these broad conceptions and examine the considerable nuance within the fantasy sport community. Later in the book (in Chapter 5), we will examine how the majority of participants play for free while a much smaller number wager substantial amounts of their take-home pay in grand attempts to win high-stakes leagues. This chapter delves into the role of specific demographic variables in influencing who participates in fantasy sport and that larger, critical question of *why*. We will explore how men and women play with different frequency and for different reasons—and the fact that these reasons change when they move from single to married status (or vice versa). We will examine the way younger players are motivated to play for significantly different reasons than are older players. We will explore many different notions of how a player's personal and social identity (Sherif and Hovland, 1961) creates a wide variation among fantasy sport participants. Perhaps everyone speaks the same sports language and follows the same games. Nevertheless, understanding key differences among the participants helps to illuminate the diversity among the wide swath of North American participants that the fantasy sport industry now encompasses.

Importance of studying demographics

Deconstructing motivational and consumption differences within the play of fantasy sport participants is critical from both cultural and marketing standpoints. From a cultural standpoint, fantasy sport participants tend to be regarded as a somewhat fringe group, despite the activity's popularity. (Subcultures frequently are pigeonholed into narrow constructs; consider, for instance, the *Star Trek* fans frequently mocked as "Trekkies."). Overall, of course, sports fans have enjoyed a broadening of their archetype as the number of people who follow the games continues to increase. Consider that in 2006, the average rating for an NFL game in the United States was 66% higher than the network prime time average; in 2012, the NFL rating is 151% higher than that average (Gregory, 2012). As sports have become the largest events in media—the Olympic Games have been called the "biggest show on television" (Billings, 2008, p. 1)—society accepts that sports fandom overlaps with virtually all circles of modern life. Thus, while fantasy sport still is considered niche (see Ruihley and Billings, 2013), the truth is that it is embedded within many forms of modern culture, especially in the United States. Insights that expand the narrow characterizations of fantasy sport participants are critical for defining the industry as an accurate, robust form.

Understanding consumers is also an important facet of any organization or business (Laurent, 2013). From production and pricing to placement and promotion, knowing more about the consumer assists with the most important aspects of selling a product. Demographic, geographic, psychographic, consumption, and product usage attributes all factor into sophisticated analyses, a process briefly visited in Chapter 2 and known as segmentation. Segmentation is an important part of understanding any large consumer base and can be defined as "dividing a large, diverse group with multiple attributes into smaller groups with distinctive characteristics" (Schwartz and Hunter, 2012, p. 6). Such specific demographic groups have "similar needs and desires" (Schwartz and Hunter, 2008, p. 6) and will respond to marketing efforts in similar manners. Scholars such as Mullin, Hardy, and Sutton (2007) have noted the potential problems with assuming heterogeneity outside of demographic distinctions while assuming homogeneity inside these demographic groups. As such, it becomes important to test motivations for groups such as fantasy sport participants from a macro level (as in Chapter 2) with a direct comparison to micro-level demographic trends (discussed in the current chapter). Since fantasy sport has an estimated 35 million consumers (Fantasy Sport Trade Association, 2012a), placing its participants into a single, static composite can be a costly management mistake resulting in shortsighted sociological understandings.

One of the first tasks prior to segmentation involves gathering the information needed to determine whether the market is "quite heterogeneous" (Fullerton, 2010, p. 62). Without question, the fantasy sport industry of the twenty-first century is demonstrably more heterogeneous than in its early years, yet it still is referred to in a homogenous manner, ranging from the 1980s conception of the quintessential fantasy geek articulated by Barmack and Handelman (2006) to modern profiles of the obsessive fan in a football jersey surrounded by multiple media screens and countless reports of statistical minutiae. To provide as much useful information as possible about this customer base, the following sections focus on several breakdowns including areas of age, race, gender, marital status, and favored fantasy sport. Each section will report, analyze, and discuss general sports consumption and attitudes, fantasy consumption and attitudes, and fantasy sport motives.

Highlights of overall sample

Our sample of 1,201 North American participants is an active group of fantasy sport participants. Results indicate that a relatively high 41% (n=506) of fantasy participants are involved in three or more different types of fantasy sport, with 31% (n=371) involved in two different sports, and 27% (n=324) involved in just one fantasy sport. The top fantasy sports in terms of participation are football (93% of sample), baseball (59%), and basketball (37%). Regarding participants' favorite fantasy sport, football again was at the top of the spectrum (n=833; 69.4%), followed by baseball (n=232; 19.3%), and hockey (n=89; 7.4%). Table 3.1 offers comprehensive frequencies and rankings in these areas.

From a consumption standpoint, the participants should be classified as heavy consumers of sports media. Results indicate an average sport consumption of 17.8 hours (SD=12.9) per week and specific fantasy-oriented sports media consumption of 8.7 hours per week.

Breakdown 1: fantasy sport and age of participant

Because of generational differences resulting from the digital divide and the mainstreaming of fantasy sport play in the mid-1990s, age is a rich and useful variable for examining media consumption and attitudes—particularly for fantasy sport, because it has a generally youthful appeal. Since fantasy sport activity is most likely to begin in high school or college, it is an activity largely divided by age, with those 35+ considerably more likely to have participated in some sort of newspaper-based fantasy sport league before migrating online, and those younger than 35 likely to have never experienced fantasy sport in anything but an online format.

Table 3.1 Top participated fantasy sports

Sport	Number of participants	Percentage of sample
Football*	1,115	93%
Baseball*	714	59%
Basketball	439	37%
Hockey*	271	23%
Professional golf	103	9%
College sport	97	8%
Auto racing	73	6%

* Top three favored fantasy sports.

Consider the varying role of the Internet by age of user. The Pew Internet and the American Life Project annually reports generational age breakdowns of online activities. In a 2012 report on general Internet use and home broadband connections, Pew (2012b) revealed that American adult Internet use is at its peak, with 85% saturation. Within that group of Internet users, 84% frequently go online to find information about a hobby or interest and—more specifically relevant to this book—52% seeking out news or information related to sports (Pew, 2012b). Another Pew report (Pew, 2012a) highlights generational breakdowns, finding that a staggering 97% of those aged 18–29 use the Internet, with the percentage declining from that point as age rises. Other groups use the Internet at the following rates: ages 30–49, 86%; ages 50–64, 81%; and ages 65+, 53%. Pew also has explored generational differences in the pursuit of hobbies online. Their report found that adult male Internet users under the age of 50 were among the "most likely groups to pursue their hobbies online" (p. 2). This age of 50 appeared to be a point of demarcation for the Pew study, which found that, for instance, 86% of people under the age of 29 sought out their hobbies online while only 62% of people 65+ said the same.

Age breakdown, as a segmentation strategy, also is evident in many media guides/kits provided by media organizations. For example, *Sports Illustrated*'s SI.com media and promotional materials give a breakdown of the consumer ("SI Audience Profile," 2012). This audience profile highlights areas of gender, household income, education, employment, average age, and the specific age percentage of 18–34 years. The title of this audience profile states, "SI.com is the #1 place to reach young, professional, affluent, educated sports fans" (para. 1). In another example, ESPN's Department of Integrated Media Research has conducted research focusing on the "Life Stages of the Sports Fan." This sports media empire placed emphasis on age demographics within the following areas: sports avidity, sports participation, time spent with various forms of sports media, types of sports programming viewed, and co-viewing behavior. In one section, the report claims "all [the aforementioned areas] differ based on what life stage a sports fan is in" (Enoch, 2011, p. 2). All had significant differences by age, with some being substantial deviations. For example, 72% of all teenaged males reported an interest in professional basketball, yet only 43% of those 65+ reported an interest in this sport. Similar contrasts could be reported throughout—women over the age of 65 were almost twice as likely to report an interest in the Olympics than were women younger than 35.

The link between age and fantasy sport consumption has been specifically addressed in academic research, yet only once and with a non-representative sample. Brown, Billings, and Ruihley (2012) examined age differences between younger (18–34) and older groups (35+). Results indicate that the younger fantasy sport participants are a more engaged demographic. Reasons for this engagement-based age-oriented claim included:

* Younger participants consume an average of 4.2 more hours of sports programming per week than do older participants (19.3 hours compared to 15.1 hours).
* Younger participants have significantly higher self-identification of being fans (6.44) than do older participants (6.12) based on the seven-point Likert measure developed by Seo and Green (2008).
* Younger participants were more likely than older participants to view themselves as having more sports knowledge based on the concept of Schwabism (Ruihley and Runyan, 2010) and willingness to share that knowledge based on the measurement of mavenism (Feick and Price, 1987; Walsh, Gwinner, and Swanson, 2004).
* Younger participants had significantly higher motivation factor scores when using fantasy sport for (a) entertainment, (b) passing time, and (c) surveying the media and technological landscape for fantasy sport information.

Understanding how different age groups adopt and use the Internet along with seeking out hobbies or interests online can meaningfully assist sales, advertising, and marketing-based selections and strategies. Uncovering the differences between age groups in consumption, fantasy motivations and other related factors is important to consider when dealing with any sports organization, especially when the organization evolves from technology to a high degree as in fantasy sport. This research highlights further age comparisons focusing specifically on the fantasy consumer. To gain a clearer picture of the fantasy sport participant, we explored comparisons of sport and fantasy sport consumption, as well as attitudes. This exploration utilized age and generational information. Analyses are offered based on two methods of dividing the data: (1) comparing two age groups of 18–34 years and 35+; and (2) comparing four age groups consisting of 18–24 years, 25–34 years, 35–44 years, and 45+. The former analysis was offered as a form of consistency for comparison to the previous work from Brown, Billings and Ruihley (2012); the latter was offered as a means for comprehending more subtle age differences consistent with Internet-based divisions illuminated by Pew Research (2012a and 2012b). In both cases, the use of a more representative sample in this current survey will greatly enhance the generalizability of findings.

Comparing motives based on age

Utilizing statistical analyses (i.e. Analysis of Variance; ANOVA) to compare the combined motivational means of the two age groups (18–34 and 35+), seven motivation factors were measured on a seven-point Likert scale, with three motivating factors emerging as statistically different between the two demographic groups. The differing motivations consisted of surveillance (Younger 5.53/Older 5.25), camaraderie (Younger 5.74/Older 5.44), and social sport (Younger 6.01/Older 5.43). The factor of pass time (Younger 5.05/Older 4.79), while shown to be different by the numbers, was slightly outside the acceptable range of statistical significance. A full list of motivations between the two groups is offered in Table 3.2.

Table 3.2 Fantasy sport motivational differences of two-age groups

Motive	18-34 (n=845)	35 and up (n=356)	All (n=1,201)	Significance
Arousal	5.6	5.5	**5.6**	.044
Camaraderie	5.7	5.4	**5.6**	.000*
Competition	5.7	5.6	**5.7**	.039
Control	5.8	5.8	**5.8**	.329
Escape	4.0	4.1	**4.0**	.075
Ownership	4.3	4.5	**4.4**	.044
Pass time	5.0	4.8	**5.0**	.006
Self-esteem	6.1	6.0	**6.0**	.079
Surveillance	5.5	5.3	**5.4**	.001[a]
Social sport	6.0	5.4	**5.8**	.000[a]

Note: Motivations measured on Likert-type scale (Anchored by 1=Strongly Disagree to 7= Strongly Agree).
[a] Significant based on Bonferroni's correction of p.<.005.

As previewed, the sample of fantasy sport participants was segmented further into four age groups: 18–24, 25–34, 35–44, and 45+. Utilizing expanded statistical analyses (i.e. ANOVA and post hoc tests), comparisons of the motivational means of the four groups resulted in three motivating factors housing significantly different pairings. The bulleted list below highlights these significant pairings. To view all the motivation breakdowns of the four age groups, please see Table 3.3.

- Camaraderie, 18–24 (μ=5.7) significantly different from 45+ (μ=5.2)
- Camaraderie, 25–34 (μ=5.7) significantly different from 45+ (μ=5.2)
- Pass Time, 18–24 (μ=5.3) significantly different from 35–44 (μ=4.8)
- Pass Time, 18–24 (μ=5.3) significantly different from 45+ (μ=4.7)
- Surveillance, 18–24 (μ=5.7) significantly different from 35–44 (μ=5.3)
- Surveillance, 18–24 (μ=5.7) significantly different from 45+ (μ=5.2)

Comparing sport consumption and attitudes based on age

It is worth noting differences in sports consumption and attitudinal levels when one compares the two age groups (18–34 and 35+). The measured factors focusing

Table 3.3 Fantasy sport motivational differences of four-age groups

Motive	18-24 (n=229)	25-34 (n=616)	35-44 (n=258)	45 and up (n=98)	All (n=1,201)
Arousal	5.8	5.6	5.5	5.4	**5.6**
Camaraderie	5.7[b]	5.7[b]	5.5	5.2[a]	**5.6**
Competition	5.9	5.7	5.6	5.6	**5.7**
Control	5.9	5.7	5.8	5.7	**5.8**
Escape	3.9	4.0	4.2	4.0	**4.0**
Ownership	4.6	4.2	4.5	4.6	**4.4**
Pass time	5.3[a]	5.0	4.8[b]	4.7[b]	**5.0**
Self-esteem	6.2	6.0	6.0	5.9	**6.0**
Surveillance	5.7[a]	5.5	5.3[b]	5.2[b]	**5.4**
Social sport	6.2	5.9	5.5	5.2	**5.8**

Note: Motivations measured on Likert-type scale (Anchored by 1=Strongly Disagree to 7= Strongly Agree).
[a b] Marker a is significantly different from marker(s) b (within each row of the motivation) accounting for Bonferroni's correction of p.<.005.

on general sport consumption were overall fanship, satisfaction with their sports experience, and hours consuming sports. Comparing overall fanship between the two age groups revealed a significant difference, with the younger age group mean at 6.7 and the older group mean at 6.4 (measured on a seven-point scale). Significant differences also emerged in satisfaction with their sports experience; the younger group mean was 6.2 while the older group mean was 6.0. When asked about the number of hours spent consuming sports, the younger group indicated spending 18.38 hours, while the older age group indicated 16.73 hours, a significant difference, yet not nearly as wide a gap as the four hours found in Brown, Billings, and Ruihley (2012). Consult Table 3.4 for complete details.

Dividing the age groups into four groups (18–24, 25–34, 35–44, and 45+) also yielded interesting results. In a comparison of sports fanship, significant differences were abundant, with fanship decreasing as the groups aged. For overall sports satisfaction, the 18–24 group mean was significantly higher than all other groups. However, measuring the hours of sports consumption did not produce any significant differences. The youngest group indicated spending 19.1 hours consuming sports; the highest consumption of all age groups. The group with the least amount of consumption hours was the 35–44 age group, averaging 16.4 hours. Please see Table 3.5 for a complete list of differences.

Table 3.4 General sport consumption and attitudes comparing of two-age groups

Factor	18-34	35 and up	Significance
Fanship	6.7	6.4	.000[a]
Sport satisfaction	6.2	6.0	.013[a]
Sport hours	18.4	16.7	.046

[a] Significant at Bonferroni's adjusted p.<0.016.

Table 3.5 General sport consumption and attitudes comparing four-age groups

Motive	18-24[a] (n=229)	25-34[b] (n=616)	35-44[c] (n=258)	45 and up[d] (n=98)	All (n=1,201)
Fanship	6.8[bcd]	6.7[abd]	6.5[ab]	6.2[ab]	6.6
Sport satisfaction	6.4[bcd]	6.1[a]	6.0[a]	6.0[a]	6.1
Sport hours	19.1	18.1	16.4	17.5	17.9

Note: Motivations measured on Likert-type scale (Anchored by 1=Strongly Disagree to 7= Strongly Agree). Letter next to numbers identifies with labeled age group significance (Bonferroni's p < .016).

Comparing fantasy consumption and attitudes based on age

Significant differences were found when comparing fantasy consumption and attitude levels between the two age groups. While means for the factors of enjoyment and satisfaction with the activity were high, the younger group means were significantly higher than means of the older group for both factors. Both age groups had extremely strong factor scores relating to their intention to return to the activity (6.9 and 6.8 out of 7.0) and significant differences were not found comparing the two groups. The older age group devoted, on average, 9.91 hours per week to fantasy sport while the younger group devoted 8.15 hours per week to the activity.

Significant differences emerged from examining the four age groups in isolation. The mean for enjoyment was significantly higher for the 18–24 group (μ=6.6) than the mean for the group of 45+ (μ=6.4). Similarly, fantasy sport satisfaction had one pairing of significant difference between the 18–24 (μ=6.8) and 45+ (μ=6.6). All age groups had very high factor scores relating to their intention to return to the activity (μ=6.9 and 6.8 out of 7.0) meaning that significant differences were not found when pairing any two groups for comparison. When measuring average hours per week devoted to fantasy gaming, the mean increased, as did the age of each group. The lowest mean (18–24 years) was 8.0 hours while the largest mean (45+) was 12.0. (Statistical note: 45+ group mean was significantly different from 18–24 group mean and 25–34 group mean). Consult Table 3.7 for expanded details.

Table 3.6 Fantasy consumption and attitudes comparing two-age groups

Motive	18-34	35 and up	Significance
Enjoyment	6.6	6.5	.004[a]
Fantasy satisfaction	6.7	6.6	.002[a]
Future intentions	6.9	6.8	.034
Hours fantasy	8.1	9.9	.002[a]

Note: Motivations measured on Likert-type scale (Anchored by 1=Strongly Disagree to 7= Strongly Agree).
[a] Identifies significant difference (Bonferroni's p < .012) between the two groups.

Table 3.7 Fantasy consumption and attitudes comparing four-age groups

Motive	18-24[a] (n=229)	25-34[b] (n=616)	35-44[c] (n=258)	45 and up[d] (n=98)	All (n=1,201)
Enjoyment	6.6[d]	6.5	6.5	6.4[a]	6.5
Fantasy satisfaction	6.8[d]	6.7	6.6	6.6[a]	6.7
Future intentions	6.9	6.9	6.9	6.8	6.9
Hours fantasy	8.0[d]	8.2[d]	9.1	12.0[ab]	8.7

[a] First three measured on Likert-type scale (Anchored by 1=Strongly Disagree to 7= Strongly Agree).
Note: Letter next to numbers identifies significance (Bonferroni's p < .012) with age group.

Ramifications of age findings

When considering life cycles, one must note the youngest demographic as vital for both the current and future state of the activity. From an industry standpoint, understanding such an influential market can lead to success in selling and promoting the product. It is no surprise that younger consumers are technologically savvy, possessing myriad options when consuming sports media. Projecting to the future and the strength of the industry decades from now, retaining specific demographic motivational and consumption tendencies has the potential to enhance its long-term stability. This demographic, most likely the newest of sport fans based on age, proved to be slightly different from their more mature fantasy sport counterparts regarding both general sport fandom and consumption.

One of the key findings throughout both age examinations (two-group and four-group tests) was the significant difference between the youngest and oldest groups. When examined for sports consumption, the 18–34 (two-group test) and 18–24 (four-group test) groups possessed a higher self-identified fanship score as well as more satisfaction with their overall sports experience over the compared groups. A perceived drawback to being a fantasy sport participant is that this activity can disrupt "normal" fandom, forcing participants to support many players from different teams. With this type of interest, it could be easy to lose sight of individual teams and records, bringing to mind our previously cited observation by Sandomir (2002) about fantasy sport participants who "root, root, root for no team" (para. 1). This is a valid and important concern: one might assume fantasy sport is creating a new type of fan, one who does not care for team accomplishments or the team game. However, at this time and with this sample, those in the younger demographic still identify strongly as sports fans and report satisfaction with their current sports experience.

Considerable attention has focused on the sports consumption of fantasy sport participants compared with that of general sports fans. ESPN's Department of Integrated Media Research (2010) reports media consumption of fantasy sport participants as triple the consumption of ESPN-specific media offerings, compared to general sports fans (22:40 hours compared to 7:06 hours). In addition, Billings and Ruihley (2013) found a near doubling of overall sports media consumption among fantasy sport participants (18:00 hours compared to 9:36 hours). In this research, the number of hours consuming sports media by age group, while offering some levels of difference, did not rise to the level of statistical significance between young and old. While the manner and type of sports consumed may change, the differences in relationship to fantasy sport generally did not change to any meaningful extent.

There were, however, several noteworthy findings regarding fantasy sport that possess life cycle-oriented implications. The youngest measured group reported more enjoyment and satisfaction with the activity than did the older participants, a crucial distinction. Keeping the younger demographic satisfied and wanting to return to the activity is not a difficult task; they identified higher motivations relating to camaraderie and surveillance than did their older counterparts. Trying to facilitate that type of camaraderie goes beyond providing the activity of conversation, it involves creating the venue, software, chat rooms, and message boards hosting such interactions (Ruihley and Hardin, 2011b). The same postulate could be argued regarding satisfaction with a search for fantasy-oriented information. As fantasy sport participants—especially the young—survey the media landscape for information, they find a multitude of ways to garner timely and comprehensive sports-related information. Understanding that younger consumers are more likely to be motivated because of surveillance desires requires placing more emphasis on reaching those consumers in their own social and media environment, a void the fantasy sport world appears ready to fill. At the 2012 Fantasy Sport Trade Association Winter Conference, CBSSports.com, embracing the open-platform format, announced that it would allow "outside developers full access to its fantasy sports games and underlying data to develop commercial products, in hopes of developing the kind of marketplace for fantasy games that Apple's iTunes Store has created for apps in general" (Fisher, 2012, para. 1). Fisher adds:

> For developers, especially small operations, it means access to a wealth of consumer data that would have been impossible to compile or buy on their own, and a new way to reach sports fans. For users, it will mean a marketplace populated with new apps designed to enhance their fantasy sports experience. (Fisher, 2012, para. 4)

This type of access grants developers and fantasy sport stakeholders (with technology skills) an opportunity to shape and form their fantasy sport experience to look, feel, and act the way they want. A key point Fisher offered in the previous statement is that this is a "new way to reach sports stakeholders" (para. 4). Even though fantasy sport is considered a contemporary sporting experience and a technologically savvy game, it also must continually innovate. The industry cannot become stale in regard to distribution, marketing, or design; the younger demographic now demands such perpetual improvements (Bilton, 2011).

On the opposite end of the age spectrum, another telling result unfolded among the older fantasy participants. The oldest group—whether split or divided in quartiles in each test respectively—consumed significantly more hours than did their younger peers. In test one, comparing two age groups, the older group (35 and beyond) identified consumption of fantasy sport as 9.9 hours per week while those younger than 35 reported just 8.1 hours of weekly consumption. Within the four-group comparison, this gap became more noticeable, as those 45 and older consumed four more hours of fantasy sport than did their 18–24-year-old counterparts (12.0 hours compared to 8.0 hours).

Returning to the implications for businesses, there are many ways to promote a company or product on a fantasy sport website. From banner ads on the home page to promotional videos in the live scoreboard, organizations cleverly incorporate advertising. As an example, Figure 3.1 shows the marketing efforts of insurance provider Geico on a home page for an ESPN fantasy football league. Knowing that one age group is substantially more likely than another to spend more time online is important when considering the stickiness of the activity or the website. Such stickiness has been long regarded as critical to advancing an industry because it involves "repetitive visits to and use of a preferred website because of a deeply held commitment to reuse the website consistently in the future" (Li, Browne, and Wetherbe, 2006, p. 106). The more a viewer visits and is satisfied with the content of an organization's message or product, the more likely he or she is to view online advertising. As stated in Chapter 2, segmentation and targeting jointly assist organizations in effectively and efficiently reaching their

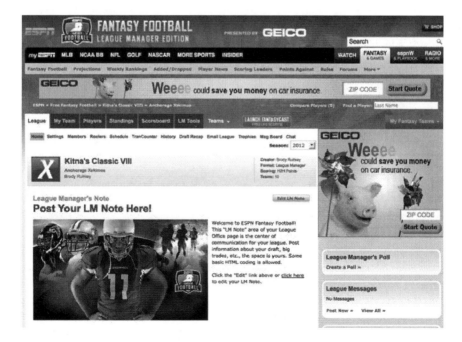

Figure 3.1 Geico advertising on ESPN Fantasy Football website

key public constituencies, all while using an appropriate amount of resources. As applied to the number of hours consuming fantasy sport media, knowing that the older demographic is spending significantly more time with the activity allows organizations to use this information when selecting advertising partners and developing those demographic-specific messages.

Breakdown 2: fantasy sport and race

Even with widespread growth and popularity, one homogenous group still represents the overwhelming majority of fantasy sport participants: Caucasian men. The Fantasy Sport Trade Association (2012b) supports this claim in its overview of industry demographics, reporting participation at 87% male and 88% Caucasian. The lack of racial diversity among fantasy sport participants inspired a column in *ESPN The Magazine* entitled "Up Front: To heck with fantasy. I'm about what's real" (Smith, 2008). In his article, ESPN's Stephen A. Smith (2008) voiced his concern over the disparity in the lack of minorities participating in this activity:

> I'm not surprised to learn that so few blacks are among the 30 million people who participate in fantasy sports. I've always thought that a lot of these guys (and 96% of them are guys) are nerds desperately in need of more sociable leisure time activities. Leisure time for black folks historically consists of direct interaction, the kind of experience you get at a family barbecue or hanging out with friends. Sitting in front of a computer screen pretending to be Bill Parcells? Sounds like work to me. (para. 6)

Smith (2008) further discusses the disparity of race in fantasy sport with Dr. Kim Beason, an Associate Professor at the University of Mississippi and the CEO of Fantasy Sport Research Specialists. Beason's research illustrates that there are specific types of jobs that are more conducive to participating in fantasy sport because of variables related to Internet access and fluidity of occupational expectations. Beason states:

> When you break it down, it appears the [racial] disparity has to do with a critical mass of individuals who are together discussing fantasy sports ... Up to now that has mostly occurred in the white workplace. And a lot of time, it's on the Internet. (Smith, 2008, para. 6)

This ESPN commentary suggests that marketing efforts, using the hip-hop culture and the ever-widening reach of the web, are ways fantasy sport organizations can broaden their diversity and attract more minorities, allowing new consumers to test and become involved with the product. Nonetheless, there appears to be a queasy undercurrent particular to Black/African-American participation in fantasy sport because of the requirement that players (a majority of whom are black) are "owned" by fantasy sport participants (a majority of whom are white). This slavery comparison may seem far-fetched to some, yet it may be a barrier of unique concern to potential Black participants.

All of these possible reasons for the lack of racial diversity within fantasy sport are best classified as hunches; further investigation is needed to address specific reasons why minorities are not participating in this activity. Word-of-mouth recruitment of friends, family members, and coworkers is a major way people become interested and ultimately involved in fantasy sport. If the only word-of-mouth activity occurring in fantasy sport is between culturally similar people, then growth is limited. In the absence of insights about nonparticipation, marketing efforts will continue to overlook large groups of people.

One academic study has attempted to address fantasy sport and race, albeit limited in scope. Agyemang and Ballouli (2010) presented research focusing on the barriers present for African-American entry into fantasy sport participation. After conducting semi-structure in-depth interviews of 15 African-American participants, they found that the major themes for nonparticipation were: economic factors, lack of interest, technological limitations, and lack of fellowship.

When conducting research on randomly sampled fantasy sport participants, it is difficult to obtain a widely diverse set of participants because a representative sample is inherently racially homogeneous. For the survey associated with this text, that was the case. Given that all but 122 respondents were White/Caucasian, filtered information by race proved unattainable. Still, race was scrutinized within a White/non-White binary to determine differences between the two groups, as one clearly represents an in-group and the other a presumed out-group (see Tajfel and Turner, 1986). Thus, all minorities were combined to produce a subsample of 122 non-Caucasian fantasy sport participants (37 Latinos, 29 Asian, 19 African-American, and 37 who classified their race as "other"). It is important to note that while the comparisons and averages are significant, there is a 9 to 1 Caucasian to non-Caucasian participant ratio.

Viewing the motives of each group, one interesting finding is that the non-Caucasian group has higher means for 8 of the 10 motives. Participating in the activity to pass time has a higher mean for the Caucasian participants, while the motive of social sport emerged with the same mean; yet on all other factors, non-Caucasians scored higher. Because of the smaller sample of non-Caucasians, however, it is important to note that only two of the higher motives for non-Caucasians (arousal and self-esteem) were significantly different from the Caucasian means, as outlined in Table 3.8.

Sometimes non-significant findings are just as important as those of significance. That could be the case when examining sports and fantasy sport consumption and attitudes by race. Comparing the means for overall sports fanship, satisfaction with their sport experience, and hours of sport consumption produced no significant differences between the compared groups. Similarly, all differences were not significant when focusing on fantasy consumption areas of enjoyment, satisfaction with the activity, intent to return to the activity, and hours of fantasy consumption. Table 3.9 provides a complete list of means.

Table 3.8 Motivation compared between Caucasian and non-Caucasian

Caucasian (n=1079)	Motive	Non-Caucasian (n=122)
5.6	Arousal[a]	**5.9**
5.6	Camaraderie	**5.8**
5.7	Competition	**5.9**
5.8	Control	**5.9**
4.0	Escape	**4.1**
4.4	Ownership	**4.6**
5.0	Pass time	4.9
6.0	Self-esteem[a]	**6.3**
5.4	Surveillance	**5.6**
5.8	Social sport	5.8

Note: Motivations measured on Likert-type scale (Anchored by 1=Strongly Disagree to 7= Strongly Agree).
[a] Identifies significant difference (Bonferroni's p < .005) between the two groups.

Table 3.9 Sport and fantasy sport consumption and attitudes comparing Caucasian and non-Caucasian

Motive	Caucasian	Non-Caucasian	Significance
Fanship[a]	6.6	6.7	.190
Sport experience satisfaction[a]	6.1	6.2	.292
Consumption hours sport	17.7	19.9	.073
Fantasy enjoyment[a]	6.5	6.6	.147
Fantasy satisfaction[a]	6.7	6.7	.984
Fantasy return intentions[a]	6.9	6.9	.411
Consumption hours fantasy	8.5	10.1	.064

[a] Note: Measured on Likert-type scale (Anchored by 1=Strongly Disagree to 7= Strongly Agree).
[b] Identifies significant difference (Bonferroni's p < .007) between the two groups.

Ramifications of race-based findings

This small sample of non-Caucasian fantasy participants produced motivational and consumption results suggesting that there is no inherent reason why non-Caucasian participants would be less likely to enjoy playing fantasy sport if they sought to participate. The motives of arousal and self-esteem were the only two *statistically significant* motives, and those favored non-Caucasians. Such findings could either (a) suggest enhanced motivations for play by non-Caucasians or (b) signal that the only non-Caucasians participating are heavy sports fans with high motivations to embrace this sport-based ancillary activity.

Regarding the two statistically significant differences, arousal involves the positive stress or eustress and self-esteem outlines a person's personal pride in his or her team. While arousal does not have a significant linear relationship with intentions to return to the activity, self-esteem does. This means that as the self-esteem factor rises, intent to return to the activity does as well. Shifting to overall satisfaction in the fantasy sport experience, both arousal and self-esteem have a significant linear relationship with satisfaction. These two findings raise questions as to why more non-Caucasians are not participating in fantasy sport, as the two motivations this group rates more highly than do Caucasians are major factors in overall satisfaction and intent to return to the activity.

The other motives (e.g. camaraderie, competition, control, escape, ownership, pass time, surveillance, and social sport) were not significantly different. In addition, there were no significant differences in consumption of general sport and fantasy activity. With the research results producing so much similarity and so little difference between Caucasians and non-Caucasians, how can the activity's racial disparity be explained? Professor Beason's aforementioned comments suggest that fantasy sport started and thrived in the white workplace, so there is a preconceived notion of fantasy sport occupying a white space within culture that makes others feel less welcome. ESPN's Stephen A. Smith (2008) argues that it is the social nature of the activity in and of itself that divides races (barbecues vs computers screens), but that hardly seems fair when classifying such large, diverse racial groups in the United States. Lastly, Agyemang and Ballouli (2010) argue that economic factors, lack of interest, technological limitations, and lack of fellowship are reasons for lack of participation by African-Americans. With the findings in this research showing no difference in fantasy interest, consumption, or social motivation, it is hard to believe that the listed reasons from Beason, Smith, Agyemang, and Ballouli would cause a 9 to 1 ratio of Caucasian to non-Caucasian fantasy participants.

Looking at the early days of fantasy sport, during the 1980s and 1990s, it would be easy to blame the white workplace and the perception that the activity was for lonely, nerdy misanthropes as a reason why other parts of America failed to embrace fantasy play. However, technological advancements, accessibility to the game, social networking fantasy features and websites, and proliferation of the 24-hour sports viewing and news cycles have removed many entry and social barriers and made the game much more mainstream, popular, and often even "cool" within many parts of society. In particular, obvious advancements in social networking, such as the early effort of MySpace and the continued growth of Facebook, Twitter, and LinkedIn, now provide platforms or devices that facilitate fantasy sport participation.

The fact remains that there is a presumed lack of interest in fantasy sport on the part of non-Caucasians. We employ the word "presumed" because it remains unclear whether non-Whites opt not to participate in fantasy sport because of (a) lack of interest or (b) feelings that they are not welcome and that fantasy sport is not for them. Further research should seek answers to these two potential problems. Industry and societal remedies will hinge on whether minorities feel ambivalent or hostile toward the activity.

Another important area for future research is the manner in which minorities are learning about and viewing the activity. Simple word-of-mouth is apparently not reaching a diverse set of people. Future research should query: do marketing and advertising campaigns send racialized messages? What are the messages? What media, channels, and television shows are being used for marketing? What are the demographics of those selections? The fantasy sport industry must answer these questions to allow future mainstreaming of the activity. If there are problems in the strategic marketing plan, demographic profiles will continue to reflect a homogenous consumer base, while alienating both potential consumers and uninitiated fans of the activity.

The industry's own leadership also may provide insights in regard to the race issue. Examining the leaders of the industry (as will be done in Chapter 4) suggests that this truly is a Caucasian man's activity. An example from American popular culture, while fictional, seems to be realistic when it comes to the demographic portrayed: on the FX television show focusing on fantasy sport, *The League*, the cast is entirely Caucasian and almost all male.

A rudimentary glance at the primary fantasy sport organizations suggests that their demographics are similar to those of the television show. The leading trade organization for fantasy sport activity, the Fantasy Sport Trade Association, consists of an all-Caucasian board of directors with 14 men and 2 women. Sirius XM Fantasy Radio has dozens of hosts for its shows and activities. But of the 43 active hosts as of the fall of 2012, 42 are Caucasian and only one, NFL running back Maurice Jones-Drew, is African-American. Among the more popular fantasy hosting organizations, ESPN highlights 9 football writers/experts, all Caucasian and just one female; Yahoo! identifies 6 writers on its website, all Caucasian males. In sum, non-Caucasians who might consider participating in fantasy sport will find few non-Caucasian role models among those in highly visible and influential positions.

Figure 3.2 The cast in FX's television show *The League*

Breakdown 3: gender and fantasy sport

Fantasy sport participation by gender is another area warranting consideration, because of the lack of female participants. The Fantasy Sport Trade Association (2012b) reports that 13% of fantasy sport participants are women. Simple math tells us that this is a segment of 4.5 million women in a 35-million consumer industry— and that if fantasy sport is to grow, the majority of potential participants are women. It was a goal of this research to compare men and women fantasy sport participants in the described areas, yet the sample only resulted in an ungeneralizable number of 36 women respondents among the total of 1,201. Lack of women participants is a finding in itself, and while results of this particular data collection did not allow significant comparisons and analysis, two previous studies have specifically examined gender and fantasy sport. We will use them to illuminate this area because it is vital for understanding some key demographic trends in fantasy sport.

Study 1

The first critical examination of fantasy sport focused on masculine privilege being reinforced within the activity. Davis and Duncan (2006) examined this topic by conducting an exploratory multi-method study of the experiences of fantasy sport league participants. Through a critical perspective, the authors use textual analysis of fantasy sport websites, personal observation, and focus group interviews to determine how masculinity presents itself in fantasy sport participation. They found that masculinity was both reaffirmed and fortified through the issues of control, importance of sports knowledge, competition, bonding, differences in gendered participation, and the use of men's sports more than women's sports. Davis and Duncan (2006) believe that masculinity through control comes into fantasy sport through the way male participants place "themselves in the shoes of authoritative and affluent team owners. Through businesslike ventures, masculinity is fortified by accepting and exercising social power" (Davis and Duncan, 2006, p. 252). The authors suggest that this control may reflect the experience and the "social power that predominantly White, male owners of professional sports teams possess on a daily basis" (Davis and Duncan, 2006, p. 252).

The work of Davis and Duncan (2006) underscored ways men "keep women in a socially inferior position" (p. 258; DiIorio, 1989). While it is fair to assume there are sexist, insecure men participating in fantasy sport, it seems premature, at the least, to conclude that such beliefs expressed in one focus group represent the thinking of every type of man involved in fantasy sport. Further investigation could lean heavily on this work and these findings to create a more generalizable look at this issue.

Ramifications of Study 1

The first study approaches the issue of gender in fantasy sport from a critical perspective. To be fair, Davis and Duncan (2006) were not arguing for generalizability of their work, but rather struck an exploratory note regarding the examination of gender normativity within this sport-based activity. Sports topics, overall, reinforce many stereotypes, attitudes, and cultural norms that typically do not provide opinions, coverage, or inclusion of men and women in any equivalent measure (see Hardin and Whiteside, 2009; Hargreaves, 1994; Wenner, 1993). The question is whether these gender issues transfer to fantasy sport participation.

Three main factors could be argued as primary in the view of fantasy sport as a sexist reinforcement of masculinity. First, differential participation rates clearly inform even the casual onlooker that the activity involves men almost exclusively. Highlighting the schism even more dramatically is the fact that most men never experience fantasy sport in leagues that include women. Given the relative scarcity of women in current leagues, men may be reluctant to invite women to participate, as a gender outlier is likely to experience the hostility of being ostracized. Women could form their own private leagues (and have), but that in turn perpetuates a troubling, separate-but-equal mindset, probably akin to what Crosset (1995) describes women dealing with in the world of private golf courses.

A second way masculine/sexist sentiments are being produced through fantasy sport is through information gathering and obtaining sports knowledge. Information seeking or surveillance is an essential component and motivation for participation in fantasy sport, as indicated throughout this and other research (Billings and Ruihley, 2013; Davis and Duncan, 2006; Dwyer and Drayer, 2010; Farquhar and Meeds, 2008; Ruihley and Billings, 2013; Ruihley and Hardin, 2011a). Consequently, sports knowledge offers men the indirect chance to "evaluate what it means to be a man" and reaffirm their masculinity (Davis and Duncan, 2006, p. 254; Hartmann, 2003). This affirmation is reinforced as participants accumulate knowledge of sports news, injuries, and player characteristics. With this knowledge, fantasy sport participants can operate better teams, conduct more efficient trades, and ultimately, have more success in an equation that is directly attributable to their knowledge. Thus, fantasy sport becomes a breeding ground of sports statistics aficionados. Women might not share this drive to compete, win, and dominate through statistics; in fact, it likely impedes their desire to participate. Many already feel like second-class citizens as sports fans (see Whiteside and Hardin, 2011) and do not wish to replicate the negative experience in the realm of fantasy sport.

A third and final factor that reinforces masculinity is that nearly all of the current leagues are built around men's sports. In the two popular fantasy sports of professional football and professional baseball, as well as in leagues focusing on men's professional basketball, golf, hockey, or NASCAR, most fantasy sport activities center on male athletes. The results of the focus group conducted by Davis and Duncan (2006) discussed this precise issue. Participant comments and the results offered explanations and emphasis on athletic ability, strength, power, speed, physicality, and aggressiveness as reasons why men's sports may be used over women's sports. However, the major reason for building fantasy sports around men's games is that the entire sports media complex is similarly built around men's games. Messner and Cooky (2010) found that ESPN's *SportsCenter* offered an all-time low of 1.4% of all coverage devoted to women's sports. Previous research reports similar stories of disempowerment and outright omission of women's sports (Dworkin and Messner, 2002; Duncan and Hasbrook, 1988; Duncan and Messner, 2000). Eastman and Billings (2001) even found women's sports as a whole receiving less time in a given month than coverage of a high school spelling bee. Given such a paucity of media coverage, it is unsurprising that few fantasy leagues are built around women's sports leagues, particularly considering the high desire of participants to consume large numbers of mediated games to see if their teams win or lose. Ruihley and Hardin (2013) discovered that nearly 80% of sampled fantasy sport participants use television to enhance their fantasy sport experience. Since men's sports conservatively could be estimated to embody more than 90% of the coverage in all sports media (Coakley, 2007; Duncan and Messner, 1998) it is easy for fantasy sport participants to use television and radio to follow the sporting events in which their fantasy sport teams are participating. The lack of coverage of women's sports may be a reason why women opt not to play fantasy sport, although the notion that women are more likely to seek out women's sports media is currently unsupported (Whiteside and Hardin, 2011).

Ramifications of Study 2

Utilizing purposive and targeted sampling techniques, Ruihley and Billings (2013) specifically targeted women fantasy sport participants, gathering responses from 348 men and 182 women with an average age of 30.1 years (men 28.4 years and women 33.3 years). Men were reported as predominantly single (n=165, 47.4%) and married (n=114, 32.8%), while women identified as being married (n=74, 40.7%) and single (n=51, 28.0%). Additionally, focusing on consumption of sports-related content, men self-reported consuming 21.3 hours while women reported consuming 11.6 hours. Research questions and findings focused on differences with fantasy consumption, fanship, how each view their sports knowledge, and motivations to participate in fantasy sport.

The results revealed significant differences in the ways men and women take part in fantasy sport. Findings showed men have participated longer (5.8 years vs 3.2 years) and in more leagues than women (3.1 leagues and 1.5 years). Self-reporting the amount of time devoted to fantasy sport per week, men averaged 4.7 hours while women averaged 3.5 hours per week. Ruihley and Billings (2013) utilized and altered Seo and Green's (2008) scale items to measure fanship. The sample's overall average factor score, based on a seven-point scale, was 6.3, yet men averaged 6.5 while women 6.1, a significant difference.

Other inquiries sought to determine whether any differences existed between how these two groups perceive their fantasy sport knowledge as measured by concepts of mavenism and Schwabism. Men were found to have higher scores on mavenism (4.8 vs 3.9) and Schwabism (4.3 vs 2.9). Statistically speaking, the existing differences in these two sports knowledge areas are statistically significant (p=.000, while accounting for Bonferroni's correction $p < .025$).

The final comparison made in Ruihley and Billings' (2013) work on fantasy sport gender differences examined motivations for participation. The motives measured were arousal, entertainment, enjoyment, escape, pass time, self-esteem, and surveillance. Somewhat surprisingly, only two of the seven measured items revealed any type of significant differences. Motivating factors of enjoyment and passing time were averaged higher for men (enjoyment 5.8 vs 5.3 and passing time 5.2 vs 4.9). All other factor averages were nearly identical between the genders. Table 3.10 reports these factors by gender.

The top motives for each gender seem to tell similar stories regarding the fantasy sport experience for both men and women. The top three motivations for men were, in order: (a) Enjoyment, (b) Entertainment, and (c) Surveillance. The top three for women were the same, yet in a different order: (a) Entertainment, (b) Surveillance, and (c) Enjoyment (Ruihley and Billings, 2013).

Concluding thoughts on gender and fantasy sport

These two foundational studies provide useful heuristics for deciphering the complicated and tenuous relationship between gender and fantasy sport. Two of the main areas addressed in both examinations were information gathering (i.e. surveillance) and consumption. Ruihley and Billings (2013) argued that "hours alone do not necessarily emphasize the importance of having sport knowledge—the most appropriate measure could be comparing consumption of non-fantasy playing sports fans with their fantasy-participant counterparts" . In later work from the authors, Billings and Ruihley (2013) did compare traditional fans and fantasy sport participants, finding that that participating in fantasy sport resulted in a "near-identical increase in consumption for each gender: 63% for men and 61% for women when compared to their non-fantasy playing sports fan counterparts" (Ruihley and Billings, 2013, in press,). This result suggests that once women become involved with fantasy sport, their time of consumption increases in almost exactly the same proportion as that of male participants. With that type of statement and result, it is important for the fantasy sport industry to redouble efforts to garner additional women as participants. While the group may be small in numbers, they have similar

Table 3.10 Motivational differences by gender (Ruihley and Billings, 2013 MCS)

| Variable | Fantasy sport participants | | | F | Sig. |
	Men (n=348)	Women (n=182)	Total (N=530)		
Arousal	4.8 (SD=1.5)	4.7 (SD=1.5)	4.7 (SD=1.5)	0.087	.768
Entertainment	5.8 (SD=1.0)	5.6 (SD=1.1)	5.7 (SD=1.1)	2.573	.109
Enjoymenta	5.8 (SD=1.1)	5.3 (SD=1.3)	5.6 (SD=1.2)	19.449	**.000**
Escape	3.9 (SD=1.5)	4.1 (SD=1.5)	3.9 (SD=1.5)	1.918	.167
Pass timea	5.2 (SD=1.3)	4.9 (SD=1.5)	5.1 (SD=1.4)	7.341	**.007**
Self-esteem	5.0 (SD=1.3)	5.0 (SD=1.3)	5.0 (SD=1.3)	0.105	.746
Surveillance	5.6 (SD=1.2)	5.4 (SD=1.2)	5.5 (SD=1.2)	4.016	**.046**

[a] = Statistically significant difference between men and women at Bonferonni's correction (p<.007).

characteristics and motives for the activity. Not only could additional revenue be generated, the process also would embrace a more inclusive role for fantasy sport in mainstream culture.

Breakdown 4: favored fantasy sport

As reported earlier, based on Fantasy Sport Trade Association research, the top two fantasy sports are American football played in the National Football League (72% of participants play) and baseball played in Major League Baseball (37%). Rates of play at major sites such as CBSSports.com, ESPN, and Yahoo! confirm this ranking. While one could view the sports as complementary, with seasons that largely occupy different months of the calendar, these sports are vastly different from each other in terms of players, schedules, statistics, and season details. A fantasy football season often encompasses 16 weeks with a single game in each, while MLB teams play 162 games with 5 to 7 games per week. Within the survey for this book, we sought to determine motivational differences based on a player's favorite sport. Within the study, players naming football as their top fantasy sport had an average age of 31.3 with the majority of the group being male (96.0%), Caucasian (89.4%), single (51.1%), and college educated (77.1%). The MLB group's average age was 32.7, with the majority being male (99.1%), Caucasian (93.1%), single (51.3%), and college educated (80.6%). Based on these overall demographic breakdowns, these two groups appear to be nearly identical. However, we wanted to analyze the motivational differences between the two groups to identify any differences in the participants' reasons for playing.

Motives and sport consumption

It seems logical to assume that NFL and MLB players might have different motivations for participating in fantasy sport. Perhaps passing time would be a greater priority for the MLB group, because of baseball's prolonged season. On the other hand, those favoring the NFL might be motivated by the excitement, arousal, and tough plays of football competition. There might be other motivational distinctions, as well, since there are so many differences between the two sports. However, no statistically significant differences were found in a comparison of NFL and MLB participants. See Table 3.11 for complete list of motivations and significance level.

General and fantasy sport consumption

Beyond these similarities, other findings confirm the relative uniformity of the two groups. When queried regarding their overall sport consumption, those favoring the NFL indicated spending 17.79 hours consuming sport, while the group favoring MLB indicated 18.29 hours. Both groups were measured on overall sport fanship, and results indicate the NFL group (μ=6.64) having a higher

Table 3.11 Fantasy sport motivational differences of favored fantasy sport

NFL (n=833)	Motive	MLB (n=232)
5.7	Arousal	5.4
5.7	Camaraderie	5.5
5.8	Competition	5.5
5.8	Control	5.7
4.0	Escape	3.9
4.4	Ownership	4.3
5.0	Pass time	5.0
6.1	Self-esteem	5.9
5.4	Surveillance	5.5
5.9	Social sport	5.8

Note: Motivations measured on Likert-type scale (Anchored by 1=Strongly Disagree to 7= Strongly Agree).
[a] Significant based on Bonferroni's correction of p.<.005.

mean than the MLB group (μ=6.56). Participants also were asked about their overall sport satisfaction: the groups were nearly equal with the NFL averaging 6.2 and MLB 6.1 on a 7-point scale.

Non-significant differences also were found in fantasy consumption levels between the group favoring baseball and the group favoring football. The baseball-favoring group had been involved in fantasy sport an average of two years longer (11.1 years of fantasy play) than had the NFL group (9.1 years of fantasy play). The MLB group devoted, on average, 9.2 hours per week to fantasy sport while the NFL group devoted 8.3 hours per week to the activity. Enjoyment was nearly equal for both groups with rounded averages at 6.5. Satisfaction in the fantasy sport experience favored MLB (μ=6.73) over NFL (μ=6.69), but not by statistically significant levels. Intentions to return to fantasy sport in the following season also favored MLB (μ=6.91) over NFL (μ=6.88). Table 3.12 offers complete comparisons of sport and fantasy consumption between these two major sports.

Table 3.12 Sport and fantasy sport consumption and attitudes comparing favored fantasy sport

Motive	NFL (n=833)	MLB (n=232)	Significance
Fanship[a]	6.6	6.6	.059
Sport experience satisfaction[a]	6.2	6.1	.487
Consumption hours sport	17.8	18.2	.704
Fantasy enjoyment[a]	6.5	6.5	.915
Fantasy satisfaction[a]	6.7	6.7	.029
Fantasy return intentions[a]	6.9	6.9	.057
Consumption hours fantasy	8.3	9.1	.650

[a] Note: Measured on Likert-type scale (Anchored by 1=Strongly Disagree to 7= Strongly Agree).
[b] Identifies significant difference (Bonferroni's p < .007) between the two groups.

Breakdown 5: fantasy sport and marital Status

Levy (2009) states that it may be easy to dismiss fantasy sport participants as "geeks living perhaps tucked away in their parents' basement," (p. 197) but studies do not support that description. As other research (Billings and Ruihley, 2013; Ruihley and Hardin, 2011a) corroborates, fantasy sport participants are more likely than the general population to be educated, employed in managerial and professional occupations, possess above-average incomes, and be married with children. In fact, the Fantasy Sport Trade Association reports that 73% of fantasy participants are married (Fantasy Sport Trade Association, 2012a). Although not aligning with the industry estimates, one of the interesting breakdowns of the data in this book is a near 50/50 split as far as marital status. Of the 1,201 participants 582 (48.5%) were married while 619 (51.5%) were not—providing two robust groups for comparison.

An analysis was conducted comparing sport and fantasy sport attitudes and consumption between single and married participants. When comparing general sport consumption and attitudes, significant differences rose for overall sport fanship, sport satisfaction, and hours consuming sport. Those married (μ=6.5) had a lower mean fanship factor score than those not married (μ=6.7), a lower mean measuring overall sport satisfaction (married, 6.1; unmarried, 6.2), and fewer hours consuming sport (married, 16.6; unmarried, 19.1). Similar to trends in general sport fanship and consumption, it appears single people spend more hours enjoying sports than do their married counterparts.

When comparing the same two groups regarding fantasy consumption, there are no significant differences in the areas of fantasy enjoyment, satisfaction with the activity, intent to return to the activity, and hours of fantasy consumption. However, three differences did emerge in motivations to participate in the activity. The unmarried reported higher motivation scores in pass time (married, 4.8; unmarried, 5.1), surveillance (married, 5.3; unmarried, 5.6), and social sport (married, 5.7; unmarried, 6.0) than did married people. For a list of all motives and means, consult Table 3.13.

Table 3.13 Fantasy sport motivational differences of married/unmarried

Motive	Married (n=582)	Not married (n=619)	Total (n=1,201)	Significance
Arousal	5.5	5.8	**5.6**	.013
Camaraderie	5.7	5.6	**5.6**	.936
Competition	5.7	5.7	**5.7**	.418
Control	5.8	5.8	**5.8**	.928
Escape	4.1	4.0	**4.0**	.391
Ownership	4.3	4.5	**4.4**	.151
Pass time	4.8	5.1	**5.0**	.001[a]
Self-esteem	6.0	6.1	**6.0**	.098
Surveillance	5.3	5.6	**5.4**	.001[a]
Social sport	5.7	6.0	**5.8**	.000[a]

Note: Measured on Likert-type scale (Anchored by 1=Strongly Disagree to 7= Strongly Agree).
[a] Significant based on Bonferroni's correction of p.<.005.

The prior four sets of analyses in this chapter stressed the importance of understanding one's market for more effective and efficient use of marketing staff and resources. Deciphering marital breakdowns is no different. In this sample, the single participants are motivated to participate more than their married counterparts are in the areas of passing time, surveying the information landscape, and socializing. The higher motives for pass time and surveillance have many potential implications for the fantasy sport professional. More passing of time and seeking out information can indicate that single participants will "stick" more to the fantasy sport websites and host sites (Li, Browne, and Wetherbe, 2006), meaning they will seek out information and be less likely to mind passing time while completing that task. A host site armed with this information as well as data on its consumers can tailor advertising and marketing campaigns for that audience.

Conclusion

These five demographic breakdowns resonate with the words of Linda Ellerbee, broadcast journalist who once said: "People are pretty much alike. It is only that our differences are more susceptible to definition than our similarities." The differences between types of players—young and old, single and married, Black and White, male and female—are statistically significant and should not be ignored. However, it also is crucial to note that there were far more mean splits between groups that were not statistically significant. A fair conclusion would be that there are motivational differences between people of different ages, races, genders, favorite sports, and relationship statuses, and yet these differences might not signal holistic deviations among fantasy sport players.

Research about who chooses to play reveals profound racial and gender splits, with seven eighths of participants being White/Caucasian and male. Such differences loom large when compared to overall population statistics. Yet, once people of different demographic groups opt to play, they find similar reasons for participating. Even some of the statistically significant differences, particularly in regard to race and gender breakdowns, could be the result of participants' minority status within the activity. Consequently, differences by demographics are meaningful and insightful, yet should be regarded as trends more than absolutes. Participants of various identity-oriented heritages and backgrounds are notably different, yet not holistically so; these different groups are siblings, but not twins. When taken jointly with Chapter 2, these details offer a full quantitative understanding of *who* is playing fantasy sport as well as *why* they continue to participate. The chapters to come will feature additional statistics, with a more qualitative tilt toward understanding specific views of fantasy sport play both inside and outside the industry.

4 The major players

An inside look at the Fantasy Sport Trade Association

In Chapters 2 and 3, we described the fantasy sport participant in great detail. Note that we are not referring to the "typical" fantasy sport participant, who becomes harder to pin down as the activity becomes increasingly mainstream. Broad generalities—e.g. "male" or "sports uber fan"—may represent the majority of participants but fail to describe millions of other fantasy sport users. Nevertheless, we have pinpointed motivations for playing these games within games, and identified how these trends differ based on issues such as gender, race, age, and marital status. The next logical step involves the exploration of the people and companies involved in delivering these fantasy sport games (and numerous ancillary products) to the masses. This chapter offers some extended description from people who devote their careers to facilitating a multitude of fantasy sport games. Similar to the people who play them, the gatekeepers of this industry defy monolithic description. Are there "statheads?" Yes. Are there obsessed fans? Yes. Are there people who are forging new trends each and every year? Absolutely. There also are people who work 80 hours a week regularly competing among other professionals who produce content and fantasy products in their free time. There are people who have become celebrities from having their work showcased on mainstream broadcast and basic cable outlets. There are marketers, managers, web designers, writers, and specialists in many other areas. They are all highlighted in this chapter, which provides an in-depth look at members of the Fantasy Sport Trade Association (FSTA).

To offer a proper glimpse into the inner workings of this association, we conducted 26 interviews with many key members of the FSTA during 2012. The people we interviewed ranged from on-air personalities (such as ESPN's Talented Mr. Roto, Matthew Berry) to industry leaders and trailblazers (such as FSTA President Paul Charchian) to award-winning writers and online editors (including a Yahoo! Fantasy Sport triumvirate of Brandon Funston, Brad Evans, and Andy Behrens). However, before we turn to these major players and their views of the fantasy sport industry, it will be useful to examine the history of the industry as seen through the eyes of those involved in its evolution.

The evolution of the fantasy sport industry

While its origins stem from the 1960s, fantasy sport, particularly fantasy baseball, enjoyed a small, yet devoted and growing following in the 1980s (Hale, 2010). The 1990s appeared to be a major tipping point for the industry, largely because of the mainstreaming of the Internet—in hindsight, a perfect fit for fantasy sport play because one of the major hindrances for early fantasy sport adopters was the lack of access to statistical data and the lack of desire to continually calculate scores for each contest. The early 1990s brought new mainstream media developments (Leith, 2004), such as *USA Today*'s offshoot, *Baseball Weekly*, which provided voluminous information for sports fans. Fantasy baseball participants were among those statistics-starved readers. Howard Kamen and Steve Gardner from *USA Today* spoke of the ebb and flow in the relationship between the fantasy industry and that publication, one of the few US newspapers with a national readership. They noted that before fantasy play migrated to the Internet, fantasy sport participants needed to acquire daily and weekly statistics from the newspaper, and *USA Today* was more than happy to fill the void. As Steve Gardner recalled, "*Baseball Weekly* developed to give people who were really interested in baseball even more of the stats. That's the origin of the *USA Today* as a part of the fantasy industry." *Baseball Weekly* initially had a freelance writer, John Benson, who wrote a weekly fantasy column. John Hunt followed, founding the high-profile experts' league called the League of Alternative Baseball Reality (LABR—pronounced labor), which exemplifies the evolution of fantasy sport from a print standpoint. Before the mid-1990s, newspapers could offer the content fantasy participants craved the most: statistics. Moreover, they could do so without devoting space specifically to fantasy sport, as they were already committed to printing daily box scores and cumulative statistics. When fantasy participation migrated to the Internet, the statistics naturally moved with the games, as websites would automatically enter the statistics and determine scores, outcomes, and standings (Turner, 2004). As a result, participants would no longer turn to newspapers and magazines for statistics; the Internet was a virtually instant leader in that regard. Print media would have to adapt by offering a form of fantasy sport "color" commentary consisting of expert advice and analysis (Phan, 2005).

Fantasy sport was growing, and leagues were forming on popular websites such as ESPN.com and Yahoo! The first fantasy oriented television show was offered, and its co-anchor, Brady Tinker, described how it unfolded within those formative years:

> BT: Back in the 1990s, we did a show through the NFL Players and the Major League Baseball Players Association on Fox Sports [for] the whole country. We were in 78 million homes, [but] we were a little ahead of our time. We did good work. The company I was working with at the time was Prime Sports and they thought the big business that they were doing was these $50–$100 entry games or $1 per trade … instead of trying to make more money off of the television. We could have made a lot more money off the TV at the time [with a different business model].

Others did recognize that the financial incentives of fantasy sport centered on hosting league websites and then charging administrative fees, while embracing the attention economy to provide advertisements and to link pay-expert services. ESPN's Senior Director of Product Development, John Diver, noted the company's humble beginnings in fantasy sport:

> JD: Nineteen ninety-five was really the year that the Internet and fantasy games started for ESPN, and the first thing we did was [create] fantasy football—that was our first game. Two thousand signups, playing $20 a team. Then the big one was fantasy baseball in 1996.

By the mid-1990s, enough entities existed to be viewed as a viable industry. The Fantasy Sport Trade Association (FSTA) was formed in response to the need to legitimize what was now being built at a relatively rapid rate. *Fanball* founder Paul Charchian described how events evolved to the first meeting:

> PC: We started having consumer-based conventions for fantasy football in Minneapolis. We had them in the Metrodome, in Mall of America, and we were pulling in a lot of people from the industry. People were coming and were like, 'We're all here! We should start to formalize these get-togethers and start working on some industry things.' I believe it was 1998 that the FTSA was created. Back then it was a realization that we were big enough to have the need to speak as an industry.

Fantasy sport media stopped being primarily about access to statistics and more about what Steve Cohen, SiriusXM's Senior VP for Sports Programming, termed "uncovering these hidden gems for the fans and telling them who the next big-time players are going to be." Instead of consulting media outlets to decipher what happened in the sports world and then interpreting the resulting impact on fantasy sport, there was an enormous desire to forgo that initial step. Fantasy sport began to emerge as a primary entity, one that happens to use statistics derived from other games with other outcomes. The largest response to these fan cravings was the creation of information companies like Rotowire and, a year later, Rotoworld. Rotowire founder, Peter Schoenke, described the growth:

> PS: I started Rotowire in 1997, although, for the first four years, it was calledRotoNews.com. I started it in Chicago with two buddies that I went to college with at Northwestern. About two years after we did it, we were the eighth-biggest sports site on the Internet; we were bigger than NBA.com. We couldn't keep the servers up. It was the rare Internet success story.

By the end of the decade, major media outlets had to decide on the degree to which their entities were in (a) the sports information business, (b) the fantasy sport information business, or (c) the fantasy sport gaming business. Some, such as ESPN, placed more resources in the fantasy area, while others, such as *USA Today*, did not. As *USA Today*'s Howard Kamen explained:

HK: We collectively didn't realize the potential there for fantasy and, quite frankly, we got passed … [It's] important to understand that up until just a few years ago you had an entire organization that was the print side of *USA Today* and you had an entire organization that was the dot-com side. For a long time there wasn't a ton of communication.

USA Today columnist Steve Gardner concurred, noting that company decision makers "never really were able to catch the game crowd, the people that wanted to play, and get them on our site." Kamen articulated the resistance:

HK: There just was not an understanding by the management teams that this was something that could be a money maker. It was seen as 'Oh, it's a little niche thing that a few geeky guys are playing.' In order to be successful here, you have to be able to have the content that is intertwined with the games, and you have to be able to own it. [As a result], a lot of the online piece [for *USA Today*] is now licensed from *Rotoworld*.

Thus, divisions started to form between outlets offering sports statistics that were highly useful for fantasy (*USA Today*), outlets that offered fantasy-specific sports information (*Rotoworld, Rotowire*), and outlets that offered "one-stop shopping" by hosting the actual games along with analysis (ESPN, CBS Sportsline, Yahoo!). The fundamental—and often business-defining—question was whether to (a) charge for content via options such as premium subscriptions and league fees or (b) keep content free and make the business profitable through the sheer mass of people accessing advertising on fantasy pages. Different organizations found different niches. Senior Editor and former writer, Brandon Funston, spoke of the model for Yahoo!:

BF: Yahoo! seeded their fantasy sports division by going free when ESPN was still charging money for their fantasy leagues. A huge amount of people came in at that time, and once you develop your habits in a fantasy league, you never leave. Yahoo! really helped themselves in the fantasy space by zagging when everybody else was zigging.

Meanwhile, corporations such as CBS Sportsline (later renamed CBSSports. com.) sought smaller numbers of people who were willing to pay $100-$150 for a league with premium services and, arguably, more committed fans. People stayed on their sites even with other free, readily available comprehensive options because of loyalty and a perception that participants there were more dedicated. Underlining this point, CBSSports.com reports that 83% of its current fantasy participants have played six or more years with the site. One spokesperson for CBSSports.com used the following analogy:

CBS: The analogy of a gym is a good one. If you belonged to a gym that didn't have a membership fee, you might go sometimes, but you might not be as motivated to go because it's free. You aren't paying anything. As opposed to the gym memberships that most people pay for, you've kind of got that nagging sense in the back of your mind that I'm paying for this. I should use it.

Rotowire's Peter Schoenke explained that the free versus pay dilemma was not exclusive to the game servers:

> PS: We were free back in those days. Then, after we did all that we were like: How do we make money on all this? The dot-com advertising bubble had crashed, so, in 2001, we went pay mostly. It grows every year. We were sort of the first movers in the information space and kind of the best of breed and people like ESPN, Fox, Yahoo!, NFL.com, all use us for player news and information.

A primary competitor for Rotowire in that marketplace is Rotoworld, currently drawing 3.7 million unique visitors and 108 million page views per month. Rotoworld has implemented a hybrid model in which the majority of the offerings are free, yet premium services are promoted to keep the company financially viable. Rotoworld/NBC Universal Director of Fantasy Content Brett Vandermark outlines the Rotoworld model and the often difficult challenge of selling content without games or direct ties to megasporting (see Eastman, Newton, and Pack, 1996) events:

> BV: We're not a game site, so it's all about revenue—always. NBC has a big digital sales team now. But, how do you get them to sell Rotoworld? They've got the Super Bowl, the Olympics, hockey. They can sell those in packages. For Rotoworld, it's tougher for them. [We have to get] the writers to understand what you're trying to do: to have the best news available, but also to promote these premium products that we have because that is how you get paid. Yes, the free news is why people come. Those have to be great, but since significantly less people come to our premium side, it's at least got to be just as good or better, because that's how you get paid.

Seeking and hiring writing talent became a priority. There was no dearth of people willing to write fantasy sport columns, meaning the pay would often be $100 or less per month. However, as the industry evolved, expectations for writers changed, and successful columns became known brands that people would seek out for information and expertise. Yahoo! writer, Andy Behrens, discussed the evolution from the desire for mass opinions to smaller, stronger, Twitter-sized opinions:

> AB: When I was hired at Yahoo!, most fantasy content was basically a couple of super-long columns a week … There was no job such as 'blogger' [but] I think basically what fantasy experts were doing 15 years ago was mostly blogging. Within a couple of years, that became 'produce as much content as you can in smaller, more easily digestible nuggets.' [Now] the job has definitely changed from writing 5,000-word columns to where you're expected to be on video, you're expected to be on radio.

With the burst of creative, insightful writers came the need to form an ancillary association to the FSTA, the Fantasy Sports Writers Association (FSWA). President and Chairman Mike Beacom explained why the group was necessary:

> MB: There was a general feeling that the FSTA was not representing editorial needs in the industry. It did hand out some awards for Best Magazine etc., but it was a true trade association. It basically dealt with business issues, not so much on the editorial side. So, there was a need there. If we don't have awards that are credible and believable, they have no value. If people trust the process, there's value in winning the awards. There's legitimacy.

The ultimate prize in establishing legitimacy, though, involved moving fantasy from a predominantly print and online product to one that was viable for television. While smaller sports networks offered basic 30-minute "start-or-sit" types of fantasy football shows, ESPN formally entered the fray in 2006, hiring Matthew Berry, also known as The Talented Mr. Roto. He, along with Rob Stone, Ron Jaworski, and Danni Boatwright (then famous from a stint on the popular CBS program *Survivor)*, comprised the primary players for *The Fantasy Show*, a short-lived series that proved not to be viable. ESPN had a fantasy presence, yet was concerned about how to translate that to the viewing audience. ESPN's Matthew Berry elaborated:

> MB: The show aired Thursday afternoons on ESPN2. Critically, everyone liked the show, but in that time slot, getting huge ratings was a challenge. The internal feeling was that fantasy would work on TV; we just needed to tweak the format and find the right time slot. Next year, we started *Fantasy Insider* on ESPN News and *Fantasy Football Now* on ESPN.com. The success of both those shows proved there was a huge appetite for televised fantasy content on Sunday morning, both on TV and digitally. Currently, we air *Fantasy Football Now,* Sunday mornings, on both ESPN2 and ESPN.com. The show has won an Emmy and the ratings have been terrific.

Initially, fantasy sport was relegated to being discussed primarily within fantasy-specific shows. However, there was a sense at ESPN that it could be interspersed within tent-pole programs, if presented in an appealing format in smaller, easily digestible "bites" of information. Berry summarized the essential questions as the network was starting to move fantasy sport to this new format:

> MB: How do you do fantasy on television when it's not a pure fantasy show? Creatively, how do you make it work in segments in shows like *SportsCenter*, *NFL Live*, and *Baseball Tonight*? How do you make it interesting, informative and fun for a viewer who may or may not be there for fantasy advice? How do you make it so it enhances the program rather than detracting from it? Those were the discussions we had all the time.

Berry noted that his role has evolved since he first joined ESPN; his initial job required considerable advocacy behind the scenes, but that has become less necessary given the growth of the industry:

> MB: The first two years I was there, I was actually in a management role. Much of my job was meeting with the various stakeholders and saying: 'We need to hire more people. We need more heads. Fantasy is growing and only going to get bigger. We can do more. This is where I think our coverage and business can improve.' In 2008, I switched to a talent role. I don't do nearly as much behind the scenes. Frankly, I don't need to. We have people whose job it is to be proactive in terms of pitching fantasy and trying to integrate fantasy into all of our other programming. Fantasy has come a long way. People understand the value of fantasy and how important it is to our fans that watch ESPN or consume ESPN media.

Perhaps the final major tipping point for fantasy sport happened in 2010, when SiriusXM launched a 24-hour channel exclusively devoted to fantasy sport. SiriusXM's Steve Cohen discussed how this was a natural next step in the development of the Sirius sports media products:

> SC: When we launched Sirius NFL Radio eight years ago, we launched a Friday night fantasy football show hosted by Adam Caplan and John Hanson. The show was a big hit on the channel, [so] when the opportunity came for me to convince the folks here to launch a channel, I had quite a bit of documented research that I was able to bring to that meeting to convince them to allow us to launch this channel. We launched in the summer of 2010. [Almost instantly,] we got more listeners calling our talk shows on our fantasy sports channel than we did on any other SiriusXM produced sports channel. [By December, 2011] we had an average of over 28,000 calls a day.

Through this combination of tipping points, the fantasy sport industry had been legitimized, revolutionized, and mainstreamed. In 2003, 15 million Americans were playing fantasy sport in the United States. One decade later, that number has more than doubled. The top-rated ESPN2 show is *Fantasy Football Now*. Billions of dollars are pouring into an industry that, not long ago, could have been best described as a fringe group of people creating games in their free time.

Misconceptions of fantasy

While we know that fantasy sport participation grew continually over several decades, interviewees also spoke quite candidly about how fantasy sport was a "tough sell" to many constituencies, including potential participants, advertisers, and mainstream media organizations. In a group so wholly committed to fantasy sport, it is noteworthy that a number of key interviewees expressed doubt that "fantasy sport" is the best term to describe their business enterprise. For instance, here is FSTA President Paul Charchian's stance:

> PC: If 'Roto' had picked up steam [it would have been better]. If this had been Rotofootball and Rotobaseball, I don't think it would have been a problem. But, because the word 'fantasy' was in there, it got tied to the Renaissance Festival in people's mind. So, everyone thought fantasy football players were walking around with a 20-sided die in their pocket.

Charchian's remarks resonated with those of many others who articulated a rocky path to legitimization, filled with barriers from those wishing to relegate fantasy sport to niche status. In general, the term *fantasy* was problematic, because of its cultural connotations as something that is inherently not mainstream. Examples of "fantasy" offerings with loyal followings could include everything from *Star Trek* and *Dungeons and Dragons,* to a vast array of books that, while selling consistently for decades, failed to move beyond a core market of fantasy fiction fans. Of course, while fantasy sport players created fictional leagues, they used real sports statistics of real players subject to real management techniques. They hardly were comparable to, say, admirers of comic book superheroes. But they were marginalized within the overall sports media because of the "fantasy" term, along with perceptions that fantasy sport could alter or dilute the overall sports media brand. Said Fox Sports' Jim Bernard:

> JB: One of the misconceptions is that mainstream thinking, boardroom thinking, of 'oh, fantasy that's *that* group.' 'That group' is slowly becoming a powerful and valuable group: a group you can sell to.

Brett Vandermark spoke of the two vocations he must straddle because of his connections with both the NBC Sports brand (known quantity/established) and the Rotoworld brand (unknown quantity/unestablished):

> BV: I use 'fantasy geek' as an example. It depends on who you are talking to as to whether I introduce myself as NBC Sports or Rotoworld. If it's a girl … she's probably not going to know what Rotoworld is. It's going to be 'Rotoworld, what's that?' Well, it's fantasy sports. And she, more than likely [will respond with], 'Oh, that stupid fantasy football game that the guys spend all their time with.' So I just say NBC Sports with her. But, if I'm talking to a guy just out of college, [the response will be], 'Oh, yeah. Rotoworld!' Even five years ago, I think it was more of an 'Oh, that's weird' or 'That sounds stupid.' But, [now] there is no hiding from the fact that this is a big deal.

Echoing such sentiments, Paul Charchian notes that "even today, many credit card processors and banks refuse to work with our companies. There's a certain social misconception that we are nerds who grew up playing *Dungeons and Dragons*." For fantasy sport writers, the two audiences of fantasy participant and sports fan overlapped enough to allow publications to write with dual purposes, which was necessary when one side of the equation (fantasy) was seen as potentially diluting the other (traditional sports fans). *USA Today*'s Steve Gardner explained:

> SG: When *Baseball Weekly* was launched [in the 1990s], people knew at the time that fantasy was one of the main reasons that people were buying it. But, fantasy was a dirty word, and if you said *fantasy*, you had already turned off 80% of your potential audience. If you went back and looked at them now, so many of the things that were written, you could see, playing time battles, pitching rotations, injuries and things like that—a lot of those things were written to where you can get some serious fantasy information from this, but to label it *fantasy* was taboo. It was a big step to actually have a fantasy column.

Other interviewees offered examples of other pervasive misconceptions within the fantasy sport industry. Steve Gardner commented on how the work of fantasy sport specialists goes far beyond the image of the fantasy geek:

> SG: The standard mindset is that somebody who is interested in fantasy sports is just blogging from the proverbial mother's basement and doesn't really have information, they're just spouting opinions. Fantasy today is not just taking numbers and putting them on spreadsheets. It's analyzing trends. A lot of thought goes into it, and I think that's one of the misconceptions: that it really does take a lot of work. It does involve a lot of thought. It's not just spouting opinions. Derek Jeter is better at shortstop than Nomar Garciaparra? You need to come up with *why*. People that are reading you are not going to take your opinion at face value just because you're out there saying it. You have to show them why you think Derek Jeter is better than Nomar Garciaparra or Alex Rodriguez. If you can do that in a convincing way and make sense, people will take you much more seriously.

Also noted was the differentiation between the work of fantasy industry insiders, as they offer research, analysis, and opinions, and the amount of labor required of the typical fantasy participant. According to Fox Sports' Adam Slotnick:

> AS: There is the misconception that it's incredibly difficult and time consuming to play. It is what you want to put into it. There are those hard-core fans that are going to play the daily baseball games and pore over every single stat and spend hours. [But] it's about getting the more casual, or middle-of-the-road fan to realize this game can be and is fun. It really is what you put in and what you want to get out of it—and communicating that to the user.

Beyond the definition of what fantasy sport is and what it involves, Matthew Berry speaks of the influence of the activity in many other realms of gaming. Berry opines: "I think probably a lot more people play fantasy than even actually realize it. If you [play ESPN products such as] Tournament Challenge [March

Madness], Streak for the Cash, Pigskin Pick 'em, or even Super Bowl Squares, that's fantasy." It appears the imprint of the games, whether called roto, fantasy, simulated, or any other term, has made a lasting impact, particularly on American society. FSTA President Paul Charchian makes this case:

> PC: Something we're finding that's small, but starting to appear more and more now, is taking the concepts of fantasy sports play and applying it to nonsporting elements that would attract females specifically. We're seeing fantasy *American Idol* leagues and fantasy *Survivor* leagues. Even if they're not billed as fantasy leagues, if you go to the official website of a favorite lifestyle TV show, you may find that there's a game on there … running on a proven fantasy sports model.

Niches Within the Fantasy Participant Population

As the industry gained approximately 20 million participants in North America between 2003–2013, the diversity of fantasy participants expanded as well—making it increasingly necessary to define industry roles in an exponentially complex fantasy sport media machine. Discussing the impact on primarily print outlets like *USA Today*, Howard Kamen described the difference between the hard-copy statistics the newspaper offered in the 1990s ("It was really the only place to go") and the unique insights and game hosting that became premium offerings in the 2000s. Even now, the *USA Today* staff dedicated to fantasy sport numbers just three—and that group was difficult to attain. Said Kamen:

> HK: Until 2008, there was no fantasy desk; it was basically Steve and I and a couple of other people just kind of writing on our own time. Then, we had a merger of the dot-com staff and the print staff. At that time, we were able to convince the sports editor to go ahead and create a fantasy sports position. We then brought in a new management team to run what is now called the *USA Today* Sports Group.

Realizing that the majority of *USA Today*'s online traffic originated from Google searches and other engines, the leadership taking over the corporation in 2008 embraced elements of fantasy sport offerings. According to Kamen:

> HK: The new leadership team understands that fantasy sports have to be a part of [the new *USA Today* model], so the question is how do you accomplish that? You can do your homegrown talent and bring in a staff of 30 people and try to start from scratch or you can go out and make an acquisition and buy your way back into the game. My guess is it's going to be the latter.

Meanwhile, the major fantasy-only information purveyors, Rotoworld and Rotowire, struggled to create balanced financial models and structures. The companies faced a different type of competition than that encountered in most other parts of corporate

America. Simply having the most people assigned to the work (Rotoworld has 25 full- and part-time people while Rotowire employs 15 people full-time) and producing the most robust, interesting offerings did not ensure a stable share of the fantasy sport market. Rotowire's Peter Schoenke offered a comparison:

> PS: If you're in the insurance industry, there's probably not a lot of people knocking on the door saying 'I'll write for you for free for your insurance company.' But, some guy tomorrow could start some blog and even if he's not making a penny of it, he'll be a viable competitive threat to you. He might put 20 hours a week into it just because he wants to, even if he's losing money off of it. If we're in the insurance business, that's not happening, but here, it's 'whack a mole.' You think you've got this good product; you're the leader in one area. Then some free guy comes along and you're [suddenly trying] to figure out how to stay competitive.

The goal was to innovate and provide information in the clearest, most easily digestible format available. Rotoworld's Brett Vandermark explained one issue he faced when he took over in 2009:

> BV: Rotoworld used to be whoever writes the last article gets to lead the site and just chuck everything on there [on a scroll]. Too many people come there to just haphazardly throw things up. It's got to be scheduled ... We want people to have fun, but with the amount of information that's out there, there has to be some structure.

The biggest issue these information-based companies faced involved many of the same problems faced by most Internet companies (such as Facebook and Google): How does one capitalize monetarily on being the leader/go-to offering in a certain market? Again applying the "whack a mole" concept to indicate constant innovation, Schoenke detailed how Rotowire has managed to remain an industry leader:

> PS: We were all free when we launched and *mindshare* was the word, and it was all about [Internet advertising]. Then [Rotowire] went all-pay and everyone said we were crazy. I came to these conferences and people would be like, 'you're nuts,' and then that kind of came around to where now even a lot of newspapers have finally said there's this paid/free hybrid that can work. So, you kind of thought you had that figured out, but now there's mobile apps–you've got to have an app. People actually pay for stuff, especially in the Apple environment. 'I'll pay $2 for a cheat sheet or $4 for a draft kit.'

The desire to fulfill a niche part of the market was even true for the biggest media conglomerates hosting the majority of fantasy sport leagues. Some, such as CBS Sportsline, made the decision to remain as pay-only sites. The decision ensured that it would not be the industry leader in overall number of participants, but could be the industry leader in terms of hard-core, dedicated participants. Others opted to go with the broadest swath of people, most notably including Yahoo! and ESPN. John Diver explained ESPN's decision to be a relatively basic, free site that is widely available and consumed:

> JD: On the first Sunday of the year, at about 12:45 ET, when everyone's trying to make that roster move, if you hit submit and it spins and comes back, [it's over.] So, our job from Day One has been: Make it scale. You can have the greatest features in the world, but if they don't work, it doesn't matter. Scale is Job 1.

Even the giants of the industry can have problems with the functionality of scale, which happened to Yahoo! in the fall of 2012. When its fantasy football website went down immediately before the 1 p.m. ET kickoff, fans were enraged (Laird, 2012). Yahoo! issued an apology, via Monday emails, sent to every fantasy football player, noting that "Our first priority is having the best experience for our users, and today we fell short." The long-term ramifications of this single yet large-scale failure are yet unknown.

Nonetheless, scale of fantasy play is important because, as ESPN's Matthew Berry concurs, "the more people that play fantasy sports, the more they're interested in sports, and the more they're interested in sports, the better it is for ESPN." John Diver goes on to explain the overall concept of ESPN as it relates to his job:

> JD: Part of our job is to create habits. We want people to have bookmarks, go check their fantasy basketball page, go look at tomorrow's lineup, make sure they don't have any bench players, make sure no one's hurt, pick your Streak for the Cash, go look at your English Premier Soccer League team. If someone has 45 minutes a day that they sit in on their computer or cellphone, we want to try to get a percentage of that.

While ESPN's model was sweeping in scope, Yahoo! had already secured millions of fantasy participants in a free model that seemed widely pleasing to most people (at least until the November 2012 online failure), making it difficult to get people to switch to ESPN. Diver explains: "Every year I think our biggest challenge and goal at ESPN is to pass Yahoo! in unique users. We are about 600,000 short; the marketing guys are like, 'Oh, 600,000. No problem.' And we're like 'it's not that easy.'" Thus, ESPN tries to attract new participants with new games, currently numbering 42 in all—most of which are "minigames" in addition to the most popular, longer-lasting games such as fantasy football and baseball.

The goal of many of these initiatives is to offer variety in the overall fantasy sport landscape. This is true of the people involved in the industry as well. Matthew Berry is famous not because he is on television; rather, he is on television because he carved a unique niche that was beyond the binary of "start" or "don't start" this player. He ultimately became a brand in the fantasy sport world, a personality with guest appearances on the FX program *The League* as well as

ABC's *One Life to Live*. He achieved all this by letting people experience his personality and humor amid the sports advice. Berry explains how he created his role in the fantasy world:

> MB: You can't 'out-info' the Internet. I do my research, but I'm not going to out-stat somebody else. I'm not going to out-scout someone else. I think the people that are fans of mine enjoy it because I take that analysis and make it succinct in an entertaining, interesting, funny way.

While Yahoo! and ESPN sought the greatest number of fantasy participants, other outlets also worked to position themselves within the overall landscape. Given that CBS had largely secured the market in terms of early adopters and heavy users, Fox Sports opted to seek out the exact opposite: the first-time or casual participant. Noted Jim Bernard:

> JB: We took a conscious effort to get the casual, lighter fan. You can set up a league with us in five minutes. Really. You can take the defaults, take the presets and do it really easily. Then, to cater to the hard-core player, you can hit a lot of buttons and open up advanced fields and make all the decisions that you want to. You don't have to see those; you can basically accept the default. We made that choice to try to take the intimidation factor out.

However, such a model must still secure a fair share of heavy fans that represent the major web traffic and, in turn, the greatest amount of revenue. Fox's Adam Slotnick explains this balance:

> AS: We understand that the bread is really buttered by the hard-core fan and that's going to drive engagement in our sales metrics, [but] in terms of the first-time player, we have a great pipeline because of the MSN relationship. We are exposed to a lot of users that either have casually played or have not played at all. So, we're trying to introduce them. That being said, the conversion rate is a lot lower than what it might be with a targeted audience. It's a challenge.

As Bernard summarizes, "Obviously, fantasy football drives the bus [but] we try to support the broadcast side, so we have NASCAR, baseball, and football products." Between offering the right amount of sports, ensuring overall network synergy, and developing a go-to audience, all mainstream media outlets appear to be invested in fantasy sport, at least for the immediate future. Meanwhile, a key question is whether fantasy sport represents a steadily growing, still inchoate part of sports fandom, or whether it is peaking—an inevitable bubble about to burst.

Growth in the Market

This question of whether fantasy sport has peaked or is near capacity seemed to be on the minds of the interviewees. Yet most had a bullish forecast for fantasy sport, exemplified by Yahoo!'s Brad Evans: "There's going to be trickle-down to the next generation. I don't think it's peaked; I don't think it's plateaued." Many people had statistics to reinforce their assertions that fantasy sport play is still on the ascent. Notes FSTA President Paul Charchian:

> PC: [We have] roughly 2 million new players every year [and this has happened] for a dozen years. It doesn't seem to be stopping. Logically, we assume that at some point it's going to plateau. But, kids are getting more involved in fantasy sports, and they're playing with their parents. We poll all the current players and ask, 'When do you think you'll stop playing?' Eighty percent of current players have no intention of stopping within 10 years and half of those, 40% think they will play until they *die.*

Given the statistics reported in Chapter 3, opportunity for future growth seems plausible: The percentage of fantasy participants peaks in the 25–34 demographic (FSTA 2012b). If this divide is more of a web-based digital phenomenon, then the older demographic percentages will rise, and the overall number of participants will increase, as new people fill the younger demographic categories. This is already resulting in a massive increase in the amount of fantasy sport information consumed, as Brett Vandermark notes with an example from Rotoworld's status in early 2012:

> BV: This will be the 19th month where [Rotoworld has] had a minimum of 20% growth in page views year over year. This is the 19th straight month we'll have a minimum of 15% growth in unique users year over year. And these are not small numbers to begin with. There are months we had in 2011 where we had 800 million page views. [In 2012], I expect 1 billion. When you have 3½ to 4 million unique users per month, there's a lot of room to grow. I don't mean mobile; I mean our premium products.

As a brief footnote to Vandermark's prediction, on December 21, 2012, Rotoworld did, indeed, reach 1 billion page views. Such growth, both in terms of the number of participants and in the amount of fantasy-based products being consumed, is partly the result of a concerted effort to move fantasy sport into the mainstream of all sports media. SiriusXM's Steve Cohen underscores attempts to make people realize that "fantasy sports make fans bigger, better, wiser sports fans." One way their radio station did so was by getting Jacksonville Jaguar running back Maurice Jones-Drew to participate in a weekly program, showing that professional participants are interested in the fantasy angle as well. Notes Cohen:

> SC: Does it get any better than that? An All-Pro running back that you get to talk to about what's going on in the league, and pick his brain on defenses and players going up against those defenses and all that?

ESPN's Matthew Berry offers other examples of attempts to make fantasy sport trendy, such as Sirius XM's fantasy football show hosted by Playboy Playmates:

"If you told me five years ago Playboy Playmates would be playing fantasy sports and playing it in a real way, I wouldn't have believed you." ESPN made an overt choice to focus less on getting people to switch from another website to their own and more on gaining new participants, particularly those who already were listening, watching, and reading ESPN media. This "grow the pie" strategy invariably becomes an issue of branding the activity. Berry notes how ESPN attempted to redefine the fantasy sport participant within its network plan, specifically among their heaviest consumers: young males.

> MB: We wanted to change the perception of fantasy sports. We didn't want it to be geeky or nerdy; we wanted to make it just one of those things that guys do. What do guys like? Guys like movies where stuff blows up. They like fast cars. They like attractive women. They like cigars. They like going to Vegas. They like poker with the guys. They like pickup ball. Oh, and they like fantasy sports. Getting more people to play it and referencing it as something that everyone does helped move it more into the mainstream.

Part of the attitude about potential growth involves the ability to expand untapped markets. There appears to be a delicate balance between expanding the overall fantasy sport brand and giving people what they crave the most: baseball and, in particular, football coverage. As Steve Cohen says, "You've got to play the hits, right? Until fantasy basketball, fantasy hockey, fantasy NASCAR, etc. become larger factors in the fantasy world, we're going to give as much time as it deserves." Fox Sports' Adam Slotnick takes a slightly different tack, noting:

> AS: I don't think the growth rate has slowed. A better assessment is perhaps that it hasn't fully matured. There's a lot of integration with TV or radio or just other mainstream sports. I think we're starting to see more and more of a comfort level [with fantasy play in a larger variety of sports].

It appears that the newest frontier experiencing the largest growth in US fantasy sport play is basketball. It exhibited a heavy increase not only in fantasy play, but also in overall media ratings and web traffic after the 2010 "Decision" of LeBron James to join the Miami Heat to create a triumvirate of NBA Dream Team caliber players. Rotoworld has especially noticed this increase, believing it has to be more than just the LeBron James effect. States Brett Vandermark:

> BV: Everybody knows football was made for fantasy. But why basketball? Nobody has been able to give me an answer why basketball's suddenly working so well. But, it has; it's caught up. We are growing in baseball, but not [like] basketball. That's interesting, because fantasy started with baseball. But basketball's with baseball as far as web traffic. It's getting closer. With us, it's getting really close.

Fox Sports also is heavily invested in NASCAR (auto racing). But finding a way to make auto racing a major player in the overall fantasy landscape has proven difficult, as Jim Bernard explains:

> JB: NASCAR as a fantasy sport has a very loyal, rabid fan base. A lot of people are NASCAR fans. But, they are a [niche, largely Southern] group, where football just seems to be in every office, every person. It just has such a wider spread, where NASCAR is just that group.

Still, the overall consensus of the interviewees incorporates the concept of a rising tide lifting all boats, whether that increased interest comes from the core fantasy sports such as football and baseball, the rising fantasy sports of basketball and NASCAR, or the less popular fantasy sports such as hockey and golf. Product providers share in that consensus, particularly for major media outlets that offer fantasy sport as just one segment of a much broader sport media landscape. As ESPN's Matthew Berry extrapolates:

> MB: We know that fantasy players are ESPN's most hard-core fans, our most ardent fans, or the ones that are consuming the most media on ESPN. We would love it if they all played fantasy sports on ESPN.com. But, even if they play on another website, we know that they come to ESPN for their sports news information and analysis regardless of where their fantasy game is played out. So, the more people that play fantasy, the more people are interested in sports and the more people interested in sports, the better it is for ESPN in general.

Participant background and demographics

As mentioned many times previously, the fantasy sport participant (and, hence, the *potential* fantasy sport participant) is typically one who knows a great deal about sports but may also be seeking a new level of fandom. As established earlier in this book, both mavenism and Schwabism impact the fantasy sport participant an inordinate amount when compared to the traditional sports fan. Steve Cohen discusses how SiriusXM reaches that demographic in its radio offerings:

> SC: It's a much higher plane in terms of the intellectual level that we discuss sports. We want to make you more knowledgeable. We want you to know why this was effective and why that was not the smartest call in this instance going up against that defense. We want you to know the strategies [that can be employed beyond mere player ability].

Yahoo!'s Andy Behrens notes how the potential crossover happens with his company, which uses the overall Yahoo! Sports website to funnel people into potentially reading fantasy sport columns. He states, "There will be a fantasy link on the front page and suddenly we've got 1,000 people commenting. None of them are fantasy players … it's not somebody clicking over from the sports front page or from the MLB front page." The prime example at the time was news about Tim Tebow, who was a major part of the sports media landscape even among people who would not classify themselves as sports fans. According to Behrens, an entirely new audience was suddenly reading Tebow-related fantasy sport articles in their desire to consume anything related to the popular football player.

Industry experts consistently cited teenagers and college students as their largest untapped audience, because their overall sports fandom is still being discovered—and is generally ascending. Similar to the approach of advertisers, the fantasy sport industry endeavors to establish long-term buying trends with this age demographic. Once fantasy sport participants are established with a fantasy league host, they rarely switch to another website. They will seek information columns from a wide variety of Internet locations, but in terms of game play, as ESPN's John Diver confirms, "Any kind of design is learned behavior … People get familiar with the interface." Diver outlines ESPN's strategy:

> JD: We've focused more in the last few years on trying to get that 18-year old who is going to college. He's got nine buddies. We get them to sign up and play fantasy football with us, and we have them for the next 40 years.

Nevertheless, most respondents readily admitted that fantasy sport play is not for everyone—not even for many people who would classify themselves as major sports fans. Some sample fantasy sport and, for various reasons that will be detailed in Chapter 6, opt not to continue in the activity. One seminal issue appears to be conflict when a person has a difficult time bridging the gap between being a fan of a team and being a fantasy sport owner. Given that Lee, Ruihley, Brown, and Billings (2012) found that 41% of all fantasy participants favor their fantasy teams over their favorite teams (seemingly making their very fluid fantasy teams their de facto new favorite teams), the paradox does exist with a minority of participants. Some attempt to synthesize the two potentially conflicting loyalties. Explains SiriusXM's Steve Cohen:

> SC: If you play fantasy football with your heart as opposed to your mind, you're going to be a lousy fantasy football player. [They're] just fans of, say, the Kansas City Chiefs who say, 'You know what, I'm going to build a fantasy football team around my favorite team.' You're doomed for failure [when you prioritize your favorite team over better fantasy choices].

FSTA President Paul Charchian explains what typically happens to people when they first decide to participate in fantasy sport play:

> PC: Twenty percent of first-year players will simply drop out. It's just not right for them; they know in their first year, they never play again. Of the [remaining] 80%, about half end up being social players: people to whom winning and losing isn't their measurement for enjoyment: 'I'm here to show

up for the draft, I'm here to smack talk and if I win, great.' The other 40% end up not only staying but also wanting to win ... they are buying premium services ... with a clear goal of trying to win.

The words "North American, White, and male" certainly apply broadly to players in the current fantasy sport landscape, but the single word that best describes fantasy participants may well be *avid*. Steve Cohen makes this case:

> SC: You'll hear these sports talk shows 'I don't want to talk fantasy sports.' You know why? It's because most of these guys can't keep up with the knowledge that fantasy fans bring to their talk show. Fantasy fans know all the starters. They know all the backups. Most of these talk show hosts in terrestrial radio don't know who these guys are.

Relationship with the mainstream media

Of course, the most certain way to secure new participants would be to utilize mainstream media sports offerings. But respondents noted that while circumstances have undoubtedly improved over previous years, there was a long struggle that is still being waged today. Fantasy Sports Writers Association (FSWA) President, Mike Beacom, outlines the case the fantasy sport industry has been attempting to make:

> MB: Most would argue that attendance dictates coverage. Well, sometimes the opposite is true—coverage dictates attendance. That's true in fantasy. If you cover things, sometimes that helps recruit players; when you have players you have business.

In a similar vein, Matthew Berry described how he had to make a clear, methodical, comparative statistical case to create inroads for fantasy sport coverage at ESPN:

> MB: I think there was a belief that 'It's a game, it's a niche, it's a small little thing.' But, in fact, the numbers and studies that we would give when talking to various stakeholders at ESPN would counteract that. Once people became aware of the size of the fantasy playing audience, and the amount of our fans that were engaged in it, fantasy became a much bigger part of the conversation.

There is ample anecdotal evidence that fantasy sport is being accepted as a major player in the sports world generally, and particularly within the NFL. While the NFL now embraces fantasy with enthusiasm (even offering fantasy games on nfl.com), FSWA's Mike Beacom offered a glimpse of the league's past attitudes:

> MB: [Years ago], I was supposed to do a fantasy story on Green Bay's weapons in the passing game. I called the Packers to get permission to talk to

an assistant coach and … I listened to 10 seconds of laughter before I got an answer. At that time, the NFL just snubbed its nose at fantasy. The NFL really didn't have fantasy. It wasn't branding it [but now they do].

Fox Sports' Jim Bernard and Adam Slotnick spoke of their own evolution within the overall Fox Sports structure over the years. One battle was over the amount of on-screen graphics and the amount of information on running sports tickers/scrolls. Graphic designers tended to opt for a more minimalist approach that made the screen more aesthetically pleasing. Jim Bernard argued otherwise:

JB: I remember eight years ago, they were just going to put just scores [on the television screen graphics]. [We said], 'No, you can't. These guys care. You've got to say who scored that touchdown.' Certain times the graphics do have it, certain times they don't. We like to keep pushing it forward. You'll see in the halftime shows, they definitely have bullet points that are directed to the fantasy guy.

Much like Matthew Berry's ESPN approach of blending expertise and entertainment to "go mainstream," Fox Sports was coaxed toward greater fantasy sport coverage through the sheer magnitude of statistical data highlighting its growing popularity among core sports media viewers. Notes Slotnick:

AS: There's definitely a maturation of the industry as a whole. We've gone through many different iterations of our games with many different partners, internal and external. Now, we are at a point where we are internally building the games, and I'm actually confident that I can say that they're solid, they're stable. Now that we've reached that point, we're in a much better position internally to make the argument with the editorial desk. We have the research numbers to back it up, too.

None of the respondents demonized decision makers within their own companies. Rather, they raised valid questions about the degree to which a fantasy sport offering would cannibalize a mainstream media offering. Both ESPN and Fox used their Sunday morning NFL television pregame coverage as exemplars, both arguing that while the viewership certainly overlaps, it is not to the degree that most experts would predict. ESPN's John Diver offers his justification for increased fantasy sport coverage in television pregame offerings:

JD: On Sunday morning, there's two people that are watching: gamblers and fantasy guys. There's not a whole lot of fans, like Packer fans, because everything we do [on an NFL pregame show] is very macro—we don't really focus on one specific team. If you want that stuff you go to your local TV station [or website], but the acceptance of the TV producers to put fantasy on air has grown tremendously.

Fox Sports' Adam Slotnick articulates his reasoning on some of these same issues, arriving at much the same conclusion:

> AS: We have this internal discussion: Are we programming to that audience or potentially counterprogramming for that audience? We have the NFL Fox Pregame Show, the number 1 pregame show in America. If we were to do a fantasy show that went up against it, would we be doing ourselves a disservice on the whole? I'm not sure what that answer is, but my inclination is that we probably wouldn't, because my guess is that the people who are watching the ESPNs and the Yahoo!'s aren't watching the NFL on Fox pregame show to begin with ... I think they're two completely different audiences.

Print-based media largely saw fantasy sport coverage as an appendage to traditional media that could be offered on their websites; they did not offer systematic print newspaper coverage of fantasy sport until quite recently. *USA Today*'s Steve Gardner explained its evolving fantasy coverage from a meager beginning, recalling that it began with a simple shout from above: "We need a fantasy column. We should have this. Do you want to write it? Since you're the baseball editor for online, how about if you just write a fantasy column and take over that for a little bit?" Later, Gardner noted some conflicts in which fantasy coverage could be viewed as impeding other sports coverage, particularly when fantasy columns proved so popular that *USA Today* began its fantasy baseball blog before establishing its regular baseball blog. Gardner illustrated the potential internal conflict at the paper:

> SG: You'd have trade deadline day, and there were deals made. And, I'd have the fantasy analysis up of the trades that were made before the baseball site got the announcement that the trade had been made. They were getting upset with me for posting things.

Thus, television media were offering very small amounts of time for fantasy coverage, while print media relegated much of their coverage to the more expansive opportunities available online. However, Yahoo!'s Brandon Funston argued against the notion of the Internet as offering an infinite amount of space, maintaining that fans still desire coverage on high-traffic space—parts of a website people find in one or two clicks rather than five or six. Speaking of Yahoo!'s main page, Funston offers:

> BF: It's a huge land-grab situation where everyone's fighting to get something on that front page. It's such a windfall when you actually get it. [Management is] always looking for unique spins. They want to keep people interested in clicking on what's on the front page. If we get something on there, we get huge numbers, and it's not your typical sports fans.

In sum, respondents nearly universally felt that (a) relationships with mainstream sports media decision makers were better than ever before, but that (b) fantasy sport would always struggle for acceptance and time within media outlets and within sports organizations as a whole. As FSWA President Mike Beacom argues:

> MB: Will every person that covers fantasy football ever get to hang out on a Tuesday after practice? Probably not; the NFL's media demands continue to grow every year. It's a matter of space and bodies and fantasy probably is always going to take a back seat, even if we're looking at traffic. Numbers used to win out, but I think more than that the NFL looks at credibility. Who do they really trust in the locker room and in front of the players? Fantasy is probably going to have a long climb there, fair or not.

Yet, the people interviewed felt the case had been made for at least a modicum of mainstream acceptance. Yahoo!'s Andy Behrens summarizes the current situation best, noting that "it just doesn't feel like a little cult anymore, and I don't think it feels that way to a lot of decision makers."

Fantasy sport journalism

One of the current debates touching on both fantasy sport and the broader media field focuses on who is reporting on fantasy sport and the credentials these people bring to their careers—specifically as they relate to the traditional expectations of journalistic standards. While there are no current university degrees in fantasy sport, there are degrees in journalism, and many universities have established programs in sports journalism specifically. Schools of journalism are not necessarily producing the best practitioners of fantasy sport writing, however. Rotowire's Peter Schoenke describes what it looks for in a potential hire:

> PS: A lot of how we hire people pertains to their fantasy aptitude so to speak. Not necessarily that they're a great player, but that they know the information and they know the game. They know the sports really well and they're able to apply that to whatever they're doing. A lot of our writers have been guys who were, like, a real estate attorney or a technology person for an airline company. This is their way to do sports, so they write and freelance for us on the side. There's a bunch of other people who get out of college and are looking for jobs and they want to write about sports and the Internet and fantasy is a great outlet for them, and then they moved up. So, it's really kind of all different characters. We had a guy who worked for us who was our minor league analyst for a while, [and] he ended up getting a job with the Brewers; another worked for the Seattle Mariners.

FSWA President Mike Beacom notes that competent, compelling writers who are not likely to move to other jobs, or toward retirement any time in the near future, are now filling most of the top jobs. Moreover, these relatively young experts can canvass meaningful swaths of the industry:

MB: I'm in my mid-30s. Most of the guys in [the industry] are probably 35–45. There's a lot of life on those tires. Look at [ESPN's] Nate Ravitz. Nate is probably my age or a little older and now manages fantasy content for ESPN.com and manages ESPN Insider. This is a guy who came from the fantasy industry. So, in one person you've got a guy who wrote fantasy who's now in charge of two divisions for the largest sports media provider in the world—and he came from fantasy.

There is a fair amount of disagreement on whether what fantasy sport writers do constitutes "journalism" in the traditional sense. Yahoo!'s Brad Evans believes what he does could most aptly be called "educated guesswork," differentiating his role in the following way:

BE: It is a different medium. I don't consider myself a journalist, I consider myself an analyst, and I think there's a difference there. We're taking the data. We're mining all the information we can, and we're making an educated, analytical viewpoint and providing a perspective to our audience in a fun and entertaining way. We're just an extension of entertainment.

Evans's colleague, Andy Behrens, confirms this assertion, noting their key focus on entertainment and the fact that they are not generating information so much as spinning the information already available:

AB: I don't think any competitive fantasy player is getting their news that way anymore, waiting for the weekly column that drudges up all the nuggets from around the league. Now people are expecting you to give very strong opinions based on specific news items. They're not looking at you to report or parrot news, they're looking to you specifically for strong opinions. Some of them are looking to be entertained.

Yahoo! Senior Editor, Brandon Funston, notes how this plays out in terms of what is expected of "traditional" sports journalists as opposed to what Yahoo! Fantasy Sports typically provides. Funston believes the deviation largely resides in the realm of breaking news:

BF: If you're a Jay Glazer versus a Charles Robinson or someone like that, their reputation is staked on how many stories they break. For us, we're not breaking anything, and as long as you get the information in a decent amount of time before Sunday kickoff, that's all that matters.

However, *USA Today*'s Howard Kamen disagrees with the belief that fantasy sport is all analysis and less timely reporting, at least from his vantage point. Notes Kamen:

HK: I would argue that breaking news is a really big part of fantasy sports, because you need to know when a guy is a game-time decision [based on their injury status]. Is he playing? Who got hurt? But, from the perspective where *USA Today* sits, we're not in a position to be breaking news necessarily on fantasy.

Kamen's *USA Today* colleague, Steve Gardner, offers a unique bridge between these positions: He is a member of both the Baseball Writers Association of America and the Fantasy Sports Writers Association. This "foot in each world" experience leads Gardner to believe that "I've got to apply journalistic principles across the board to feel like I'm being consistent in what I'm putting out there— whether it's on the fantasy blog or whether it goes in the newspaper or *Sports Weekly*." The differences, according to Gardner, pertain more to the journalistic process than to overall expectations and standards:

> SG: It's easy for me to set everything up, and boom—go to those people for the inside information. Whereas, writing the fantasy column and doing analysis, you can ask some people what they would do or how they analyze things or what their place in the fantasy realm is, but you've got to draw your own conclusions.

Yet, as Howard Kamen notes, Steve Gardner is more the exception than the rule. Most people writing within the fantasy world today are the real estate freelancers and tech people to whom Rotowire's Peter Schoenke alluded. Kamen believes this ultimately does permeate issues of journalistic standards, or at least holds the potential to do so. Offers Kamen:

> HK: Steve was already a journalist and a writer and an editor and doing radio, so he came to writing the fantasy column for *USA Today* from a different perspective. Somebody who maybe is in school right now or writing for a blog doesn't have any sort of experience and/or training, so the standards potentially are different.

Arguing that fantasy sport is no anomaly and that all forms of journalism deal with the same standards-laden issues, writer Mike Beacom explains just how murky all journalism labels are in today's digital world:

> MB: What's been blurred isn't the quality but who really fits and who just doesn't? Before, to really be considered a writer you had to be attached to [an established outlet or publisher]. Now, it's almost like self-publishing books. Are you really a published author? Anybody that writes something is going to call themselves a writer today.

Thus, with the lines blurred, the best description of what many fantasy sport writers do, according to Yahoo!'s Brad Evans, is to "find a different way to skin a cat." The best writers offer nuanced angles, aggregate data, and provide insight that cannot simply be drawn from free online charts. Evans explains more of the day-to-day process of what he does:

BE: Instead of being the average-Joe sports writer who's in a locker room interviewing athletes, we're reading material. So, we're taking a lot of primary sources and applying it to what we write. We're constantly combing through local newspapers online or some of the info sites out there, fantasywise [such as Rotowire and Rotoworld]. So, we're constantly combing through information on a regular basis and, of course, watching games.

Yet, even with this contrast, Brandon Funston notes that a major part of his job involves ensuring that a certain bar is reached for overall standards, even if that bar is subjective and different for every online fantasy site. As an example, Funston offers the following:

BF: When there's something breaking and we don't know 100%, we're always willing to say [credit original sources]. We pull out certain stats from Fan Graphs.com or Pro Football Focus, and we always attribute the fact that we got this from them.

The other way writing has been assessed is through the Fantasy Sport Writers Association, which Mike Beacom leads. The association gives out annual awards and inducts top industry leaders (approximately five each year) into the FSWA Hall of Fame. Beacom explains the focus on awards and honors:

MB: One of our goals early on was to try to raise the level of journalistic excellence. To say to people 'We're here.' We can do that through awards. We also can do that through trying to set standards for our membership and how writers conduct themselves.

The overwhelming majority of the people interviewed, when asked about whether fantasy sport writing is within the realm of formal journalism, either denied that it was, or explained that while there are similarities, the two fields are largely different. Merely insisting that it is different from other forms of journalism does not necessarily make it so. Yet their attitudes provide insight into the role fantasy writers believe they play on a day-to-day basis. Concludes Beacom:

MB: Fantasy writing is different from sports journalism in that there's more need for entertainment. If you're covering a game or even if you're writing a sports feature, you're still going to relay on a set of journalism standards that fantasy writers can get around. There's more inside humor. You can go places that may not be appropriate—and I'm not talking about vulgarity or sexism or racism—I'm talking about more playful types of things that you can do inside of fantasy content that a newspaper isn't going to let you get away with.

Conclusion

In contrast to the two preceding chapters, Chapter 4 aimed to give the reader an inside view of the fantasy sport industry, outlining past benchmarks for growth as well as identifying areas that continue to grow at the time of this writing. The historical aspects and major tipping points were discussed and outlined through the lens of the industry pioneers. From key questions of free versus pay formats, to credentials and the criteria for fantasy sport journalism, insiders offered their opinions on instances when fantasy sport thrived and also moments when it has struggled. While one could fairly perceive an optimistic bent in these comments by industry leaders, our goal was to get an inside perspective from this burgeoning industry. One could question some industry choices and business models, yet still appreciate the efforts that were necessary to win a place for fantasy sport content and games within the overall sports media spotlight.

Another goal of this chapter was to establish that the fantasy sport industry is populated by many full-time working professionals who outnumber part-time contributors with meager or questionable skills. The industry is not a collection of unattended computers running games. It is composed of real people who have dedicated their careers to advancing this activity into a billion-dollar industry. Most of these leaders enjoy sports as other fans do, love the fantasy atmosphere, take pride in their work, and constantly defend themselves against naysayers in traditional sport media. It is important to note the influence of a relatively small number of people: FSTA meetings (held biannually) typically feature 150–200 participants. This entity nonetheless delivers the overwhelming majority of gaming options and ancillary content to a vast array of players. Ultimately, a small group of people—no larger at its core than a single football team—activated an industry now measured in the tens of millions of participants. This group of influential industry leaders continues to shape not just fantasy play, but the sports media empire as a whole.

5 Money changes everything (or does it?)

Free, low-stakes, and high-stakes fantasy play

In economics, there is a concept referred to as the 120% rule. It is a theory based on the notion that no matter their income, people always believe an extra 20% will make all the difference in defining their happiness. A person making $20,000 per year envisions an easier life if only he or she could make $24,000. A person making $1 million per year imagines the magical things that would materialize with an income of $1.2 million. Tax cheats may rationalize similarly, telling themselves that freedom from those pesky taxes surely would supply that extra 20% and the happiness they envision.

The 120% rule has applications outside of economics as well. Teenagers presume their nights out with friends would be much more fun if they could stay out 20% later. Journalists try to convince their editors that they really could tell the "full story" given 20% more space. Employees imagine achieving that elusive balance between work and personal life if they just had about 20% more leisure time. Applying the 120% rule to sports, one might feel that it is not enough just to enjoy playing or watching a game: one might want to put a little extra into it, adding "juice" to the athletic outcome. This could involve making bets on the side, fun wagers among friends, horse racing's "trifecta," or NCAA basketball's March Madness.

For some fans, fantasy sport embodies the 20% windfall. While watching one's favorite "real" team allows for a great deal of enjoyment, fantasy sport could provide that 20% bonus—in fact, even when one's "real" team loses, there could be a fantasy-oriented silver lining—consider the high ratings for enjoyment cited by fantasy participants in Chapters 2 and 3, even when we know that each fantasy game produces one winner and one loser. This brings us to a smaller subset among fantasy sport fans: the high-stakes participants. If fantasy sport provides an extra 20% of enjoyment for the traditional sports fan, then we might view these participants as seeking *another* 20%. Though an eclectic group, high-stakes participants share a common bond: they not only love fantasy sport, but they also seek to dominate it.

In Chapter 3, we offered contrasts between different types of participants based on their gender, race, age, and marital status. In this chapter, we will analyze differences among people who play for free, those who pay for services of a host site, those who play for a relatively small amount of money in the form of a prize fund, participants not playing for a prize fund, and those who play for more—sometimes, a whole lot more. (That last group comprises a small percentage of participants who are nonetheless fascinating to study.) This chapter will compare survey information from participants who play for free and those who pay for the services of the host site. In addition, we will contrast those who have prize funds attached to their experience and those who do not. Finally, we will examine fantasy participants in high-stakes leagues. The first two comparison groupings (free and low-stakes participants) will utilize data collected in surveys designed specifically for this chapter. The high-stakes participants were interviewed for this book at a pair of 2012 fantasy football drafts: the National Championship of Fantasy Football and the Fantasy Football Players Championship. Both leagues involve participants paying thousands of dollars in hopes of winning hundreds of thousands of dollars. Both held their drafts in Las Vegas in September of 2012, and the authors of this book were there to explore a fundamental question: beyond the obvious financial impact, what "value added" experience do they gain in high-stakes fantasy sport that they feel cannot be attained through free or low-pay leagues? In essence, we asked them: "You paid thousands of dollars and flew to Las Vegas for the draft, so are you getting your 120% of fantasy sport enjoyment?" But first, we must understand the considerably larger group: people who play fantasy sport for free.

Free vs pay leagues

The percentage of participants playing in leagues requiring no entry fee is quite high, with 52.3% of the respondents in our survey reporting that they play for free. Since nearly all of the rest play for $50 or less, these two groups comprise not just a large slice of the pie; but virtually the whole pie. However, our classification difference is significant: there are fundamental differences between a free activity and one that involves cost, even if the fee is nominal.

For instance, in a much-cited study, Ariely (2009) offered subjects a superior product, Lindt chocolate truffles, for 15 cents while offering a comparatively inferior product, Hershey's chocolate kisses, for 1 cent. A decisive 73% opted for the superior Lindt truffle. Ariely then lowered the amount of each by 1 cent. The 14-cent truffle was suddenly soundly defeated by the free Hershey's Kiss, which became the choice of 69% of the people. Such studies underscore the relevance, prominence, and significance of offering a product for free. Free requires no forethought. Free is equated with limitlessness.

It is not a surprise that new and casual fantasy sport participants are more likely to participate in free leagues, as shown in Table 5.1.

According to our own survey results reported in Table 5.1, the free participant is not only younger (average age 30) but has been involved in fantasy sport for 8.3 years, while the person who pays at least some fee for participation is more likely to be older (average age 33.8) and a relative veteran, averaging 11 years of fantasy play. Additionally, pay participants estimate spending significantly more time maintaining their fantasy teams than do free participants (9.4 hours per week vs 8.1 hours per week) yet, interestingly, both free and pay participants estimated equal amounts of weekly time devoted to sports as a whole (17.9 hours per week).

Table 5.1 Demographic differences between pay and free fantasy participants

Motive	Pay	Free	Significance
Age	33.8	30.0	.000[a]
Years in fantasy	11.0	8.3	.000[a]
Fantasy hours[b]	9.4	8.1	.011[a]
Sport hours[b]	17.9	17.9	.998

Note: Motivations measured on Likert-type scale (Anchored by 1=Strongly Disagree to 7= Strongly Agree).
[a] Significant based on Bonferroni's correction of p.<.012.
[b] Hours per week.

When presented with statistics showing that the majority of participants do so for free, most outsiders to the fantasy world wonder: how do these fantasy sport websites make money without an entry fee? The answer is multifaceted, and focused on two main areas: the attention economy (see Anderson, 2009 for an extended explanation), and premium services, typically involving access to more robust statistics and expanded expert analysis.

Regarding the attention economy, new media have brought free access to myriad information sources while creating fierce competition for eyeballs within the advertising community (Davenport and Beck, 2002). Lanham (2007) finds that as a result, no one is lacking for information, but our ability to focus on things is fragmented amid the inundation of textual and visual stimuli. Thus, a dominant website is one that can command our attention for not just seconds, but prolonged minutes. Sports media have discovered that fantasy sport information can more than double their web traffic—and can get people to focus on the same web page for a considerable amount of time. This is rare in the Internet age, and advertisers willingly pay to promote their products on such sites (Anderson, 2009). It also helps explain why the largest entities in the fantasy sport industry are not stand-alone fantasy websites, but Yahoo! and ESPN, which merge fantasy content with other sports content. This makes it difficult to ascertain the overall impact of fantasy within the full website, but clearly, trends in web traffic and unique visitors make offering fantasy sport—even with free entry—a very worthwhile proposition. Add in other fantasy games that do cost money (such as ESPN's *Streak for the Cash*) and the result is a well-oiled synergistic machine in which the economy of free is in full effect.

The other way the free fantasy sport industry manages to turn a profit is with premium services. For instance, Rotowire offers information to ESPN.com. However, for $129.99, a participant can gain two years of access to advanced statistical matrices and projections as well as even more depth and insight than one finds with Rotowire's free product. Such premium services can be found on a season-by-season basis; for instance, Rotoworld is owned by NBC Universal, and offers the majority of its content free, but it charged $14.99 for advanced information pertaining to the 2012 NFL season. At the time of this writing, the newest entries into this landscape are mobile applications, which are typically offered for free, yet have the same form of attention economy/premium services combined business model at the core.

Returning to motivational research, one fundamental question of this chapter involves the degree to which motivations of free participants (defined as those that do not pay for hosting) differ from those who pay some amount for hosting services. Some may assume that there is little difference, given that even when people pay, there usually is little money at stake. That is a fair observation. Consider the case of a fantasy baseball player whose season lasts approximately 25 weeks: a $50 investment amounts to just $2 per week. A fantasy football participant may have a 14-week season, making a $50 investment equate to just $3.57 each week. League fees often fail to make up even the majority of fantasy sport financial investment, as access to pre-season rankings and other magazines and materials may account for a larger share of a fantasy participant's investment. Yet, the previously noted "power of free" (see Anderson, 2009; Ariely, 2009) must be examined in this matrix.

As seen in Table 5.2, relatively little changes when paying for hosting fees becomes part of the equation. The motivations for fantasy play seem to be relatively the same in magnitude and in ultimate hierarchy from the most to least prominent reasons for play.

Comments from free participants

After collecting the data, we focused some attention upon the qualitative responses of those who exclusively play for no financial incentive, with the goal of determining the extent to which this group participated for demonstrably different reasons. However, results showed that free participants have some of the same incentives as everyone else, corroborating the quantitative findings. Of particular interest was the question pertaining to whether playing for free still presented a unique challenge that would keep participants invested. The majority of free participants still found ample reason to participate. For instance, one person noted the enjoyment of "besting others who think they know about sports when they really don't know anything." Another explained, "I love the challenges week to week in football and day to day in baseball. Bettering my own team by trading players and being first to waiver wire for new players. The thought process to set my lineup, (i.e. player, matchup, location, weather conditions). I like to win!" The notion of being the "smartest person in the room" is still alive and well, even when participants play for little money. As one respondent declared, "I enjoy the strategy of analyzing statistics and feeling like I will find advantages that other owners will not. I love winning and displaying my passion for the sport." Others paired this desire with the enjoyment they ultimately find within the activity: "[I love] proving my superiority in decision-making and prediction ... for an additional dimension of enjoyment of the actual sport." Playing for free did not lessen the perceived challenge of play, nor did it lower the level of bravado among the participants:

I love the managing, [and the] competitiveness between people and just that it shows, more or less, who knows more about that sport. I feel extremely confident in my knowledge of sports and players, so I love playing fantasy sports to show others my understanding of sports.

Table 5.2 Motivational similarities and differences of pay versus free leagues

Motive	Pay (n=563)	Free (n=628)	Significance
Arousal	5.6	5.6	.299
Camaraderie	5.7	5.6	.119
Competition	5.8	5.7	.098
Control	5.9	5.7	.011
Escape	4.2	3.8	.000[a]
Ownership	4.5	4.3	.004[a]
Pass time	4.9	5.0	.147
Self-esteem	6.1	6.0	.016
Surveillance	5.4	5.5	.312
Social sport	5.8	5.9	.378

Note: Motivations measured on Likert-type scale (Anchored by 1=Strongly Disagree to 7= Strongly Agree).
[a] Significant based on Bonferroni's correction of p.<.005.

In addition, several free participants reported that they receive enhanced enjoyment from having more of a clear interest in a multitude of game outcomes. This prolongs their overall entertainment because, as one respondent explained, "It makes sports more interesting, especially when all your teams suck and are put of contention early." Another respondent offered a concrete example as a transplanted New Yorker in a different region of the country:

> I am a New York Jets' fan that lives in South Florida. The television networks shove the terrible Dolphins down my throat each week. I have no interest in their games or matchups between Jags and Bucs … unless of course I have a player going against them, which makes it bearable. I also love that it is a yearly competition between me and my friends.

Another person echoed that sentiment:

> I enjoy having a vested interest in each game being played each week, instead of just having my world revolve around my city's team. It makes me learn/care about the happenings of players all across the league and allows me to interact with people about a sport I enjoy and compete with them on a regular basis.

However, the most common type of comment among free participants pertained to friendship and camaraderie. This was sometimes combined with other motivations, such as "pass time," e.g., "Passes the time and is a way to interact in a friendly way with friends. It is a fun way to talk some trash to friends and just some good safe fun." Sometimes camaraderie appeared to be an incentive in itself: "It is a great reason to stay in touch with close friends, even out of season. Between drafting, playing and awarding trophies, the camaraderie is nonstop." One female respondent explained the degree to which fantasy sport has permeated her family relationships, mostly for the positive:

> I participate in fantasy football as a family activity. Everyone on my mom's side of the family is in a league and it's all for fun. It's friendly competitiveness, and keeps us close (at least during football season). I also enjoy participating because I learn more about sports and can hold my own when having a conversation with men about sports.

In sum, the free participants still enjoy the activity, finding themselves highly engaged and highly personally and emotionally invested—but not financially invested. As one respondent clarified, "Bragging rights matter as much or more than the cash payout does." Most expressed sentiments that were roughly the same as those of participants who play for money. Offering a summary that might have come from virtually any participant, free or pay, one respondent simply stated, "I love sports and I love statistics so [fantasy sport] is a marriage made in heaven."

Prize fund leagues vs non-prize fund leagues

Nonetheless, many fantasy sport participants play in leagues in which prize funds are attached. This can mean a prize attached to a hosting payment (i.e., pay $100 for a chance to win $100,000) or a payment separate from the hosting costs that are applied to distributing prizes at the end of the season. In this scenario, one may have to pay $12.50 as one's share of the hosting cost and an additional $37.50 to be applied to the league's prize fund. With a 12-person league, this pays the $150 hosting fee, creating a $450 pool of funds to be distributed to the league's top finishers. Such funds can provide just enough incentive for people to care about the league, respect the competition, and want to win. Many fantasy sport participants complain about people dropping out of the league prior to the season's end, creating an unbalanced competition schedule for other teams later in the season. Requiring some kind of payment toward a prize fund, or having a tier-structured payout, is regarded as a mechanism for keeping people participating throughout the entirety of the season. An opportunity to pocket an extra $250 of your buddies' money is also a nice prize for those who put time and effort into winning their leagues.

It is important to look at these two groups—those that have a prize fund (prize fund participants) in their leagues and those that do not (non-prize participants)—to determine whether they have differing experiences. Results from our survey data suggest that there is no significant difference in age (average 31.0 and 31.8 years), devoted fantasy hours per week (1.2 hours' difference), and sports consumption hours per week (0.5 hours difference). One significant difference is the years of participation in fantasy sport; those playing with a prize fund have played fantasy sports for an average of 9.9 years while those without a prize fund have participated for 7.8 years. Consult Table 5.3 for complete information.

Table 5.3 Demographic differences between prize fund league and non-prize fund leagues

Motive	Prize	No prize	Significance
Age	31.8	31.0	.218
Years in fantasy	9.9	7.8	.000[a]
Fantasy hours[b]	8.9	7.7	.106
Sport hours[b]	18.0	17.5	.639

Note: Motivations measured on Likert-type scale (Anchored by 1=Strongly Disagree to 7= Strongly Agree).
[a] Significant based on Bonferroni's correction of p.<.012.
[b] Hours per week.

In terms of motivations for their fantasy participation, there is some difference in the reasons why these two groups participate as well as what they receive from their experience. Of the ten motivations analyzed, five showed significant differences between the two groups. Those differing motivations, each higher for those participating in leagues with prize funds, consist of arousal, camaraderie, competition, self-esteem, and social sport. The arousal, competition, and self-esteem motives make obvious sense; there is money on the line. Most do not wish to lose money, preferring to take others' in such an environment; simply the lack of losing money equates to the power of free noted earlier. Beyond these obvious factors, social areas of camaraderie and social sport are particularly interesting findings. Since data collection did not specifically address social motives and prize fund leagues, one is left to speculate on the reasons for the difference. One possible explanation for social motives being higher for those in prize-funded leagues is that the participants are more attentive (i.e. following scores, more competitive, staying on the league scoreboard and message board longer). Table 5.4 highlights the major motives.

Table 5.4 Motivational similarities and differences of prize fund leagues and non-prize fund leagues

Motive	Prize (n=563)	No prize (n=628)	Significance
Arousal	5.7	5.4	.001[a]
Camaraderie	5.7	5.3	.000[a]
Competition	5.8	5.4	.000[a]
Control	5.8	5.7	.185
Escape	4.0	3.8	.133
Ownership	4.4	4.3	.424
Pass time	4.9	5.1	.207
Self-esteem	6.1	5.8	.002[a]
Surveillance	5.4	5.5	.281
Social sport	5.9	5.6	.002[a]

Note: Motivations measured on Likert-type scale (Anchored by 1=Strongly Disagree to 7= Strongly Agree).
[a] Significant based on Bonferroni's correction of p.<.005.

The non-significant findings tell important tales as well. The motive averages of control, escape, ownership, passing time, and surveillance were all too close to be statistically significantly different. For those involved in prize funds, and those who are not, to have nearly the same averages for control and ownership is useful information because these factors are basic functions of fantasy sport participation. Drafting, setting a lineup, and trading are essential to the overall enjoyment in fantasy sport. Both groups being equal on the pass time motive is critical because, as mentioned, some participants become frustrated with those who fail to pay attention to their lineup or abandon the activity toward the end of a season. If the pass time motive were heavily skewed in one direction, possibly toward the non-prize fund participants, one might be able to link early departure to this motive. Additionally, surveillance is a motive that is nearly equal between the two groups. Information providers have to think highly of the fact that those playing for money and those who are not still opt to participate for reasons related to information surveillance.

With significant differences in motives of arousal, competition, and self-esteem, it could easily be assumed that surveillance would complement those motives because of the heavy emphasis on information in this activity. To be competitive, raise your self-esteem, and have that type of positive stimulation, one must be aware of the important information a fantasy participant needs. Surveying the landscape resembles such a philosophy. In this data, the non-prize fund participants also have high surveillance motives, again raising the question of why this is not falling as the others did. It is possible that in today's technology-friendly environment and with numerous sports media outlets, each group has equal opportunity and equal desire to seek out information.

Table 5.5 features ratings between free and pay participants on several other factors for play.

As highlighted in the table, there was very little difference between those playing for free and those with money as part of the equation. There was one significant difference, in the factor of Schwabism—measuring the degree of sports knowledge one wishes to convey to others in the league. People who played for money were significantly more likely to exhibit higher levels of Schwabism than those playing for free, perhaps an unsurprising result when taking into account some of the desires of high-stakes participants that will be outlined later in this chapter.

Table 5.5 Other factor similarities and differences of pay versus free leagues

Motive	Pay (n=563)	Free (n=628)	Significance
Enjoyment	6.5	6.5	.760
Mavenism	6.0	6.0	.870
Schwabism	5.1	4.9	.041
Fantasy satisfaction	6.7	6.7	.655
Future intent	6.9	6.9	.710
Sport satisfaction	6.1	6.1	.819

Note: Motivations measured on Likert-type scale (Anchored by 1=Strongly Disagree to 7= Strongly Agree).

As mentioned in Chapter 4, industry professionals state that content is becoming easy to find and understand. In the early days of fantasy sport, one would have to search for box scores, try to comprehend byzantine math algorithms, or purchase very specialized magazines. Today, in the case of CBS Sportsline fantasy games, one can access a player profile and read his latest news, outlook, or injury report with a single click (as seen in Figure 5.1).

Figure 5.1 Player profile showing information from multiple sources

The outliers: high-stakes fantasy participants

Within the tens of millions of fantasy participants is a subset numbering in the thousands: the high-stakes participants. We decided to study them as the potential ultimate outliers. Examining these "high rollers" of fantasy sport allows us to explore the extreme end of the financial motivations fantasy sport can encompass.

We conducted 48 interviews with people who participate in the National Championship of Fantasy Football and the Fantasy Football Players Championship, each with main drafts in Las Vegas while offering satellite drafts in other locations, such as Chicago and New York City, with many more participating online. Fisher (2012) described such drafts, characterizing the atmosphere as "simply intoxicating" (p. 14). Each featured numerous six-figure prizes that come from not only winning one's division, but then also conquering other division winners in the final stages of competition. The results regarding the degree to which money changes motivations for play were mixed; as seen later in this chapter, people play these games at the highest level for a variety of reasons. Nonetheless, it is fair to say that people who participate in these leagues represent a uniquely different type of fantasy sport participant. We met one person who plays in 150 leagues per year and has made fantasy sport his full-time job; we met others who basically concede their financial losses just to be a part of the spectacle that is high-stakes Las Vegas gaming. As summarized by Stacie Stern, general manager of Head2Head Sports, "There's such an adrenaline rush. The excitement and anticipation that surrounds all of this is really big. And so many people involved say it's one of their best days of the year, that the live fantasy experience is really unlike anything else" (Fisher, 2012, p. 14). However, to understand high-stakes fantasy gaming, one must first be familiar with its origins.

The World Championship of Fantasy Football (WCOFF)

While people have been participating in high-stakes fantasy sports games virtually since the games were invented, the landmark development of nationwide (some would argue worldwide) high-stakes play occurred shortly after the turn of the millennium. The World Championship of Fantasy Football was formed more than a decade ago. Cofounder Lenny Papano explained the origin of the plan:

> Emil Kadlec, my partner, called me one night. I think it was November of 2001. I was in my office and he was like, 'What are you doing?' I said, 'Watching the World Series of Poker.' And he goes, 'Man, I'm watching the World Series of Poker too,' and without missing a beat he goes, 'that's what we should do for Fantasy Football.' We sat there the first night and we were like, 'If we were participants, how would we do it? We'd want it in Vegas because there's like championship fights in Vegas. We'd want it at the MGM Grand or Caesars.' We wound up doing the first one at the MGM Grand. We just sort of went through a wish list and then we were like, 'Man, are we nuts? Do you think people would really do this? Kind of a field of dreams, like

build it and they will come?' We built it—552 teams, something like $1,350 per team. Build it and they will come.

Gradual but steady growth occurred with WCOFF and by 2007, the league boasted 864 participants. Once people saw the success of WCOFF, it was clear that imitators would soon emerge as competition for the main league. Others saw what had happened and experienced regret for not developing the idea first. As one participant told us:

> Before high-stakes was even invented, I ran a local league at $1,000 per team on a local level. This was 15 years ago. I kick myself every day because I could have put up a website, got a couple of people to put up $50,000, $60,000 a piece. Emil and them did a hell of a job. They built it up, they sold it and made a bunch of money.

In 2007, WCOFF was sold for an undisclosed sum to Gridiron Fantasy Sports, a division of 360 Sports Marketing, and the group had a new financial plan. Most of the high-stakes fantasy participants we spoke to sensed an immediate shift that was unsettling to them:

> When the original owners of WCOFF sold to the new owners the new owners had a grand vision of being this huge fantasy industry, not just fantasy football. They did a lot of advertising. They increased their price structure. They went into fantasy baseball. They did a bunch of things and they were using investment money to pay as opposed to an entry fee. They were also bringing in celebrities to do celebrity drafts. And they were fronting those players. The celebrity players almost got preferences over the original—you know the main players. VIP rooms and stuff like that. I don't think that's supposed to be part of the experience at all.

While splinter groups formed almost immediately (with one direct result being the development of the Fantasy Football Players Championship), many stayed with WCOFF, feeling it still offered the greatest value for participants. However, financial troubles soon hit the new managers of WCOFF. One person noted that "they had a business model that was built on boom times and then it was a hard economy." Others said they should have recognized the signs that the league was having financial difficulties:

> There were a number of signs: one, slowness to pay out; two, getting early-bird discounts to sign up for the next year, and then the payouts came after the early-bird signups. You kind of start feeling that maybe the money's not all there. I felt that for the last two years but I chose to ignore it. I knew what I was doing. I got very lucky I didn't get burned.

By September of 2011, the heavy investment in growth and celebrity (including, for instance, the hiring of 100 referee-outfitted cocktail waitresses) had put WCOFF more than $4 million in debt. The process of paying winners went from being slow to being nonexistent. The league folded. Lenny Papano offered a summary of the difference between the old and the new owners of WCOFF:

> We had the golden rule known as Lenny Accounting. You get X amount of dollars that come in, you figure out what the prize pool is: thou shalt not touch this money. The rest of the money? Do what you want. Pay your mortgage off, whatever, that's our money to do what we want either corporately or as individuals, what have you … I think that they didn't—not I think, I know—they didn't respect that.

Other participants we spoke to were even more frank about the problems, one noting, "They're scared; they ran. I don't blame them. They should run scared. If I was in WCOFF and I would have won $300,000 and they didn't pay me—it would have been ugly." Yet, more than half of the players we spoke with at both of these high-stakes leagues were veterans of WCOFF, meaning that even that experience did not cause them to flee the activity. One participant who was owed money for his winnings stated: "You're going to find the disgruntled. We're not disgruntled. I even lost money and I'm not disgruntled."

WCOFF established the foundation for what is high-stakes fantasy play today. While the majority of the leagues evolve around football, baseball leagues are prevalent and high-stakes leagues based on other sports are in development. WCOFF, if nothing else, whetted the appetite that clearly was there. Thus, the question becomes: what motivates that appetite for high-stakes play? Fantasy Sport Trade Association President Paul Charchian said that even he does not truly comprehend why one would opt for these leagues over localized leagues with friends, stating: "Why do I need to be the smartest guy in the room with a bunch of strangers who I can't brag to? I'd rather be the smartest guy in the room with my accounting department when they've got to see me at the water cooler all season long."

However, high-stakes play has never been more popular. Dave Gerczak of Fantasy Football Players Championship noted that it now caters to people of many different tastes with many different price points, ranging from just $77 to what they call their "high society" league requiring a $10,000 entry fee. He explained the current financial model of FFPC, which wanted to avoid the pitfalls WCOFF encountered:

> We pay out 80%. So, you're working with a 20% margin. You have credit card fees. That chops off 3% right away. So you have a 17% margin to work with. Any other industry, that's way too low, so you just really have to manage your costs intelligently. You can't just go and have a $150,000 marketing budget and expect to survive.

Gerczak believes strongly in establishing relationships with the participants, giving each of them his (and his two partners') cellphone numbers and creating trust with people who often play in more than one of the leagues offered by the company. He believes "it's almost like a concierge type thing where [if] you take care of these people, they learn to kind of love you, not love you, but really love what you do."

The participants fit no categorized profile, other than the fact that they typically have more disposable money than does the average American. Gerczak estimates that participants in the FFPC average annual incomes around $120,000–$140,000 per year. However, he was quick to note the outliers, including a New York schoolteacher who makes around $40,000 each year, but who spends $10,000 on high-stakes fantasy football. Gerczak noted that the teacher "is very good. He's done well. He's always been profitable."

The financial factor

On the periphery, it is not at all surprising that fantasy sport has drawn people who are interested in gambling aspects of sports. Levinson (2006) reported that $380 billion is wagered on sports each year. And scholars have discovered that, for instance, fantasy football increases NFL media consumption, presumably because of the money bet on the games (Drayer, Shapiro, Dwyer, Morse, and White, 2010). Thus, the gain/loss aspect of fantasy sport (see Lee, Kwak, Lim, Pederson, and Miloch, 2010) has been used to classify fantasy sport as a form of gambling (Moorman, 2008). Researchers of fantasy play have even studied—and found—money as a motive for overall play (Dwyer and Kim, 2011).

Obviously, our interviews with high-stakes participants included asking about the role of the money in overall play. While admitting that for some it is a clear motivation ("There are people who do it for a living. That that's all they do—and they make a few hundred grand a year"), others regarded the highest prizes as almost the equivalent of winning the lottery ("Everybody has a dream of winning a quarter of a million dollars doing something that most people see as just a hobby").

Many people were confident enough in their abilities that they were simply seeking to tap into the possibilities of using these innate or acquired skills for profit:

> I play in enough leagues so that luck will even out. If you play in enough leagues and you think that you're better than the rest and if I can win 25–30 % of my leagues, I'm going to make money. That's the main reason.

Playing in a multitude of high-stakes leagues was often viewed as a way to overcome the factor of luck, as some were convinced that their skills—presumably superior to those of the majority of participants—would overcome any bad luck:

> I'm making better than my stock portfolio. I probably have 20–25 % return on investment. As long as I keep breaking even, I'm happy. I'm not looking to put food on my table or buy clothes for my baby based on this. It's a hobby to me.

For many high-stakes participants, this supreme confidence in their own skills feeds into the fact that money is a high priority:

I always think I am the smartest guy in the room so it's all about the money for me. If anyone told you any different, it's about the money. When you're playing these leagues for this deal, it's all about the money.

Most participants conceded that the money changes the way they play as well as their other motivations, one noting, "If you're going to spend that much money, you're going to do your homework." Others said that the activity becomes virtually a second occupation when the financial rewards warrant the time commitment. Offered one participant:

I did some research, but nothing like I do now. It was strictly for fun. Well, once you start getting into $1,500.00 team, you take it a hell of a lot more seriously, and I research year round. I don't even stop.

Because of the intrinsic nature of gambling (producing more losers than winners), high-stakes participants often felt a sense of urgency about winning: "We all want and need to win something this year because we've taken some big hits." Others reported elevated levels of aggressiveness with picks ("The owners are a lot more aggressive in how they go after players. I think that's the big difference") while still others mentioned the desire not necessarily to win, but to stay in the game at this high level. ("If you break even, it's a good year. It allows you to play again. Originally when I went in [to the high-stakes world] $500 was a lot. Now I've [won more than $300,000], but [still] it's all about breaking even.)" Others referred to the same kind of "Lenny accounting" mentioned earlier, differentiating between their real/"do not touch" money and their fantasy sport money that was largely irrelevant to their daily existence:

Since I was writing part-time for a website I had enough for a league buy-in without touching my other money—my real money. I made a little money from the hobby so I thought I'd see if I could succeed at high-stakes.

One group talked about fractured friendships that resulted from the turbulent nature of high-stakes play, saying partners had decided the risk was no longer worth the potential reward. Nonetheless, many of the participants noted that as long as they were playing with "house money," they had managed to avoid any conflicts. ("Until last year, we had been extremely successful. We're still somewhere in the neighborhood of $98,000 in total winnings over six years' time, so the wives [can't] complain about it.")

Dramatic shifts in fortune yielded many interesting stories, including that of a married couple that won $75,000.00 playing fantasy football in a weekly league. They bought a house with the money, feeling that it was "pretty surreal to win that amount of money in one day just by sitting there watching football." Then there were the near misses. Here is one person's account of how close he came to victory at the end of 2011:

Last year, to win $7,500 [I needed Mike Wallace to do well for me]. Pittsburgh was down. Mike Wallace caught a ball and it was the last play of the game.

They were just throwing the ball to see if they could get down to do something. He caught the ball and if he would've turned and taken a single step it would've been two yards, I would've won. I lost the game by .02—.02 for $7,500! And he pitched the ball. He flea-flickered the ball. He pitched it to Antonio Brown who ran for like two yards and got tackled. It was nothing. All he had to do was turn up field and I win the game.

Questions of gambling

Financial incentives clearly play a larger role in the high-stakes leagues. The larger question becomes: to what extent does this type of play constitute gambling? Mahan, Drayer, and Sparvero (2012) report that fantasy sport play and frequent sports betting should be considered complementary habits. Definitions of gambling have percolated within news stories because of recent rulings regarding other activities, most notably poker, which a 2012 Maryland ruling (Katz, 2012) maintained was not gambling because the ratio of skill to luck favored the experienced participant. Conversely, Bernhard and Earle (2005) contend that "if we broadly define gambling as an activity that risks something of value (substantial amounts of money) on an event whose outcome is underdetermined (such as whims of a professional baseball season), fantasy [sport] clearly qualifies (p. 29)."

Respondents in our 48 interviews diverged greatly as to whether high-stakes fantasy play fit their definition of "gambling." The majority argued that it was not, though they offered some mitigating circumstances and potentially flexible definitions. One person conceded the difference between how he views his fantasy sport activity and how an outsider may view it, saying, "I'm not a big gambler. To me, this is not gambling. I'm sure, if I went to Gamblers Anonymous, they would tell me I'm in denial since I'm spending $20,000 a year on it." Others on the "con" side of the gambling debate focused their arguments on the large degree of skill involved:

> You have lawyers and very smart people writing papers and everything else that gambling is an element of chance, pull a lever, you win or don't win. You're not going to win anything in high-stakes fantasy football just pulling a lever, just letting your wife choose cute butts or uniforms.

Another respondent said that if his fantasy sport activity ever landed him in a courtroom, he would base his argument on the supremacy of skill: "What I would say in front of judge is: 'All right, if you think this is gambling, we'll take a cheat sheet, put it up on a wall. I'll put down my $1,000, you put down your $1,000. You throw darts and I'll pick players and we'll see who wins.'"

Some participants relied on the "mad money" argument, noting that, "When I send the entry fee at the beginning of the year the money's gone. If I win zero dollars, I have budgeted my life as predicated on the fact that I will not win. It's not gambling to me." Others maintained that fantasy play involves motivations that are different from those of the typical Las Vegas gambler, echoing Andy

Behrens's comments in Chapter 4 that most gamblers do not wish to invest and study for an eventual payoff many months later. One participant pointedly argued, "If you went into the casino and said, 'For $1,700 you can come back here and play fantasy football,' you wouldn't get too many bites."

Though a minority, some did concede that high-stakes fantasy sport is a form of gambling, albeit with qualifications. These qualifiers ranged from defending the skill involved ("I have to admit it's gambling. You put a certain amount of money out there and expect a return on it. But I like our odds a hell of a lot better than any other [form of] gambling") to the notion that fantasy sport supplants other, more destructive gambling habits ("I guess it's gambling [because] a lot of these guys, if they weren't playing fantasy football, they would pick up the phone and bet the games"). Other respondents argued that playing for $1,500 entry fees was not gambling because, "when I talk high-stakes players, I'm talking about guys who get into $10,000 leagues and $5,000 leagues. Those guys are going … where the money is." Still others, including Dave Gerczak of Fantasy Football Players Championship, opted not to weigh in on the subject of gambling. "I plead the Fifth [amendment]," he said.

Some high-stakes participants did mention the notion of fantasy sport filling a hole or need in their lives: "Your odds here are 900 to 1 to win $200,000, and that's pretty good odds, okay? The top 60 get money so you have a chance to win. I could lose $1,700 in a blackjack table in five minutes. This makes my money last six months." Another argued that since fantasy sport unfolds over several months, it can develop into a suitable substitute for gambling:

> High-stakes takes the place of just gambling week to week. You put in your money at the beginning of the year. You work for it all year. Just kind of replaces that urge a little bit. It's a little bit more delayed gratification because you don't get your money until January. You got some more direct control over what happens.

Echoing this sentiment, another respondent said:

> This is a less inexpensive way of doing it. You've got a true gambler, he could lose $500,000 a weekend. I can come here, pay $1,800 one time for a set of 16 weeks. I don't need to bet Chicago against Miami. It's a very inexpensive way of doing it if you [think of it as] $100 a weekend.

Nevertheless, many respondents subtly hinted at the inextricable link between gambling and high-stakes fantasy play:

> I've always been a big sports fan. I don't want to say a gambler, but ever since I was 12 or 13 years old, I wanted to come to Las Vegas. The first time I flew I was like 23 years old, it was out here, right in Las Vegas, and I'm a big sports fan, I watch football a lot. I said, "Hey, you're only using your knowledge you learned booking your games," so when I saw these contests I got into it.

The gambling/not gambling question was not the only compelling debate that surfaced in the respondent interviews. Many debated the role of luck vs skill within the overall competitions, at times expressing nostalgia for decades past. Now that the activity has gone mainstream, some participants long for the days when they were more exclusive purveyors of sports knowledge. Noted one person: "I would rather go back to old time and do your homework. Anybody can play fantasy today. You have so many different websites and ESPN's involved now. I remember when ESPN used to say Fantasy Football was a fantasy. Not anymore." Others experienced diminished success as a result of the leveling of the knowledge base and the increase in the high-stakes talent pool: "We won the second year. We won our third year. The first few years of high-stakes [were] a lot easier than it is now. Now, there's so much information and so much readily available. It's so easy to catch up and be at very least decent."

While participants differed on the proportion of fantasy games that involve luck vs the proportion based on skill, they almost unanimously believed that luck alone would not result in a financial windfall at this level. One person made the following comparison: "Poker is a good analogy because sometimes there is nothing any of those guys can do. You put your money in, you're 95% favored to win and the guy spikes the heart on the river and there's nothing you can do." Another offered the following breakdown for ultimate fantasy success: "These guys can say what they want but 50% of it is draft, 30% of it is luck, and 20% of it is your transactions after the draft—your drops and your adds. But you've got to get lucky."

Low- vs high-stakes

We also asked respondents what led them to play for an inflated amount of money in entry fees. Our presumption was that local success led them to contemplate whether they could experience national success. That element definitely was present, but not uniformly so. Many wanted to find other participants who would take the games more seriously: "Free and low-stakes games don't really interest me because you are not trying that hard. There's nothing on the line. It's kind of like practicing for a game vs playing a game. Once you're actually in the game, there's something on the line." There seemed to be a consistent theme of participants not just wanting to win their local leagues, but wanting to win a league after everyone else had tried and failed. As one explained, "When I was in home or private leagues, I always took it more seriously than everyone else, or I always *wanted* to take it more seriously than everyone else. The more money you put in, the more serious you're taking it and the more competitive it is." Another respondent concurred: "I can't stand the online free leagues because it's too easy to abandon your team three weeks in if your team is doing crappy. Having a bit more money on it creates a seriousness and a focus. It [makes it] nice to win."

However, others noted that while they had intended to keep playing in local small-stakes or free leagues, the amount of money involved in high-stakes leagues eventually changed their minds:

I abandoned local leagues so I could concentrate on high-stakes this year. We just had so much money invested. And I enjoy the local aspect of it, but … you can't spend your time bickering with your buddies about your picks when you need to be focused on what you're doing [in high-stakes leagues].

Some of the responses also revealed participants' conviction that the effort required for fantasy play merited playing for a more substantial financial reward. As one person noted, "When you win a Yahoo! league, they give you little [virtual] medals and stuff. Even in [low-stakes] you end up winning $500 and you think, 'Man, I did all that work for $500?'" Another cited $500 as an amount not worthy of maximum effort, even though investing $500 would easily place him in the top 10% of fantasy leagues: "Our local league is $500. It's hard to get your local guys to compete. It takes a certain person to compete in the high-stakes events." Another interviewee had a considerably inflated operational definition of what constituted "high-stakes":

The only one I really care about is the one I have been in for 25 years with all my guys from Kansas City. It's not high-stakes because the winner wins $7,000. It is not anything that makes or breaks any of us. It is not enough motivation that everyone works hard at it.

One can conclude that while high-stakes participants are drawn to the opportunity to win larger amounts of money, they also enjoy competing with kindred spirits who take the game as seriously as they do—something that was lacking in many local leagues. Ultimately, they sought venues such as Las Vegas to find comrades on the long tail of the fantasy sport participation bell curve.

Motivations: friendship

The notion of finding kindred spirits leads to further discussion of high-stakes participants' motivations, beyond the obvious financial incentives. Their many reasons for play could be classified in ways similar to the results outlined in Chapters 2 and 3. One of these motivations was camaraderie, a major factor for many interviewees even though it evolves a bit differently at this level. Participants sometimes enter the high-stakes arena together with people they already know. They might be close family members and friends who have this activity as a common point of contact, perhaps a shared annual vacation. As one person noted, "It's just being able to come with my cousin, Number 1. Getting away and just enjoy sports and competition." Another interview featured two friends from college who have jointly owned a team for many years, making fantasy sport the point of reference for a long-lasting friendship. One of them explained, "It's camaraderie and more of a hobby. It simply requires that every day Mark and I talk for at least five or 10 minutes about our team. It has allowed us to have a closer friendship over the years because [of these] forced interactions." Similarly, another interviewee is among a group of friends who travel together to Las Vegas each year to participate in high-stakes: "We come out here, at least for three hours you turn your [electronics] off and you focus on something. It's just a great escape. We're too busy to do anything else during the year. Fantasy football is the basis of our friendship. That's what keeps us in contact."

Others found new friends, particularly after their first year of competition:

> When I came to an event it was all about, 'Oh, I'm going to win. I'm going to crush this. It's all about money.' But then you start meeting people. The first year I met four or five people that I still talk to and then I'll see them … It turned out to be a little bit more than what I expected it would be.

What many people found through repeated competition in multiple high-stakes leagues was a sense of commonality reinforcing notions of social identity (Tajfel and Turner, 1986) and fan identity theories (Wann, 1995; Wann and Branscombe, 1990; Wann, Melnick, Russell, and Pease, 2001). One person explained what felt like a revelation: "Sometimes you get to thinking that your life revolves around fantasy so hard that you're like, 'God, am I the only one in the world?' Then you run into someone that manages 150 teams. It's like, hey, other people do this, too." Another participant drew parallels to other niche activities: "It's no different than Comic-Con. No different than Star Trek conventions. It's a community of people that get together and totally vibe on each other." Another had felt like a relative outcast, only to find that others had the same feelings and tendencies. He offered this candid assessment of the participants: "We've got a lot of guys in here that are a little, what would you say, maybe ADD [Attention Deficit Disorder]? A little bit numbers geeks. Some of them are not overwhelmingly social. They are the guys I gravitate to."

These friendships have become both long-lasting and far ranging. For some, playing high-stakes fantasy sport has become a way of life among close friends:

> You have bonds with some of these people now. Certain people, I will travel to Washington because they have season tickets to the Redskins or I will travel to Indianapolis because they have season tickets for the Colts. The competition gets stronger because you are friends with them and you want to beat their ass.

Nevertheless, sometimes the financial investments required in high-stakes play put pressures on friendships that, while typically not severed, are clearly altered:

> I used to have like a silent partner, but he bowed out. He saw I wasn't having success winning the big thing so suddenly he doesn't have the money this year. Then one of my other friends, he's been in it a long time, this year he didn't have the cash so he didn't come in, so basically they're back at the hotel hanging out so I came by myself.

Respondents also reported sometimes forming partnerships with like-minded personalities. As one participant claimed, "We do over 90 high-stakes leagues. I was smart to realize, 'Hey, I need to find someone who thinks similar to how I do." Without a doubt, participating in these leagues is not just about money for the majority of people. As National Championship of Fantasy Football organizer Greg Ambrosius concluded, "This is like Christmas morning for many of these guys." Part of this holiday feeling is undoubtedly the companionship/camaraderie aspect of the activity as a whole.

Motivations: Schwabism

A motivation that clearly appeared to be elevated within this pool of participants was the desire to be the "smartest guy in the room," labeled as Schwabism by Ruihley and Runyan (2010). Given that many of the people come from high economic backgrounds, the desire to beat the best fantasy participants in the world becomes the primary motivational force. One team of partners featured a successful engineer and lawyer who shared a love for high-stakes fantasy football and a desire to keep their friendship going. One of them explained how these factors unfold:

> We're both successful enough workwise that, while the money is nice, the money is not a life changer. The money—I'm not going to say it's irrelevant, but it doesn't have a top 10 appeal to us. Instead, it's more being able to tell people that you won $150,000 in a high-stakes fantasy football league.

Arguing that this is a "fantasy football mecca," many others felt that a generous share of bravado was part of their high-stakes experience: "Get everybody together and it's a way to compete with everybody and [establish] bragging rights." Thus, high-stakes play offers the opportunity for the optimal game experience. One experienced participant noted this implied positive correlation between entry fee amount and quality of play: "The higher the stakes get, the better these things are, there is no doubt about that. At the $5,000 and $10,000 level, nobody makes mistakes."

While many would question the appeal of fantasy sport play with people they do not know, that often is a feature of competition at this level: "You're not challenging your family anymore. You're challenging random strangers." In this situation, fantasy sport play becomes a challenge of logic, a puzzle ("It is about learning the game, how to perfect it, how to adjust to everything that is being thrown at me to succeed") as well as an engrossing use of their expertise and people skills:

> I just don't have the patience or the mindset to get into the way you have to do this. But I do understand and observe everything that's going on here. Listening to people talk, watching the way they draft, getting into the psychology of what they're doing is fascinating.

For others, fantasy sport, when played at the highest level, may not even be about sport fanship anymore. Instead it becomes a complex calibration of trends and statistics, likelihoods and probabilities. While the generalized fantasy sport participant is described in Chapters 2 and 3 as almost a form of "Sports Fan 2.0", the high-stakes participant can be one to whom the games are simply a mechanism for testing mathematical propositions: "I've watched minimal football past few years. It's all about numbers to me." Another person argued that the wide range of movable parts is what makes the overall activity so compelling: "I like the analytical strategy. The math. All those components. It uses a part of my brain that I don't get to use on a day-to-day basis." One person seemed to feel a sense of awe at the statistical aptitude of other high-stakes participants:

> The people who are really good at this year in and year out make this a math proposition. There are algorithms to every player and every team. Every field in every day or night situation. Clear vs rain. They shrink the playing field by having elements of mathematical certainty on their side and they're good at it.

As they strive to turn all of that time-consuming expertise into winning seasons and lucrative payoffs, participants can develop a form of myopia: other aspects of their lives fade into the background as the fantasy sport season unfolds.

> [I spend] probably 10 to 12 hours a week for the six weeks leading up to the season [researching fantasy sport] and then six or seven hours in season at least. That's not counting watching the games. You're gradually ramping it up as the pre-season goes along. I know I don't sleep much when I'm prepping for baseball or football. There's a lot of juice there, you're trying to learn new stuff, and it keeps you up late at night.

The desire to perfect their craft and demonstrate their mastery among other people who respect the choices and decisions involved is a primary motivator for many of the high-stakes participants. Said one highly involved person:

> When you're playing chess against somebody that you're better than and you know you're going to beat them all the time, you want to play somebody tougher. So you want to keep upping your game and beat the best.

Motivations: excitement, entertainment, enjoyment and eustress

Many people reported a thrill from participating that is particularly relevant for high-sensation seekers (Perse, 1996; Zuckerman, 1979), a group of people often linked to elevated media use (see Hoffner and Levine, 2007). The four "E" words combine to offer the equivalent of a "rush" or a shot of adrenaline that they feel with high-stakes play. Whether it fulfills a need to gamble or a related need to compete, for some it definitely delivers a "high." As one participant said:

> The money is honestly secondary. It's more that I've been an athlete all my life. It's more the competition. I don't get a chance for competition other than playing local league softball these days or things like that.

Within this motivation, the trip to Las Vegas and the draft of players becomes essential to the experience of play, and the actual results of the games become secondary. Noted one person:

> It's a different rush [than casino gambling]. Preparation for me for this is a big part of it too—like the month of doing practice drafts and studying. Once the draft's over then the season's just like, "Oh, OK." But getting to this point and being here for the draft, that's really to me the rush of the whole thing.

Another participant clearly prioritized the rush of competition in general above all other factors, citing his unique circumstances:

> I think my need for higher stakes is because I've hit the lottery—twice. First time for $16.8 million. I won the Pick-Six. And then the second time I won $1 million on scratch-off. The need for that rush is what draws me here because once you've had that, $500 doesn't cut it.

Of course, one could take a less positive view of the rush that results from sitting around a table drafting players to formulate pretend teams. One respondent felt that the high people got from playing fantasy sport was a less desirable substitute for what they wish they were doing with their lives: "It's kind of funny and maybe even a little sad that you look around and it's all pretty much middle-aged guys, you know? They can't play anymore."

Motivations: escape

Given that Billings and Ruihley (2013) found that the one motivational aspect of sports fandom that does not elevate because of fantasy play is the factor of escape, it was interesting that some cited this as the most important reason for participating at the high-stakes level. It appears that while fantasy sport may not, in isolation, offer greater degrees of escape, combining it with a trip to a desirable location can make it so. One person said the combination of factors made this activity "the greatest weekend of the year": "To be honest with you, it's the prize, it's loving football, it's a four-day pass away from the wife. We come with about nine, 10 people to the Venetian every year for 10 years. That's our four-day pass." Another interviewee, who sees the weekend as an eclectic combination of his favorite pass times, expressed similar sentiments:

> I always liked coming to Vegas. At that time, I think the grand prize was just $100,000 to start out with. So tempting. Three or four days in Vegas with fantasy football and all of these people coming together? I said, 'You can't beat that,' so that was almost like fantasy football heaven.

Sometimes it was more than just a "guys' getaway weekend." We encountered, for instance, a husband and wife who treated it as a couple's retreat from the rest of their lives: "We assume we lost at this point. [But] if we win, we're good ... If we win, we're great." When asked if being a woman in a very male (98%+) activity made participation stressful, the wife minimized these presumed stresses, citing escapism as a positive, and concluding, "I feel fine. I feel like I know football. I've watched football since I was a kid. I've had my own fantasy team for 11 years in our family league. I feel like I can compete against the best of them. It's not intimidating. I've played sports where I was the only girl as a kid."

Still, the majority of interviewees, men citing escapism, noted that the combined pressures of their occupations and family commitments made fantasy sport a welcome respite. One participant stated, "I am an attorney. Everyone has something. The one thing I do have is this and it keeps me sane." Another explained, "I'm a sports fan. With two young kids, this is my outlet. I don't have time to go join a basketball league and play two, three nights a week where I used to before I had kids. This is what gets my competitive juices flowing. It took over for me playing sports."

The fact that the majority of participants are middle-aged and beyond their competitive athletic years was again cited within this element of escape, albeit a lesser escape than playing sports was in the past.

> I love playing baseball. I love playing football, and as you get older, your skills aren't as good as they used to be. And I think it's a natural progression where you can still compete at a high level, but it's the mental part of the game instead of the physical part of the game.

Yet another person observed that for some people, escapism is a priority that trumps all the preparation involved and even the prospect of winning back at least some of their money. He said:

> [There are] people that draft that will have no chance when they walk out because they don't understand the game. I have friends that draft teams with their favorite players on it with no intention of winning. No intention of cashing. Just having fun and having your players—that's their enjoyment. Their goal isn't to win. Their goal is to have their favorite players and have a great time. Escape from the world for a while. That's it.

Priorities: fantasy vs favorite teams

Scholars have established links between traditional and fantasy sports play (Brown, Billings, and Ruihley, 2012; Karg and McDonald, 2011). As mentioned in the opening of this book, those loyalties can either align or, most often, divide. Lee, Ruihley, Brown, and Billings (2013) found that 41% of all fantasy participants indicated they would prefer a win by their fantasy team over the regular/favorite team they follow. We presumed that this percentage would be even higher for high-stakes fantasy participants when considering the amount of money involved. While interviewing 48 people does not provide a generalizable sample, nor does it feature an overall percentage, it is fair to conclude that the majority of the people interviewed would rather their fantasy team win. Some said they did not even have a favorite NFL team anymore. When presented with this dilemma, responses included:

> Oh, fantasy, definitely! Those slobs make millions of dollars whether they win or lose. I don't feel sorry for them if they lose. This is my Super Bowl for my family.

> I've got to answer honestly. I mean, I've rooted against the Cowboys if I had a player that was going to help my fantasy team win. At the end of the day, the Dallas Cowboys don't pay my bills. Fantasy football could win me some money where I could do some good things.

> For $150,000 I will take winning the league. Division? You're talking $7,000, $8,000; you have to give the Jets the Super Bowl. But for $150,000, you have to take [the fantasy win].

> We would be in two different leagues, and one player is on our team and the other league, the player is on the team you're playing. It's a win/lose [proposition]. You don't know who to cheer for.

One person offered a nuanced response, citing favorite players and yet no favorite team. As a result, he concluded, "I guess I tend to root for the players that I draft, but I draft them because I like them. I like their skill set, I like their situation. I am a fan, but now I am more of a fan of just fantasy." While some authors (see Billings and Ruihley, 2013) cite elevated fandom from fantasy sport play, others think the dramatic increase in consumption (threefold according to Enoch, 2010) of sports media is not the result of increased investment in the outcome of regular non-fantasy games. Rather, as one high-stakes participant commented, they see the fantasy vs traditional divide as a chasm that is not easily bridged: "The true sports fan would hate fantasy sports. [Fantasy] diminishes your love for sports. The fantasy team overrides. At least for me the gambling side of it takes over the level of the team." Other participants registered differences in the mediated sports product as they attempt to cater to what has become the equivalent of the radio term "P1," or primary listener/huge fan. As one person explained:

> The NFL's not stupid. They play fantasy football on NFL.com. It's the next generation of people who are going to … add revenue to the league. Now you've got somebody who's 18–20 [years old] who's watching the stats scroll along the bottom—watching a game that's 41 to nothing! Why? Because he's got a player involved and he needs that player to catch another pass to win, whatever it is. I think the NFL and other people are smart enough to have seen how fantasy football impacts their bottom line.

Conclusion

Thus, we return to the notion of low vs high-stakes and their similarities and commonalities. What we find is that within the general notion of pay vs free, we see differences in age, number of years playing, and amount of media consumption. These are not differences to be disregarded. Free participants are significantly more likely to be younger, having invested fewer years in the activity, and spending less time with media related to the activity. However, only the motivational factors of escape and ownership change when smaller amounts of money enter the equation, with free participants experiencing less of both through their participation. One way to interpret these results is that the higher stakes matter, but that money is merely one of many salient factors, along with issues such as pride, competitive superiority, and overall sport-based credibility.

Major differences came to the forefront when we examined those participating with money in a prize fund. Areas of arousal, camaraderie, competition, self-esteem, and social sport all had higher averaging motive scores for those experiencing fantasy sport with a prize fund attached to winning. The areas of control, escape, ownership, pass time, and surveillance all were statistically equal. Implications and ideas surrounding these results were discussed.

Including high-stakes fantasy participants in the debate does not directly offer data points of reference, as they were not quantitatively surveyed. Nonetheless, qualitative data arising from the 48 people interviewed lead us to the following conclusions:

- Financial motivations diminish other motivations for high-stakes participants.
- High-stakes participants are less likely to find camaraderie within local leagues, finding more camaraderie in high-stakes leagues.
- High-stakes participants are more likely to participate based on dimensions of Schwabism.
- High-stakes participants are more likely to experience a "rush" from competition.
- High-stakes participants are less likely to have a favorite professional team.
- If high-stakes participants have a favorite professional team, they are more likely to root for a fantasy win than a win by their favorite professional team.

A debate undergirding the money issues (e.g. paying for hosting, paying into a prize fund, and high-stakes) concerns the degree to which understanding high-stakes fantasy sport play actually matters. It could be seen as nothing more than an interesting diversion into a subculture or, conversely, it could be seen as the ultimate representation of the motivations activated by playing fantasy sport. As FSTA President Paul Charchian argued:

> You're dealing with probably in the neighborhood of a 1000th or a 10,000[th]. They're playing for only one reason: cash. They're playing with strangers, so it's not camaraderie. There's so much money involved, it's not because they want to go to a draft party or something. There's nobody playing in a

$1,500-entry league that is going to mail it in. They know what they're doing and they're going to be making the best moves they can every single week. So, it's even more of a game of skill at that level.

This quotation underscores our conclusion: among free participants or those spending small amounts of money, motivations for play seldom differ; but when one examines the high-stakes fantasy sport experience, it obviously is a whole new ballgame.

6 Enough is enough

Exiting and burnout of fantasy sport participants

In his 2008 best seller, *Outliers: The Story of Success*, Malcolm Gladwell explores the characteristics of those who achieve greatness within a given realm of society. One principle Gladwell (2008) highlights is the "10,000 Hour Rule" (p. 39), a concept founded on the belief that it takes 10,000 hours for a person to master an activity. Using examples ranging from Microsoft's Bill Gates (whose private Lakeside School purchased a time-sharing computer terminal at a time where most colleges did not have one, allowing the then-eighth grader to perform actual computer programming) to the Beatles (who once played grueling eight-hour sets at a Hamburg club), Gladwell contends that greatness is defined by repetition, familiarity, and practice.

Of course, Gladwell is speaking of outliers—by definition, a rare and often transcendent group. Most people in the world will fail to reach the 10,000-hour threshold for two main reasons: lack of willpower/focus, and burnout. The majority of this book has been devoted to those who love playing fantasy sport, dissecting their reasons for doing so. However, not everyone finds fantasy sport compelling, and many more play for a certain amount of time before opting to pursue other things. While the overall trajectory of the number of fantasy sport participants as well as the amount of money within the industry continues to escalate, it is important to note that this is the result of an ebb and flow—the number of people joining the activity continually outnumbers the number of people who opt to exit the activity. Yet, much can be gleaned from the examination of people who terminate their involvement in fantasy sport. This chapter features an in-depth analysis of this segment of the fantasy sport community: those who burn out on fantasy sport, quit the activity, or opt to participate in a different format or manner.

This book has clearly established an upward trajectory for fantasy sport in terms of popularity, attention, and revenue. We have described the people inside the industry who work with, participate in, or cover fantasy sport activities. We also have endeavored to understand people's demonstrated affinity for the activity, translating real sporting outcomes into competition among peers, family, and friends. We have scrutinized the motivations of participants (Chapters 2 and 3), talked to those who have made careers of fantasy sport (Chapter 4), and heard from fans who play for love and/or money (Chapter 5). However, the burnout group deserves further exploration—and often is overlooked, simply because they lacked longevity in the fantasy sport world. While it is crucial to understand what attracts so many to this activity, it is equally important to discover why others turn away from it.

Burnouts and people who abandon fantasy sport once shared many characteristics of the present participants, consumed the activity, or competed side by side with friends or family. But due to a variety of variables, they decided to (a) quit the activity, (b) suspend their participation in the activity, or (c) opt for other formats, styles, and mechanisms to participate in a different way. At first glance, one might dismiss this group, since they no longer are avid participants. Yet analyzing their feedback provides valuable information for fantasy sport providers, offering insights on the reasons some people decide fantasy sport is not worth their time and attention. Consequently, this chapter combines studies from three primary sources. First, the Fantasy Sport Trade Association (FSTA) commissioned a study from Ipsos Public Affairs (Ipsos) that specifically queried respondents about their reasons for abandoning fantasy sport play. This information will provide a useful heuristic for understanding baseline motivations for *not* playing fantasy sport. Second, we will content-analyze a dataset made available for this book by a mainstream fantasy provider. The dataset features open-ended questions asked of people opting to quit playing at the host site. Given that some were rejecting the activity while others were rejecting the fantasy sport gaming provider, the provider will remain anonymous. Lastly, areas of quitting and burnout will be linked to motives discussed earlier in this text, with appropriate implications extrapolated. Our goal is to better understand those who participate in what could be termed fantasy sport exodus, either in the form of burnout or by not returning to a league provider.

Our approach offers a sort of "exit interview," yielding the types of candid, useful responses that employers could seek from departing employees (but rarely do). When people make a decision about whether to continue an activity, they have essentially offered themselves a choice: change vs continuity. The people studied in this chapter have clearly opted for change. The ancillary questions are (a) why did they quit? and (b) did they quit the activity entirely, or just decide to have it delivered to them in a different fashion?

Operationalizing burnout

Before delving into the specifics of each dataset, we must outline the meaning and application of the term "burnout." In sports contexts, burnout primarily concerns an abrupt end to physical activity or participation in a traditional sport. Some might think of a child with significant athletic talent who nevertheless becomes weary of the effort it takes to excel at a particular sport. Others may think in terms of physical burnout associated with overtraining or specialization—for example, a 12-year old baseball pitcher who breaks down physically after throwing too hard and too soon. Or, sports observers may recall some of the top athletes who walked away at the height of their success, such as Bjorn Borg's sudden retirement from tennis in 1983 or Barry Sanders' early exit from the NFL in 1998.

Sports sociologist, Jay Coakley (2007), defines burnout as "a condition that occurs when stress becomes so high and fun declines so much that a person decided to withdraw from a role or activity" (p. 644). In their ethically focused examination of sports burnout, Lumpkin, Stoll, and Beller (2003) address the concept, referring to it as "too much, too often, and too soon of a supposedly good thing" (p. 121). The majority of research in this area traditionally focuses on the youth athlete, attempting to discern why or how a certain athlete tired of an activity prematurely. Such a focus is natural, as most would presume that these are cases in which the young body was willing, but the spirit was not. Issues of motivation, exhaustion, self-determination, stress, overtraining, and self-esteem tend to rise to the top of reasons why athletes of all skill levels discontinue participation in a sport (Goodger, Gorely, Lavallee, and Harwood, 2007; Schaufeli and Buunk, 2003). Given some of these top predictors of burnout, we might not be able to draw a perfect correlation between participation sport burnout and fantasy sport withdrawal. But it is important to try; especially since fantasy sport is an activity in which one could participate at virtually any age. Fortunately, the divide between participating in enacted sport and participating in sport-related activities is not so rigid that it fails to provide insight. Embracing prior work in this area can assist in understanding burnout in this relatively new field of fantasy sport research. Lumpkin *et al.* (2003) offer reasons for burnout on many levels of competition (e.g. youth, interscholastic, intercollegiate, and professional sports). Some of the listed reasons are quite applicable to participation in fantasy sport and are detailed in Table 6.1.

As is clear from Table 6.1, many similarities exist between participation sport and fantasy sport withdrawal. Research in the area of athletic burnout primarily studies the individual, offering recommendations about how to handle similar individuals within similar experiences. The examination of fantasy sport burnout in this chapter will also focus on the individual experience, examining both motivation for participation and reasons for withdrawal. In addition, the analysis will include suggestions and implications for the industry and its stakeholders.

Industry-wide understandings of burnout: the Ipsos composite

A report generated by Ipsos (2010) was provided to the Fantasy Sport Trade Association. In addressing the question of *why* people were quitting fantasy sport participation, an interesting first question dealt with *when* they exit fantasy sport play. Using 581 fantasy sport "quitters," the information focused on when people quit fantasy sport, number of years' participation prior to quitting, and reasons people chose to leave the activity. Each will be explored here.

Year of quitting

The first analysis focused upon what was deemed the "year of quitting." The good news for the fantasy industry is that the Ipsos report indicates an astounding 75% of those who have ever participated in fantasy sport are still actively engaged in

Table 6.1 Reasons people quit fantasy sport

Reason for burnout	Participation sport	Fantasy sport
Overuse	Overusing and overtraining the body; causing the person to be fatigued.	Involved in too many leagues in one sport or too many sports in a year.
Poorly qualified people	Coaches not qualified to lead the person in a particular sport and/or exhibit poor leadership characteristics.	There are not poor coaches in fantasy sport, but there are poorly qualified competitors. Many leagues end a season with several competitors leaving the league mid-season.
Overemphasis on winning	Too much emphasis on winning can remove any fun or learning that may occur.	Too much emphasis on winning can remove any fun or camaraderie that may occur.
Loss of intrinsic motivation	Athletes just do not care anymore about becoming the best they can be.	Participants lose interest in the league and are not motivated to compete.
Changing interests	Athletes change interests, especially at a young age.	Participants change interest with life or sport interest changes.
Loss of friends and social activities and desire to spend more time with family	Dedication to a sport can be very time consuming.	Fantasy sport can be very time consuming.

*Categories and participation sport comments cited Lumpkin et al. (2003, p. 122).

the activity in some form. Such a retention rate is virtually unparalleled in other leisure activities—for example, a relatively small segment of people who ever sample a television show continue to watch episodes on a regular basis for years to come. In an era of short attention spans, with consumers constantly moving from one activity to another in an effort to alleviate boredom, three out of every four participants have continued to carve out time in their schedules to prioritize fantasy sport gaming.

The bad news for fantasy sport industry leaders was that in 2007 and 2008, a significant spike occurred in people leaving the activity (14% of "quitters" left the activity in 2007, while that number increased substantially to 24% in 2008). While a portion of this increase is very likely attributable to the economic recession the United States entered in 2008, such a trend line nonetheless concerns fantasy sport providers. As industry leaders commented in Chapter 4, retaining current fantasy sport participants requires considerably less effort and resources than recruiting new players. Thus, the activity appears to be adding new players each year, yet with a higher percentage of people quitting the activity in more recent years. Such a pairing of results seemingly indicates that people joining the activity now are less likely to decide that it is a perfect match with their interests, when compared to people who already have started and continue to play. Subsequent analysis must provide more information to analyze these overall trends. If there continues to be a rise in people leaving the activity, organizations must determine why, which was what Ipsos explored later in its work.

Participation prior to quitting

The second Ipsos analysis examined participation length of time (in years) prior to quitting fantasy sport; the mean amount was 3.7 years. However, 41% of those quitting stopped participating after one year or less, skewing the data in that regard. If one sets aside these single-year participants from the overall total (assuming that they were merely "testing the waters"), the mean number of years before quitting for all others inflates to nearly seven years. Thus, it appears that there are two key decision points regarding whether to exit the activity: one comes when players have competed for one full season, and the other comes as they decide whether fantasy sport represents a life phase for them, or a lifestyle.

Similar to taste-testing a food or test-driving a car, these people actually gave the activity some form of examination, ultimately concluding that fantasy sport was not for them. As consumers, they tried the product and chose to reject it. However, just as any good marketing research can provide useful avenues for future growth, examining the reasons for quitting allows an exploration of whether (a) the activity truly was not for them, or (b) the activity *in its current format* was not for them. If the latter proves true, adjustments and adaptations could lead some who are part of the fantasy sport exodus to give the activity another chance in different circumstances. On the other hand, there is a real possibility that interest, opinion, and lifestyle factors (Shank, 2009) could play a major part in people's dissatisfaction with fantasy sport. Knowing whom *not* to market to can save an organization significant resources; meanwhile, the industry could target those more likely to take the proverbial second bite at this consumer apple.

Overall, 35% of quitters participated in fantasy sport for four or more years, with 10% playing ten or more years. Knowing that a major motivation of fantasy sport participation is socializing, camaraderie, or competition among family, friends, and peers, a type of snowball effect should be considered when analyzing why fantasy participants opt to leave the activity. For instance, a league with meager, low-level participation may decide as a group that it is no longer worth the time and effort involved. Thus, all of the participants would join the fantasy sport exodus. In addition, sometimes the leader of an activity succumbs to burnout. If the leader is regarded as a market maven, that single departure could affect the opinions of others. Entire leagues could fold—even when populated with people interested in continuing their fantasy sport participation—because the activity is "not the same" without the leader or because they know of no other league to which they can transfer. The longevity of some leagues could often be viewed as intransigence, in which league members rarely interact with other leagues, causing insularity and a potential notion that one is not as much a fantasy sport participant as he or she is a fantasy sport participant *just for this particular league with these particular people.*

With 35% of those leaving fantasy sport having participated for four years or more, one has to consider the potentially influential role of the market maven. As described in Chapter 2, market mavens have been labeled as amplified consumers. They are attentive, involved, and interested consumers that enjoy sharing their information and expertise (Chelminski and Coulter, 2007; Clark, Goldsmith, and Goldsmith, 2008; Feick and Price, 1987; Higie, Feick, and Price, 1987; Stokburger-Sauer and Hoyer, 2009). The market maven is an influential consumer who considers the desire and need to share marketplace information. Applying the mavenism concept to fantasy sport, Billings and Ruihley (2013) found fantasy sport participants to associate with mavenism, significantly more than do traditional, non-fantasy sports fans. Whether it involves an outcry via social media or loyal fans venting their views on a billboard, traditional sports fans find ways to voice their opinions. If these traditional fans can wield their influence in such ways, one has to assume that fantasy sport consumers also would react similarly.

Reasons for quitting

With fantasy sport participants increasingly identifying with mavenistic practices, it is important to analyze why such fans choose to leave the activity. This was explored by Ipsos (2010) and is outlined in Table 6.2.

Table 6.2 Reasons People Quit Fantasy Sport (n=581)

Reason	Percentage of quitting
There was too much time involved in managing fantasy team	26.0%
Lost interest in fantasy sport	16.0%
Friends dropped out of leagues	9.0%
The league was disbanded	5.0%
Participating in fantasy sport became too expensive	5.0%
Was not spending enough time with my family	5.0%
I didn't find fantasy sport to be fun	5.0%
Frustrated by too many losses	3.0%
Lost interest in sports in general	3.0%
I was not spending enough time on work obligations	3.0%
There was too much focus on individual players	3.0%
The product changed	2.0%
I didn't like rooting against my favorite teams	2.0%
Fantasy sport is just too geeky	2.0%

This third analysis from Ipsos (2010) helps to explain why people leave fantasy sport, as it urged participants to consider their primary reasons for quitting the activity. The items that participants ranked first, in their own lists, were gathered, averaged, and ranked from highest to lowest percentage. The top five reasons proved to be:

1   Managing fantasy sport teams required too much time/was too time-intensive (top motive for 26% of those quitting the activity).
2   Lost interest in fantasy sport (top motive for 16%).
3   Friends dropped out of leagues (top motive for 9%).
4   The league was disbanded (top motive for 5%).
5   Participating in fantasy sport became too expensive (top motive for 5%).

The top ranked reason is part of the fantasy genetic design, making it an interesting primary factor. Hours set aside to prepare for a draft, research lineup decisions, analyze trades, study free agent players, and follow results of players on a fantasy roster are elements of the activity at its most fundamental core. While passing time appears to be a key function of many participants currently in the activity, this motivation proved to be a double-edged sword for 26% of those who quit. They essentially argued that fantasy sport was *too* effective at passing time, to the point that it was detrimental to overall life balance. Thus, the abundance of easily obtainable sports data poses problems for those at both ends of the commitment spectrum: casual players are overwhelmed by the endless sources of usable data, while highly involved players (as we have seen in previous chapters) feel that fantasy play has gotten too easy for the masses. The industry's response appears to be a broader array of options. Chapter 4 explained how Fox Sports, for instance, seeks casual players who could begin the formulation of their teams in a mere five minutes; meanwhile, CBSSports.com appears to seek the deeply committed players. Perhaps one way to lure back people who have quit the activity might be to more clearly label various provider goals to match personal interests. Decisions about time commitments are in the hands of the participants. It is not a requirement to spend a lot of time researching and following player performances, although most would argue there is a clear positive correlation between being successful and the amount of time devoted to the activity.

The second, third, and fourth reasons for quitting are different from the time management issue just discussed, because each concerns maintaining interest in the activity. A fantasy sport provider must hold interest, keep the product fresh, and avoid having people drop out; yet these reasons represent a segment of the population whose interest appears to be waning. It can be argued that each season brings a fresh perspective, with new drafts, new players to choose from, a new team to follow, the employment of different strategies, and updated story lines. Nonetheless, one could argue that the product has changed very little. A player may have sharper management skills, but the rest of the game still largely involves the same draft formats, scoring systems, and schedules that were used in the 1990s. Such consistency provides continuity, yet also could account for these delineated forms of burnout. Updating areas of scoring, enhancing graphics, increasing scoreboard quality, utilizing social networking areas, or offering product features could all be potential remedies for these concerns. Given the proven formulas for success, it could be that people may feel they already know the outcome of many contests because expert advice can project winners fairly accurately. Factors involved in player exodus certainly justify inquiry into what motivates the fantasy sport participant, discussed at length in this text.

The fifth reason people leave the activity concerned cost factors, again a telling statistic given that the majority of participants play for little or no investment. However, these comments appear to stem from providers that charge for access to their sites along with ancillary products that could be viewed as essential for success. If participants leave fantasy sport because of costs, perhaps they are unaware of the free offerings by many providers. Still, the fact that they are exiting an activity, and not simply the provider, indicates that they did not consider the price point a value. Another possible explanation for departure based on price could be the implementation of prize funds in many leagues. There may be a $50 USD entry fee into a league, with $12.50 USD going toward the league provider and $37.50 USD contributed to a prize fund to be distributed at the end of the season. At the end of a losing season, a player naturally may reflect on the money invested and feel reluctant to invest even the smallest amounts of money in coming years.

Burnout recap

As mentioned, the Ipsos (2010) data provide many implications for fantasy advocates and associates to consider. As we focus here on those who have chosen to leave fantasy sport entirely, it is important to reiterate that this activity is not for everyone. A participant might have been filling a last-minute league spot for a friend, joined a league because the rest of the family was participating, or capitulated to office pressures to join a fantasy sport league for fear of being left out of group dynamics. Whatever the reason for joining, it is worth focusing on the exit. After a test drive in the time-consuming and quick moving vehicle that is fantasy sport, why did these people decide to quit?

The point of no return: a study of NBA league lermination

The Ipsos analysis is important, as it gauges consumer opinions and actions of an entire industry. Shifting to a more specific and targeted examination, one fantasy host provided the authors of this text data on why people chose not to rejoin National Basketball Association (NBA) leagues. The data provided had not been analyzed by the organization beyond rudimentary spreadsheets. Since this information is primarily negative and gives reasons why participants chose not to return to the host organization, we will exclude the name of the host from this discussion. For the purposes of sharing the data in this chapter, the provided open-ended responses were coded, grouped, and summed. While this may not include people who have completely abandoned fantasy sport, these are consumers who have chosen not to return to a provider for a variety of reasons. It should be noted that the league they left was a free hosting league, meaning financial considerations (at least in terms of league entry) were not pertinent to the overall discussion. The general findings are extrapolated upon in Table 6.3.

The fantasy provider sent a survey to people who played fantasy basketball in 2010 and did not return to the activity in 2011. The survey simply asked participants to explain why they did not return to participate the next year. The top reasons among the 431 respondents that were pertinent to the overall discussion are listed, followed by a discussion of each.

- The logistics and format of the draft or the league (81 mentions; 18.79% of mentions)
- Lack of advertising and communicating start of the season (51; 11.83%)
- Time restraints (44; 10.21%)
- Participation in other sport or site (39; 9.05%)

Logistics

Each of the listed top reasons has major implications for those involved in the industry or hosting league play. The number 1 reason pertains to the actual product (i.e. the host site, the platform, the design, etc.). It can be easy to transfer blame to the consumer or cite personal differences with the activity as a whole, yet it is significant that these people have made this option the top reason for exiting. While not an uncommon reason, exiting a league or host because of

Table 6.3 Coded responses for not returning to anonymous fantasy provider NBA league

Code	Count	Percentage
Logistics/format/draft	81	18.79%
Advertise/communicate start	51	11.83%
Time restraints	44	10.21%
Reward	41	9.51%
Other sport/other site/following friends	39	9.05%
Competition (seriousness, champions, other)	38	8.82%
Lack of interest (sport or game)	34	7.89%
Technical difficulties/customer service	18	4.18%
Lack of other participants	15	3.48%
Player profile missing	9	2.09%
Apps/technology	8	1.86%
Communicate how to play	3	0.70%
Money/price	2	0.46%
Vague response (uncategorized)	*48*	*11.14%*
Total	**431**	**100.00%**

league rules, format, or draft experience is troublesome because that power, control, and design are in the hands of the fantasy provider. One comment about this type of logistical frustration:

> Rules that govern the playoff tiebreakers are completely absurd. My team had the 2nd best record in the league, but had the 3-seed simply because the best team in the league was in our division. The best team in the other division, despite having a record worse than mine, got the 2 seed. We tied our playoff matchup 4-4, and the other team advanced based upon the tiebreaker of them being the highest seed. How much sense does that make? (Fantasy Host Data, 2011)

Another comment states, "Didn't like the fact that players can only play so many games at a certain position. At the end of the season, all my players were frozen" (Fantasy Host Data, 2011). These comments are anecdotal, yet they show the passion that people have for the nuance of the game; both dealt with feelings that the whole system was unfair, which appears to be an essential concern in all fantasy sport play. When grouped with others sharing the same logistical concerns, the non-returners compile a case for the industry to continually change formats and styles, not just for innovation's sake but also for the sport-based goal of fair play. The suggestion offered here is not to haphazardly alter game systems based on small aggregate survey responses; however, overarching trends that question issues of fundamental fairness and equity should be continually studied and, potentially, remedied. Understanding and identifying issues that are frustrating to non-returners may save others from experiencing the same issues.

Lack of advertisement or communication

The second highest-rated reason people did not return to this particular hosting site/league was simply not knowing that the league was getting started. One could argue that the die-hard consumers will know the season start date, but 11.83% of comments dealt with being unaware of it. One participant suggests that the host provider:

> Send an email reminder two weeks before [the] NBA regular season kickoff. I forgot about getting people together until it was less than a week away from the first game. I quickly tried to get enough people for a league, but I couldn't. (Fantasy Host Data, 2011)

Another participant comments on a notice of an incomplete league:

> We got kicked out of our draft because one person failed to create an account. If I would have received a notice from [fantasy provider] I could have corrected this issue ... I could not get another draft time for three or four days which ... was ridiculous. Therefore, I took my entire league [elsewhere]. (Fantasy Host Data, 2011)

These comments focus on the need for enhanced communication. People are busy, and adding fantasy sport to their already full schedules may require multiple reminders to raise fantasy sport participation above the overall clutter of their lives. In addition to busy personal lives, the sports calendar and media attention to all sports—even during the off-season—are constant, fast-paced and continually expanding. With such a wide range of media selections, some consumers can become so engrossed in one sport that they do not focus on the start of another. Communicating, advertising, and marketing the beginning of fantasy leagues in the appropriate channels can greatly increase the rate of people who opt to return to the activity.

Time restraints

Ipsos data listed the time-consuming nature of fantasy sport as the top reason for terminating activity, and time restraints again appear in this study, ranking third in this fantasy provider dataset. Comments cited everything from new babies to new spousal commitments. The standard comment could be encapsulated in this participant's view:

> My decision was based solely on my available time, which with the arrival of my new son, and added responsibilities on my job [was not plentiful] … I love fantasy games, and football fit more in my schedule than basketball, mainly because it does not require a daily update. Basketball would require my daily attention, and I just don't have the time [because of additional familial responsibilities]. (Fantasy Host Data, 2011)

Other comments suggested that a participant would return if the fantasy provider could "add three hours of time to each day and one extra week per month" or "add an hour a day to my life" (Fantasy Host Data, 2011). Not possible, but there *are* some practical ways to shrink the amount of time needed to participate fully in a fantasy league. As many participants mentioned, daily leagues are difficult and take up a lot of time. Setting a lineup once per week, similar to most American football and baseball leagues, is a suggestion fantasy sport providers might consider.

Even without major alterations in format, giving users the option to have a daily or weekly league would provide the sense of personalized variations many consumers now expect (see Anderson, 2006). Control and access to league formatting and rules are not options that should be based on money. Rather, the industry will have to address more continuums beyond pay vs free to encompass issues such as minimal vs maximal time commitment as well as flexible vs inflexible league setting formats.

Selection of other sport or provider

According to Chapter 4, many in the fantasy sport industry believe that once a person begins to play with a given fantasy sport provider, he or she is highly unlikely to switch. In this category of responses, the participants are not really leaving the activity, but are leaving for other fantasy offerings, other providers, or following league members to another league home. One commenter argues that he "would just say that I like [other provider] leagues better ... I think [the other provider] league home pages are better and easier to follow. They are set up better" (Fantasy Host Data, 2011).

Regarding other sports, many participants simply stated that they enjoyed other sports and were not that interested in fantasy basketball, possibly indicating that reasons for quitting or switching may be different for more established fantasy sports such as football and baseball. Many comments resembled those of this participant:

> I follow football, hockey, and NASCAR. I tried to get into basketball because some guys at work were really into it. [I] watched a few games, tried fantasy basketball, but just could not get into another sport. Where I live, we have hockey and football. I also know quite a few people who race cars. I have too much else to do and don't have time for another sport. (Fantasy Host Data, 2011)

Matching to motives for play

Factors that motivate people to participate in fantasy sport may figure prominently in the reasons they list for exiting the activity. This is true of any relationship that people enter because of a perceived "value added" and exit because they feel there is no longer "value" to the association. Chapter 2 provided an outline for the motivations of participation in fantasy sport, and Table 6.4 details the top four motivations as measured by average scores, participants' top motives, relationship to enjoyment in the activity, and relationship to overall satisfaction with the activity.

The two motivations that appear in all four rankings are self-esteem and social sport.

Quitting and competition

While not the highest ranked reason for leaving the activity or provider, lack of competition and frustration with too many losses are prevalent in the responses of the exiting consumers. Matching these reasons for departure to participant motivation comes in the form of self-esteem and competition variables, with

Table 6.4 Rankings of participant motivation

Measure/ranking	Average factor score	Top participant motive	Relationship to enjoyment	Relationship to overall satisfaction
Rank 1	Self-esteem	Self-esteem	Self-esteem	Self-esteem
Rank 2	Social sport	Social sport	Arousal	Social sport
Rank 3	Control	Camaraderie	Social sport	Arousal
Rank 4	Competition	Control	Pass time	Surveillance

competition being the variable easiest to match. As shown in Table 6.4, competition is one of the top variables based on average factor score. If consumers enjoy the competitive aspects of fantasy sport and do not feel they are being challenged enough, or are dominating the league year after year, where is the fun? This lack of competition also emerges in the participants who manage a roster for a partial season. While they may have had a valid lineup against some, the lineup may have been filled with injured or bye-week players for others. This creates a major imbalance in competition.

While some quitters complained of too little competition, many others were frustrated by too many losses. One of the top motivations that was seemingly universal (as seen in Table 6.4) involved self-esteem. Emotions and competitive spirit are integral facets of the fantasy sport experience. Participants may be frustrated with themselves for not performing at a high level or aggravated by losing to peers. Further, fantasy sport is an activity that is marketed and advertised as a way to test one's sports knowledge against that of others. Introduced by Ruihley and Runyan (2010) and tested further in the fantasy sport industry by Billings and Ruihley (2013), the concept of Schwabism applies to this area of self-esteem and competition. Schwabism hinges on one's belief that one is an expert on sports statistics and information (Ruihley and Runyan, 2010). Billings and Ruihley (2013) used this concept to measure how much a participant considers himself or herself a "know-it-all" about sports in general or fantasy sport activity. The results of their analysis indicate that feelings of Schwabism are significantly more prevalent in fantasy sport participants when compared to traditional fans. Trash talking and joking occur frequently when one's favorite non-fantasy team loses a big game or has a terrible season. This typically irritates the person whose team is being criticized, and most fans tend to take it personally. Now consider that in fantasy sport, fans are trying to establish their "know-it-all" bona fides by competing against others who are trying to do the same thing. Outcomes establishing that one does not, in fact, know it all can shatter a person's self-esteem in short order.

Quitting and social aspects of fantasy sport

A top five reason for exiting in both the Ipsos and fantasy provider data was following friends to another site or having friends drop out of the league. The motivation of social sport focuses on debating, discussing, and sharing one's opinions with others. Thus, it naturally follows that when close acquaintances leave the activity, some of the enjoyment is lost as well. With this issue, one must examine the role of a fantasy sport provider. It would be difficult to expect the provider to create friendships; however, it can foster communication ultimately leading to friendship or league commitment.

Ruihley and Hardin (2011b) explored this very notion of fantasy sport communication with an examination of message boards in the fantasy sport experience. Their analysis revealed reasons why people use message boards with fantasy sport. Major reasons identified were areas of logistical conversation, socializing, surveillance, and advice or opinion. In addition, the analysis found higher overall satisfaction with fantasy sport and greater intent to return to the activity for those utilizing message board features, as opposed to those not using message boards. Ruihley and Hardin (2011b) provided discussion points to fantasy sport providers centering on promotion, content, and stickiness. From a promotion standpoint, fantasy sport providers can advertise and market the social aspects of the activity by highlighting social networking opportunities (e.g. Facebook, Twitter, and message boards) available through the host site. Content is another important area that can be bolstered by social networking. Ruihley and Hardin (2011b) state:

> Knowing that [fantasy sport users] turn to other participants to socialize and gather information and advice can lead to a plethora of content for fantasy-sport-hosting organizations and web sites. Fantasy sport organizations can create specific message boards on a national level to address information and advice concerns. (p. 247)

A final consideration centers on stickiness. Stickiness has been defined as the "repetitive visits to and use of a preferred web site because of a deeply held commitment to reuse the web site consistently in the future" (Li, Browne, and Wetherbe, 2006, p. 106; Ruihley and Hardin, 2011b). The very nature of fantasy sport promotes participant behavior consisting of viewing a scoreboard, posting on a message board, or socializing in a chat room. With these types of activities, web traffic on fantasy sites can increase if participants stay on the site or constantly check in. If the content captures the attention of the consumer, this technological dependency can be beneficial to all parties. Maintaining and updating web presence is just one way an organization can address communication and customer retention. However, technology could be viewed as a double-edged sword as the more information and layers of knowing are featured in fantasy sport, the more some might feel they cannot maintain proper knowledge levels to compete with an ever-more-knowledgeable fantasy sport participant base.

Conclusion

The goal of this chapter is to illustrate just how important the "quitters" can be. Insights gleaned from those who exit the activity bolster claims about what the activity purports to be motivationally. For instance, if people end their fantasy sport involvement because they no longer feel camaraderie, it follows that they initially entered the activity searching for and expecting camaraderie. The larger question pertains to whether those who exit the activity are gone temporarily or permanently. If fantasy sport truly is tied to specific age demographics that ebb and flow depending on family and work responsibilities, it appears that relationships with fantasy sport could follow a model similar to the "Life Cycle of the Sports Fan" explained in Chapter 3 (Enoch, 2011). A confluence of circumstances can lead people to leave the activity. Given that there are so many variables at play, understanding a fraction of those reasons will reveal more about the consumer. This chapter represents a largely unstudied area of fantasy sport research, but one that will increasingly be pertinent to understanding the long-term trend lines associated with participation in fantasy sport as well as satisfaction and enjoyment gained from that participation.

7 Projecting the future

Pitfalls, opportunities, and the trajectory of fantasy sport

Writing about the future is always a quandary of trend vs fact, wish vs reality. The prognosticator who radiates confidence today might be humbled tomorrow, yet there is value in defining overall trend lines and combining these trends with overall patterns—in the case of fantasy sport, patterns of media use, sport fandom, and game play. This chapter attempts to develop the keenest possible sense of what the future holds for fantasy sport, while acknowledging that one major change in circumstances (e.g. a work stoppage in a given sport, or rulings regarding fantasy sport and gambling) could dramatically shift virtually all portions of what has become the fantasy sport empire.

There are a number of ways we attempt to project the future position of fantasy sport in the United States and beyond; from a methodological standpoint, our approach is a hybrid collection of data. We will incorporate the survey of more than 1,000 participants, interviews with the Fantasy Sport Trade Association, and insights gathered from participants and industry leaders in overseas markets, framing the chapter through a "wisdom of crowds" approach (Surowiecki, 2005, p. 1). As explained by Surowiecki (2005), a great deal of insight can be gleaned by incorporating joint perceptions of the masses. He notes:

> We generally have less information than we'd like. We have limited foresight into the future. Most of us lack the ability—and the desire—to make sophisticated cost-benefit calculations. Yet despite all these limitations, when our imperfect judgments are aggregated in the right way, our collective intelligence is often excellent. (p. xiv)

Although we do not claim to match his prophetic acumen, we adopt an approach similar to that of political forecasting wunderkind Nate Silver (2012), who believes prediction is a "shared experience rather than a function that a select group of experts or practitioners perform" (p. 14). In fact, the majority of our insights come from the broad-based survey of participants, as we seek to discern what Silver refers to as the signal (truth) and the noise (distractions from attaining truth).

This approach appeared to make sense as we analyzed trends within fantasy sport, since the group participating in the online survey was wide in geographic scope (at least in the United States) and sophisticated in terms of fantasy sport knowledge. Such a group warranted the belief that "under the right circumstances, groups are remarkably intelligent, and are often smarter than the smartest people in them. Groups do not need to be dominated by exceptionally intelligent people in order to be smart" (Surowiecki, 2005, p. xiii). This also is aligned with Silver's (2012) concept of prediction:

> Information is no longer a scarce commodity: we have more of it than we know what to do with. But relatively little of it is useful. We perceive it selectively, subjectively, and without much self-regard for the distortions that this causes. We think we want information when we really want knowledge. (p. 12)

Conjoining these beliefs in our own pursuit of knowledge beyond mere information, we asked our sample of 1,201 participants an open-ended question about the future of fantasy sport. Combined with the comments from qualitative interviews with industry leaders, the responses offered some clear directions that we believe represent the next iteration of fantasy sport play. This chapter will explore these issues in terms of (a) overarching trend types, (b) potential stumbling blocks/pitfalls to additional permeation of fantasy sport within the overall constructs of sports media, and (c) potential for international play and trends for new gaming formats and structures.

Macro-level trends

Among the 1,201 fantasy sport participants in our survey, a total of 704 responses were offered for the specific query about fantasy sport play in the future. Those comments were then classified using open coding mechanisms (Glaser and Strauss, 1967 for grounded theory/open coding explanations) and then creating overall classifications of comments (see Billings and Eastman, 2003 for content analytic coding classification schemes). Table 7.1 highlights the 13 classifications of comments appearing in at least 2% of the overall database (the threshold for the creation of a category).

It is clear that the comments were generally positive, an unsurprising development given that the current fantasy sport participant is likely to value the activity and recommend it to others. Predictions of (a) a larger participant base along with (b) generalized positive comments were the only two categories mentioned by over 10% of respondents.

Potential for growth

Regarding the first category, potential for growth in the number of participants (111 comments; 15.8%), many respondents expressed feelings similar to those of one who noted that fantasy gaming is "only going to get bigger as more people join the craze." In such comments, participants seemed convinced not only that (a) fantasy sport had become mainstream—hence, the notion of an already-established "craze"—but also that (b) many more people potentially would enjoy the activity,

Table 7.1 "The future of fantasy sport," according to participants' answers to open-ended questions

What does the future look like?	N	%
Larger participant base	111	15.8
General positive	106	15.1
Technological advances	70	9.9
General neutral	70	9.9
Mainstream media integration	56	7.9
General growth	53	7.5
Financial impact	42	6.0
Diverse participant base	42	6.0
Diverse information sources	37	5.3
Player-based customization	37	5.3
General negative	36	5.1
Interaction	29	4.1
Provider-based customization	15	2.1
Total	**704**	**100.0**

given a proper introduction to it. The rise of televised poker as a comparison point for the rise of fantasy gaming was a noteworthy element, with seven people specifically offering that comparison. Some compared the rise of fantasy sport to growth in online poker play, while others said it was "about to be like" poker—an interesting notion, given that most estimates place online poker as having less than one third the participants already involved in fantasy sport (Cooper, 2011).

Within this same "larger participation base" category, some participants also reported a high retention rate among new players. One summarized:

> I convinced ten new [fantasy football league participants] to play in a fantasy football league this year, and they all had a blast. This demonstrates that there are plenty of Americans who have not discovered the pure awesomeness of fantasy sports.

Many respondents explicitly mentioned the younger demographic as a group in which fantasy sport would grow, with one noting that "more and more people are getting involved … There is a whole generation of kids who are already involved in fantasy sports. Kids who will grow up playing for decades." Nevertheless, the majority of these types of responses noted that fantasy sport not only offered a plethora of different formats of play, but—perhaps more importantly—presented opportunities for many different levels of involvement: "The fact that an individual can spend half an hour or 30 hours a week on fantasy sport and still have fun with it is the beauty of the game in my opinion." Again, the element of luck and element of chance appear to be critical here as the casual participant may feel less knowledgeable than other participants in the league, but comments such as this indicate underscore that most casual players do not feel hopelessly disadvantaged.

General positive feelings

As noted previously, the other category representing over 10 % of the comments involved general positive feelings for the future of the activity (106 comments; 15.1%). Many of these comments were of a basic variety (e.g., 11 people simply reported that the future was "bright"). However, some of these comments indicated a bit more depth. One respondent called the future of fantasy sport "better than real sport," comparing fantasy play favorably with sports as a whole. In a similar vein, another felt that fantasy sport had been inextricably tethered to mainstream sports, concluding that the possibility of a greater role for fantasy sport is "very bright. As long as there are sports, it will continue to grow." Within this set of comments is that sense of synergy found between fantasy and traditional sport competitions, a concept closely related to a later category classified as "mainstream media integration." One respondent felt that the stigma previously surrounding the play of fantasy sport has largely dissipated: "Fantasy sports is no longer a nerd's game. It has grown so large that it can actually have effects on the real-life sport." Given that players such as Roddy White of the Atlanta Falcons are now publicly apologizing to fantasy owners for poor performances (Martinez, 2012), such a comment resonates.

Some respondents said fantasy sport filled a void that has always existed in some form: "People will always seek something to distract or entertain. We will always root for our heroes, and will continue to be fully invested in their success if we 'own' them in fantasy." Another participant began with a rather grandiose prediction: "The future of fantasy sports is endless at this point." Of course, the laws of economics and marketing suggest that there is a limit to participation, consumption, and profits; even McDonald's experienced a drop in monthly growth in November 2012 after more than 100 consecutive months without a drop in sales (Horowitz, 2012). This respondent quickly seemed to acknowledge a possible flaw in his "endless" prediction, adding, "The only mistake websites can make is to start charging for it." Overall, the comments in the category classified as generally positive note the enhanced permeation of fantasy sport within society. One person who again may be characterized as overstating the case suggested that "videogames and fantasy sports are replacing religion as the 'opiate for the masses.'"

Technological advancement

The next most-offered comments involved technological advancements, tied with comments classified as generally neutral (both with 70 comments each; 9.9% of the database of overall comments). Specifically regarding technology, conceptions of the digital divide (see Norris, 2001) could lead one to conclude that technology-heavy fantasy sport might leave a large segment of the aging population behind. However, underscoring the relative youth of the typical fantasy sport participant (Brown, Billings, and Ruihley, 2012), most predicted positive advancements in this regard, with comments citing advantages ranging from accessibility ("Technology is making it easier to draft, follow and play from anywhere") to enhanced speed ("As the Internet improves, [the future of fantasy sport is] pretty damned good." Formulating a direct link between growth and technology, one participant predicted that increased numbers of participants would be "directly proportional to the amount and ease of information available to participants. It is a complex game, but a unique interface of fantasy and reality … rewards participants who work at it."

As with most discussions of communication-based media, conversations about the future shift swiftly to new ways to consume content in mobile, digital forms. The consensus among industry professionals is that expanding the multiplatform system will be the largest advancement for the fantasy sport industry in the future. As envisioned by Adam Slotnick of Fox Sports:

> We're going to see growth in terms of the touch points. A majority of users are still primarily playing on their desktop or laptop. People are going to get more comfortable in the apps and sites are going to get more sophisticated and more mobile. Even gaming consoles.

Rotoworld's Brett Vandermark echoed those predictions:

> It's going to go more mobile, which makes sense. I still think there is growth. There [are] so many people. I think that fantasy sports, in general, still has growth to do and mobile is where it's most likely to occur.

Industry insiders discussed technology ranging from whether to embrace social media to how synergy between companies could advance the industry as a whole. Regarding social media, Yahoo!'s Brad Evans noted, "I am a Twitter-fiend. I have embraced the medium. I love it. It is structured perfectly for our industry. Easy accessibility. Constantly there. Interaction galore. Twitter has more utility for what we do than Facebook does."

Evans also believes online synergy with television or other forms of media may be in the offing:

> I think you're going to see an evolution in the business. Whether it's Yahoo! getting a partnership with TV or it's just organically-grown online, you're going to see more programming dedicated solely for fantasy sports, and it's going to be consumed in video form.

Many of the survey respondents offered technology-focused comments that were hybrids incorporating both predictions and ideas. The list of these technological advancements included:

- A fantasy sports network (suggested as ESPN4).
- 3D fantasy sport viewing options.
- Video feeds directly to a fantasy scoreboard for "big plays."
- Live scoring of fantasy games in the formulation of a "fantasy sport bar."

- Cameras attached to players, allowing feeds of just one's fantasy players' motions to be reformatted and streamed.
- Increased mobile options beyond checking fantasy scores and setting lineups to more advanced features such as trades and breaking news.
- Increased stadium offerings to allow the first-person fan to participate, rather than relegating the game to home-dwelling devotees, social sports addicts, and virtual world aficionados (see Billings, 2010 for operational definitions of each).

Many of these ideas were suggested as natural innovations that the industry would capitalize upon because of opportunities for sustained growth and profit. One respondent underscored these beliefs in his comments regarding the potential to expand draft options:

> One change I would like to see is the ability for live drafts to move into the twenty-first century and [allow] all people who are on the go to be able to draft from their mobile devices like you can update your roster on the go. If this became available, then fantasy sport would be king—not that it is not right now.

The possibilities were quite robust in this category, exemplified well by this respondent:

> The majority of office workers [will be] taking part in an office league, whether they are a fan or not. [As a result], at some point, fantasy fans may overtake real fans in volume. Where the future of technology goes, so will fantasy sports. That could involve taking out the middle man (sport reporters). It will bring more fans into the sport itself, continuing to make sports betting and fantasy sports [popular since it is currently] a huge untapped market. With Internet-connected TVs, you'll be able to enter in your players and league and customize the viewing experience that way. That would be the ultimate for a fantasy fan, and easiest to do with NFL since all the action is mostly on one day.

Indeed, some of these desires are coming to fruition. The combination of technology and fantasy sport is even on the minds of NFL facility improvements. As an example of attempted synergy between the first-person game day experience and the increasing need to stay in touch with technology for fantasy play, Jim Bernard of Fox Sports offered this example:

> The Carolina Panthers are redoing their stadium and one of the aspects they're looking into is the Internet, and the experience within the stadium, and how to surface statistics to cater to the fantasy player. So, it's starting to get to be in people's consciousness, a group of people that weren't conscious of fantasy are now.

Additionally, the San Francisco 49ers have a new stadium set to open in 2014 and, among an array of modern amenities, it will include a fantasy sport lounge. As described by Sanchez (2012):

> It is a brilliant marketing tactic ... cellphone signals are often overloaded at a stadium during a game so it makes it hard to check up on scores and stats around the league that could be impacting your fantasy football match-ups ... It's only a matter of time until teams around the league adopt this strategy to appeal and cater to the needs of fans in our new technologically advanced age of enjoying the sport.

General neutral

Compared to the new frontiers featured in the technology comments, it is interesting that the generally neutral comments were of equal number (70). Many of these comments were of the "I don't know" or "unforeseeable" variety, yet others expressed belief that fantasy will "stay as big as it is" or, more specifically, that the activity is peaking, yet will not dissipate in the near future. Some comments reflected the daunting array of options ("More and more sites have popped up to get info from. The hard part is picking which sites know what they are talking about and which sites are well just terrible") while others offered a sense of measured enthusiasm combined with a tempered realization of threats to the industry. As articulated by one respondent:

> Like anything else, the 'industry' surrounding fantasy sports will continue to expand until it exists in excess, and then it will continue to expand some more. This will create an imbalance, naturally, which will lead to the pulling back of the industry and so called 'experts' saying that the trend is beginning to fail. In reality, it will be an equalizing, as those who play fantasy leagues are often very committed to them.

Meanwhile, some other neutral comments could be noted as "other," as some participants attempted to explain why fantasy sport has grown. In one personal narrative that was particularly telling, a respondent linked fantasy sport activities with his valuation of loyalty. He offered:

> Since the Sonics [professional basketball team] were stolen away from us [and moved to Oklahoma City], I feel more vested with my fantasy teams than I do with any real-life teams. I grew up an Oilers [professional football team] fan and they were stolen away as well [moved to Nashville], so for those of us that have to emotionally 'vest' with a team or teams, fantasy is better since the stars don't leave in free agency for 'better' cities/markets and/ or since you never have to deal with your team leaving town. You can root more for your fantasy team to do well while consuming the product and hoping for competitive and fun games to watch in real life. Perhaps others

will make this transition as more people are jilted by their favorite players leaving their teams and/or their favorite teams leaving their cities.

Integration with mainstream media

The fifth most prominent category involved specific reference to the integration of fantasy sport aspects into overall sports media products (56 comments), a type of comment given by roughly 8% of respondents in the survey. In references to mainstream sports media, no entity is more central to the conversation than ESPN (Miller and Shales, 2011), with participants specifically noting the increased role of fantasy that Jon Diver and Matthew Berry outlined in Chapter 4. One respondent underscored this evolution, commenting that "ESPN has gone from not having a big presence in fantasy sports to providing games, having radio podcasts, and devoting hours for programming on television." Another noted that "four years ago, you would never see a fantasy sports article on the front page of ESPN.com, but now you see numerous fantasy related news bits on the front page every single day." Such comments seemed reflective in nature, noting that most of the mainstream media integration already had occurred or was taking place currently as "host sites are seeing more traffic, getting paid more for advertisements and sponsors." Fantasy is becoming, as one player labeled it, "an integral part of new sport culture; the more familiar people become with statistical analysis and its impact, the more people will open themselves up to the idea of fantasy sports."

Notable among these comments was the stark division as to whether people felt this merge of fantasy and mainstream media was a net positive or net negative. Some argued that fantasy sport is "great for TV viewership" because "it gives people a rooting interest even if their home team is no longer playing or contending." Others chimed in with assertions that fantasy sport is "gradually becoming the mainstream way for hardcore sports fans to follow sport," which ultimately makes the fantasy sport industry a "powerhouse shaping the way football is broadcasted."

Nonetheless, some fantasy participants (perhaps best described as "fantasy purists") note that integration within the mainstream is not without drawbacks. Most pointedly, some felt the result of networks' embrace of fantasy sport was a relatively uneducated group of media experts who attempt to provide informed opinions but ultimately lack the knowledge to do so. One argued that media outlets were "just talking about it [due] to its popularity." Another noted that if analysts do become better-versed in fantasy related issues, the authenticity of the actual games could be lost in the process, offering that, "The challenge for fantasy … is for analysts not to get so caught up in fantasy categories, because that kind of analysis loses the audience that isn't already participating in fantasy leagues." To summarize both the positive and negative aspects of the merge of fantasy with mainstream offerings, one person simply argued—without a value judgment—that "it is starting to feel like fantasy is more important than the actual games." Thus, the comments in this category converged in their general agreement that mainstream media have allowed for fantasy sport content more than ever before and will continue to do so; however, respondents disagree quite sharply as to whether this is a welcome development.

General growth

Sixth on the list of most frequent type of comment was a classification of beliefs regarding the general growth of the activity in the immediate future (53 comments; 7.5%). These comments tended to be less complex than some of those cited earlier, with many simply envisioning the future of fantasy sport as getting "bigger" and one succinctly saying the games will be "the same as now. Only with more everything." The reasons articulated to predict growth ranged from fantasy's addictive nature ("It will continue to grow. Once you become involved, if you are even remotely interested in sports, you are hooked.") to a general sense of escalating popularity ("More betting, more elite leagues, more people wanting to play, more pundits"). These people often had comments that linked with notions of mainstream media integration ("fantasy sports will be mentioned more and more by the athletes and media who covers the sports leagues") but also embracing an equation that increased mainstream presence = increased popularity = increased growth. One comment summarized the general sense of a "bright" future based largely on respondents' knowledge of the demographics of fantasy sport—offering percentages that are reaffirmed in the survey population and extrapolated upon in Chapters 2 and 3. This man commented:

> I truly think fantasy sports are going to be the primary driver of viewership and sports consumption in another 10–15 years. Most people under the age of 35 grew up with fantasy sports and are going to continue playing for the rest of their lives. A HUGE percentage of sports fans are already playing and that percentage [will only increase] as older traditional fans (typically less computer savvy) die off (pardon my frankness).

The remaining seven categories could be characterized as secondary based on frequency. However, these comments collectively represent over one third of the responses regarding fantasy sport and the future, making them worthy of extrapolation.

Financial impact

The next most-mentioned classifications involved financial impact and incentives (42 comments each; 6%). They noted, perhaps aptly, that the industry now represents a mature, major segment of the overall sports fan population, and yet its financial avenues are still somewhat underdeveloped or untapped. Some respondents envisioned the casual participants developing cravings for more advanced play that inevitably will involve more monetary investment. In this model, fantasy football is generally regarded as the "gateway drug" for other forms of fantasy play. Noted one respondent: "It is likely to become a much more expensive habit for many people, as so many people participate." This person went on to picture how the increased financial investment in fantasy could impact other sports entities' viability, suggesting that "pro sports are very dependent on gate revenues, so as TV/broadcast technology and increasing economic strife make it less attractive to fork out big wads of money to attend in person, attendance will plummet until ticket prices do."

Nonetheless, a plurality of comments within this category specifically related to the future relationship between fantasy sport and gambling. Some expressed the belief that the relationship already has been largely established ("The big money leagues are still somewhat underground") while others saw the ties with sports betting as an inevitable progression ("Much of sports is motivated by gambling. I think fantasy will imitate that as much as legally possible"). Many comments dealt with the belief (not supported among the overwhelming majority of fantasy sport players) that it represents a form of gambling and that this connection poses the largest threat to the industry. One person projected that "eventually (in 5–10 years) someone is going to crack down on the gambling side of it, make it illegal and ruin it for everyone. There's money to be won in it. As long as you can bet on something people will be interested." Another echoed that feeling of pending doom on the gambling side of the industry, stating that an active athlete or coach "will eventually have a similar situation like Pete Rose [gambling on baseball games while manager of the Cincinnati Reds, McDorman, 2003] where they are caught being in a competitive fantasy league." However, even with these worries, the overall tone of the comments suggested that there is still substantially more money to be made within the industry, with one participant exclaiming that he'd "buy stock in 'em if I could!"

Diverse demographics

Another category that could be seen as related to the classification of "general growth" comprised 42 responses about the increasingly diverse participant base respondents believed fantasy sport would enjoy in the coming years. Most often, the fantasy sport participant referred to a wife/partner/girlfriend as being a new player. The inclusion of the significant other seemed to be regarded as a tipping point for the industry, with one person writing that "I was even successful in getting my wife interested in the game and sport" and another believing that "it will continue to grow in popularity as more non-sports fans, such as girlfriends, join leagues as a way to spend more time with their significant other." As online information sources make it easier to play, respondents believed, fantasy becomes accessible beyond the core male sports fans that largely have already discovered the activity, at least in the United States. One respondent theorized: "The statistical side to fantasy sports actually opens the door of sports to women and other people who previously were never interested in sports, and therefore creates a new an untapped market." Others noted the intergenerational possibilities of the activity, referring to play with sons and daughters. Various factors may make it difficult for those of different generations to attend sporting events together in person, but fantasy sport—now facilitated by an abundance of free research and "cheat sheets"—can broaden participation, much as March Madness does during the NCAA basketball tournament in the United States. People predicted new formats of leagues to accommodate this amplified diversity ("people that want to manage a team with their spouse against other spouse run teams that are from Iowa, for example") as well as additional players arising from existing industry structures ("Fantasy sports [used to be played] in person and everyone had to be at one place at one time. Now it can take place online with a group of strangers"). Thus, this group seemed to endorse the belief that fantasy sport could generate interest in any segment of the population ("It seems like everyone is playing it now. People who don't know anything about football will now join in on conversations at work just based off of fantasy football info") and that boundaries based on gender, race, geography, and language are rapidly dissolving. Some predicted international league competitions, a possibility to be explored in more detail later in this chapter.

Customized play

Other themes that emerged included the role of customization, divided into two categories in Table 7.1 and relating both to provider-based and player-based changes people felt would happen in the future. Anderson (2006) writes that mainstream media increasingly compete with "an infinite number of markets, of any size. And consumers are favoring the one with the most choice. The era of one-size-fits-all is ending, and in its place is something new, a market of multitudes" (p. 5). These niches (and the personalized expectations that accompany them) unfold within the responses of many respondents. For instance, regarding provider-based customization, some expectations/desires included offerings such as "a TV setting that you can program around your fantasy team that switches over to your player's game when he is on the field and/or handling the ball" and "cameras [that] will track individual players and you will be able to have a live feed of every play that your fantasy team makes." Some desired even more integration with mainstream media offerings so that, for instance, "when you're watching a game and they flash a player's stats they can also show the fantasy numbers they have put up thus far or a projection of what they would put up on that given day."

Additionally, there were calls to combine pre-existing league formats into larger, amalgamated leagues that span multiple sports and formats. A sampling of some of these ideas included:

* "Combining individual sports (football, [baseball, basketball]) leagues into one big league where teams can trade players across sports."
* "I would like to see fantasy sport leagues get as close to managing a real team as possible. I think fantasy sports could reach e-sports levels similar to MLG (Major League Gaming), where teams of GMs [general managers] compete against each other over a season to earn larger sponsored prizes."
* "Multiple sport leagues. Leagues where the same 10–14 participants play in one year round league consisting of multiple sports and overall sports knowledge."

Overall, though, the majority referenced customization in far simpler terms ("More extreme and crazy ways to play. I'm excited") or in more generalized depictions ("More detailed, nuanced games with specific and obscure rules will come into fashion, and the games will become more diverse"). Daily leagues, such as FanDuel, were mentioned as new formats in which to participate, while even some nonsporting formats were cited as things likely to be developed or likely to expand in the future. The latter included specific references to fantasy celebrity leagues, Fantasy *Dancing with the Stars*, fantasy politics, fantasy reality television, and fantasy stock market.

Some respondents expressed trepidation as they contemplated the possibilities for the future. One feared that as games provide more nuance, fantasy sport "will go very sabermetrical. A lot of stats no one understands but pretend they do." As for final categories of exploration, some respondents (29 comments in all) believed increased interaction could be featured in the coming years, with some believing mainstream media will lead the expansion because "leagues know it's a good way to connect with people and get them invested so that they don't just watch games involving 'their team.'" Again, the prediction of fantasy "coffee houses" with people "lounging, watching, and participating in live, real-time fantasy sports" was mentioned by some; others suggested that fantasy sport will simply be "far more social than it is now." However, some of these interactivity-based comments included charges that including everyone results in a potentially watered-down product, or leagues in which motivations for play are too diverse for true enjoyment. One participant lamented that fantasy sport was becoming "commercialized and oversaturated with kids who know nothing about sports who do it because they wanna feel cool." Another called for motivation-based changes within industry structures: "There needs to be a change in the way leagues are done. With so much online action in fantasy sports, the ability to find a group of people to join leagues is easy. But being able to build a league and have the same people in year after year is near impossible." As seen in Chapter 5, one characteristic of the high-stakes player is the desire to find kindred spirits, in line with the sentiments offered in this quotation.

Plethora of information outlets

Diversity of information sources was another category that emerged from the data, with most pleased with the ability to not only access information but to do so freely, instantly, and abundantly. The free vs pay format debate addressed in Chapter 4 seemed generally to be accepted and endorsed. While human nature leads one to want all information to be free (see Anderson, 2009) the majority of respondents seemed to understand the need to make some services of a premium nature, with corresponding costs. Again, though, some felt these advancements were inherently detrimental:

> I think the fun may be taken out of the game somewhat due to the vast access to statistics. What I mean by that is the Internet has allowed for too many stats

that take away from the original game. I'm old school when it comes to fantasy sports and while some changes have been good, others can tend to water down the game and even the playing field [unnecessarily].

General negative

This comment provides an appropriate segue to the final set of comments, those that predicted a generally negative vision of fantasy sport in the future. Some merely did not see additional avenues that remained untapped: "There isn't much you can do to change it. I feel it's really reached its ceiling" and "I don't think it could get much (if any) bigger. Many people just aren't interested and I think some will get tired of it after doing it for a few years." Others expressed frustration at how the games within the mainstream games were affecting their fandom and the modes of consumption. One felt fantasy play "might actually begin ruining professional sports" and another believed fantasy "sometimes overshadow[s] the actual games. That is annoying to me. This creates fans of players, not teams." This dynamic not only could create tension between a player's actual value and fantasy value, but could filter into the athletes' performance, some respondents feared. One noted this tension, stating, "The bad thing is that the pro players may become too aware of it and it may affect their play."

Some other respondents related their bearish predictions primarily to business models. One felt fantasy sport was connected to too many high-risk propositions based on fickle civic and professional components and fluctuating tastes within sensation-seekers (Roberti, 2004). As one respondent characterized the industry:

A lot of things are high risk associated with fantasy sports, including the game itself. Too many variables and too many obstacles stand in the way of fantasy sports success ... government, big media, collective bargaining agreements, greedy owners, unorganized leagues and special interest groups are all a threat to fantasy, regardless of sport.

However, another illustrated how the high correlation between sport fandom and eventual fantasy sport participation might work in the inverse:

With the current economic situation, the payrolls of teams, the salaries of professional athletes I see the potential for a decline. I am quickly losing interest with the actual games being played and I somewhat focus on the fantasy aspect, but as my interest wanes in the actual sport so does my interest in fantasy.

When taking the comments from Table 7.1 as a whole, we discover overarching positive trends—but with a great deal of division regarding how the future will unfold. Some beliefs were very specific to fantasy sport, while other predictions encompassed larger characteristics of twenty-first century media, including more diversity, greater mobile influence, and more opportunities for media synergy. If taken optimistically, these conclusions could re-emphasize how fantasy sport play—by virtue of being an online, customized format—may be ideally suited to capitalize upon new and social media changes immediately on the horizon.

Industry leaders speak: potential pitfalls

Beyond the survey data and the "wisdom of crowds," we also gleaned insights about the future from the industry leaders interviewed in Chapter 4. Given the growth of the industry, the perceived avenues for expansion, and the ability to find workable business models, the overall feeling from interviewees about the future of fantasy sport play was, in general, quite positive. The majority saw a burgeoning interest in their product and could envision other ways to meet those needs. However, when we asked them about challenges for the industry, three issues resurfaced repeatedly.

Possible Pitfall 1: Court cases involving the ownership of statistics
Potential Damage: Major
Likelihood of Occurring: Slim

Many industry leaders noted major past struggles with professional sports leagues that "owned" the statistics derived from the games. If courts found that leagues owned the majority or all of a player's online rights, the statistics achieved within their league could be argued to be the property of that association as well. Such a claim would substantially thwart fantasy sport leagues that base their entire operations on these statistics. Still, two court rulings seem to have quelled most of the concerns within fantasy sport regarding this potentially calamitous pitfall.

First is the case of the NBA v. Motorola and STATS, Inc., which was ultimately settled in 1997. Motorola had developed a pager that would allow a person to receive live statistical updates as games progressed; STATS, Inc. became part of the lawsuit by providing the live statistical data to Motorola (Umbright, 2006). Since the NBA was seeking to develop a similar device, the league filed an injunction to stop the distribution of the Motorola pager. While the initial court ruling favored the NBA, the Second Circuit Court of Appeals ruled otherwise, allowing for more leeway in the sharing of sports statistics in a plentitude of media platforms (Cornell Law Copyright Cases, 1997), later to include cellular phones, advanced web programs and sites, and other mobile formats. This decision was a major victory for the fantasy sport industry because, as Howard Kamen of *USA Today* noted in our interview, it was "precedent setting."

A second court decision involves a 2006 lawsuit filed by CBC Distribution and Marketing, Inc. (St. Louis, MO) against Major League Baseball. Major League Baseball denied a licensing agreement with CBC, arguing that it owned all of the statistics generated by MLB games and that fantasy sport leagues violated player rights in regard to publicity (Greenhouse, 2008). As Richey (2008) defined the debated issues:

The key question in the Supreme Court case was whether CBC's use of real players' names and statistics infringed the players' publicity rights. Some legal analysts say such fantasy leagues are a form of commerce that seeks to exploit the fame of sports stars. Others argue that fantasy leagues are merely a means of organizing and presenting publicly available information in an entertaining way. If the fantasy league is aimed at communicating information, the activity is protected by the First Amendment, analysts say, but if it is primarily commerce it may not be. (p. 25)

The court decisions favored CBC, effectively ending any player or statistic copyright for the immediate future (Biskupic, 2008). The decision was rendered based upon the wide availability of the statistics in question, leading the court to conclude that such statistics accrued from games were part of the public domain.

While one could view the decisions in these cases and argue that questions of statistical ownership are now resolved, debates and legal cases continue to develop. For instance, Yahoo! filed a 2009 lawsuit against the National Football League Players Association, arguing that the NFLPA had no right to charge royalties on the statistics (Ross, 2009). The lawsuit was settled in the same year with the terms undisclosed, but it is clear that this may not be the last legal challenge regarding fantasy sport and the use of statistics it requires.

Possible Pitfall 2: Court cases equating fantasy sport play with gambling
Potential Damage: Moderate
Likelihood of Occurring: Unlikely

Another major issue that could potentially thwart a significant portion of the fantasy sport market would be if it were equated to gambling in a way that regulated it as a form of betting. FSTA President Paul Charchian argued that while that would be the most pressing threat, he believes the chances of it coming to fruition are very unlikely:

[Equating fantasy sport with gambling] would be a really catastrophic blow to fantasy sports. It's extremely unlikely. Fantasy sports isn't gambling. It's been carved out of online gambling legislation. No player has ever been the subject of a criminal investigation for gambling. No company has ever been the subject of a criminal investigation for gambling, so it seems very, very unlikely.

The legislation to which Charchian referred is the 2006 Unlawful Internet Gambling Enforcement Act (UIGEA), which delineated what did and did not constitute online gambling. Arguing that "a game subject to chance" was gambling, which was then unpacked as a game in which the element of luck/chance was greater than that of skill (Alexander, 2008). Under the act, online poker was considered online gambling and thus subject to the law; meanwhile, fantasy sport was specifically argued as not being gambling, coupled with skill-based activities such as futures trading in the stock market (Longley, 2006). Thus, fantasy sport was equated with other online contest or educational games features:

> An outcome that reflects the relative knowledge of the participants, or their skill at physical reaction or physical manipulation (but not chance), and, in the case of a fantasy or simulation sports game, has an outcome that is determined predominantly by accumulated statistical results of sporting events, including any non-participant's individual performances in such sporting events.(UIGEA, In Longley, 2006)

Beyond the claim of skill trumping luck, Charchian also cited FSTA research that indicates the top incentives for play are competitive and social reasons, with finances appearing around fifth on their lists. Nonetheless, the perception from non-legal entities continues to hinder the industry somewhat. As Charchian explained:

> It hurts us in a lot of ways that people don't necessarily see. Joe's got a great idea for a fantasy product and needs funding. He's trying to raise money on it, and people think, 'I don't want to invest in this. It's gambling.'

Even with all of the evidence pointing to fantasy sport providing an adrenaline rush that is not specifically tied to financial incentives, the Fantasy Sport Trade Association formalized standards severing any notion of a link between gambling and fantasy sport. In 2011, the Fantasy Sport Trade Association (in response to some ethical debacles such as the folding of the World Championship of Fantasy Football [WCOFF]) adopted a Code of Ethics, specifically with tenets devoted to honesty, integrity, and credibility, but also with a specific stance on gambling. Notes the Fantasy Sport Trade Association Code of Ethics (2011):

> **Gambling**
> All games must abide by all laws. No game can be used for any form of gambling. Websites whose primary function is the operation of gambling operations will not be admitted to membership. All FSTA members should focus on keeping our industry creditable, and we should work with each other. (Fantasy Sport Trade Association, 2012b, para. 5)

This stance appears consistent with the overwhelming majority of fantasy sport industry leaders. Yahoo!'s Andy Behrens does not see a tie between gambling and fantasy sport, either, noting that if there is a connection at all, it would be within the relatively new realm of daily games: "Play-to-play, quarter-to-quarter, moment-to-moment fantasy opportunities are out there now." However, the goals of a compulsive gambler diverge sharply from the objectives of the traditional fantasy games that represent the overwhelming bulk of the industry. Behrens described the contrast:

> All of my longtime fantasy leagues—nobody in them is a hardcore gambler. Nobody's betting games each weekend. I'm not betting games each weekend.

I've known some guys with gambling problems, and they were not the fantasy audience. They had no interest. They were all about winning back their $1,500 *today*.

Most recent government actions regarding fantasy sport have served to loosen tieswith perceptions of gambling, most notably the 2012 Maryland bill that untethered fantasy sport from other forms of gambling (Carter, 2012). While it took three votes and six years to make the change, fantasy sport ultimately was decriminalized (although it was never prosecuted before that). Previous problems with passing the Maryland bill stemmed from an attorney general's opinion on poker that argued that three elements jointly constituted gambling: consideration, chance, and prize (Carter, 2012). While fantasy sport participation often involves all three (with prizes that are negligible or nonexistent in most leagues), the element of chance was actually downgraded—bolstering the case that fantasy sport play was more skill than luck. Similar stances appear to be the norm in cases involving fantasy sport (see Anderson, 2010). This seems to signal a decline in efforts to couple fantasy sport with gambling.

Possible Pitfall 3: Work stoppages within a professional sports league
Potential Damage: Temporarily Major; Longitudinally Minor
Likelihood of Occurring: Inevitable

The pitfall that ends fantasy play entirely would be the canceling of games or even an entire sports season; it has happened in the past, and at the time of this writing, is occurring within the National Hockey League. Given the dominant status of professional football within the fantasy sport landscape, the one major impediment to growth would be a prolonged work stoppage within the National Football League. Such a doomsday scenario appeared to be unfolding in 2011, when a prolonged lockout threatened the start of the season (Leahy, 2011). The labor issue was resolved in late July, however, forcing a truncated exhibition season that preserved all of the regular season games—and sparing the fantasy sport industry from experiencing its worst-case scenario (Di Fino, 2011).

Nevertheless, the possibility of a work stoppage within the NFL led people within the Fantasy Sport Trade Association to prepare for possible alternative plans, or at least plans to mitigate the damage. Since most people do not sign up for fantasy leagues until early to mid-August, impact on registration figures did not provide much insight. However, entities such as CBSSports.com worked to attract participants with discounted fees, along with a "Gridiron Guarantee" that ensured a full refund if the season was canceled (Wang, 2011). As Howard Kamen summarized, the feeling within the industry is that work stoppages can wreak havoc upon fantasy leagues in the short term, but that ultimately the sports survive—and so do their fantasy counterparts:

Work stoppages will happen from time to time in sports, but I've always thought that the power of game will pull the loyal fans back. And you can't question the loyalty of the fantasy sports player. So, while there could be bumps in the road, it's not something that could wipe out the industry. Loyal fans will be back en masse from the start and the casual fan base will eventually come back, too.

Considering that the three major professional leagues in the United States all have relatively new labor contracts that run until 2017 (National Basketball Association; Coon, 2011), 2017 (Major League Baseball Association; White, 2011) and 2021 (National Football League; Davis, 2011), the possibility of labor disputes resulting in work stoppages seems relatively low when compared to previous years.

Other potential pitfalls: an industry perspective

Kamen noted three other concerns that he prioritized above statistical ownership, gambling definitions, and work stoppages. Those were (a) rules changes resulting from NFL concussions lawsuits ("If the NFL changes its rules significantly—to the point of fantasy sports player apathy setting in—or winds up shutting down due to legal issues, then the fantasy sports industry could be in trouble"), (b) the reliance on younger participants who may find less disposable leisure time as their lives progress ("Will there be enough generational support—the kids of today's players playing—to keep the industry moving in the right direction?") and (c) the need for any media-based entities (particularly new media) to reinvent themselves ("Will there be any innovation in the fantasy sports game play or are things tapped out? If the answer is, 'it's as good as it's going to get right now' in terms of rules, technology, game strategy, game types, game styles, etc., then that could eventually be troublesome").

While others within the industry echoed Kamen's third concern, in general, their outlook was very optimistic. Stated Rotowire's Peter Schoenke:

It's hard for me to think of an issue for the industry that's the dark cloud. Five years ago, I'd be like 'Everything's great, we're growing at 20% and everything's good, but here are the things you've got to worry about: you've got to worry about this lawsuit we've got with the players, you've got to worry about the football potential to go on strike, you've got to worry about.' One negative about the future it is that there haven't been a lot of innovations in terms of the way you play. Maybe a little bit—daily games have come along. But, for the most part, the vast majority of people play the traditional commissioner game when they play football.

Beyond borders: fantasy sport beyond North America

There is a reason why this book has nearly exclusively pertained to fantasy sport play in North America and particularly the United States: fantasy sport games are considerably more prominent in the United States than in other nations around the world. However, the burgeoning fantasy sport empire beyond North America collectively represents many millions of annual players. Fantasy Sport Trade Association President Paul Charchian said there is no reason that fantasy sport could not thrive in other countries. "They're just as passionate about their sports, if not more, than we are here in America and so many of the same things that we enjoy about fantasy sports could work on fantasy soccer in Argentina."

The mainstreaming of the Internet resulted in rapid expansion of internationally played games. By 2004, for instance, 1.6 million people were playing fantasy soccer in the United Kingdom and 750,000 participants were involved in fantasy cricket in India (Pfanner, 2004). Fantasy horse racing is now popular in Australia (Mactarggart, 2008) and China (Pfanner, 2004). Differential levels of play are partly dictated by national stances regarding the connection (or lack thereof) between fantasy sport and gambling definitions. This makes fantasy sport less prominent in some parts of Europe (e.g., Spain, France) and far more prominent within other European countries (e.g., Britain and the Netherlands). Indeed, the hub of European play appears to be in the United Kingdom. Pfanner (2004) explains some of the reasons:

> Outside the United States, fantasy sports leagues may be a smaller business, but they are growing in popularity. In Britain, a society that embraces sport and betting with seemingly equal enthusiasm, fantasy sports are a natural fit. In Continental Europe, they are less developed. Tighter restrictions on online gaming, for instance, have limited the spread of virtual leagues in which money changes hands, though UEFA, the association of European soccer leagues, runs a free fantasy league in which mainly pride is at stake. (p. 13)

To gain more insights into this secondary market beyond North America, Andrew Wainstein, CEO and founder of Fantasy League.com, was interviewed. Wainstein is arguably the most prominent industry expert in the United Kingdom, becoming very involved in providing fantasy sport gaming options several decades ago. As he noted in a previous interview with Sculpher (2011):

> I have a background in computing and am also a football [soccer] fan, so when I first heard of fantasy sports in the USA; I began to think about putting the two together. Our fantasy setup started back around 1991 and was effectively a postal game. Things really began to take off when we did a deal with the *Daily Telegraph* to run their fantasy football game, which of course ran through updates in the paper, with information stored on our computer. From there, things took off right away and three or four papers began running their own competitions the same season. (para. 3)

In his interview for this book, Wainstein noted that he "started Fantasy League in 1991 working from a bedroom in his parents' house, funded by a few thousand pounds in savings." As for 2012, he has 2.5 million fantasy sport participants on his website, with over half participating in a Sun Dream Team game. This represents a major swath of the market that is estimated at 3.5 million participants in Britain (Sculpher, 2011). He reports similar growth to that of the United States (15% per year) with a similarly optimistic view on the potential to garner even more participants in the future.

While the sports are clearly different from those in the United States (unsurprisingly, soccer is the most popular), the business model is largely the same. Ninety percent of participants play for free, with exceptions being a game run through a newspaper, *The Daily Telegraph*, (£6; $10 per year), along with premium games, Fantasy League Classic (£10–£20; $16–32 per season) and Fantasy League Professional (£30–£40; $48–65 per season).

One major difference between the entity Wainstein runs and that of industry leaders in the United States is that it is independent from the sports news/media industry as a whole. While fantasyleague.com has sponsored games with those entities, the website is strictly for the fantasy participant, a definite contrast to the hybrid models of the United States industry leaders such as Yahoo! and ESPN. Wainstein believes this isolated focus on fantasy games helps in terms of brand recognition:

> [We have been successful because of] a combination of things; being the original, a strong and well-known brand help, but these are underpinned by being a 100% specialist in fantasy games and by being committed to innovation and quality throughout the last 20 years.

Another major difference between the games offered by fantasyleague.com and those offered in the United States involves the degree of complexity. In the United States, most of the games being played (notably the big three sports of football, baseball, and basketball) yield a wide array of statistics that can be repurposed and reformatted for fantasy games. Meanwhile, the major game offered by Wainstein's company is soccer, which features comparatively fewer statistics within the enacted game. Wainstein explains their strategy in terms of statistics and game complexity:

> We have capitalized on the huge audiences and passion of football followers, but also have succeeded by keeping our scoring format very simple since 1991. While statistics are a bit more prevalent in football here now, the simplicity is designed to reflect the way people watch the game and means that the fantasy game scoring is transparent to anyone following a match, including just goals, assists, clean sheets and goals conceded.

There are possibilities for bridging the gaps between continents. It appears that in some ways the United Kingdom is developmentally behind the fantasy industry in North America—there is no equivalent to the Fantasy Sport Trade Association, for instance, but there is a fan forum for reviewing fantasy games: www.fiso. co.uk. Meanwhile, there also appear to be opportunities for expansion that Wainstein has capitalized upon and that the industry in the United States would be wise to emulate. Wainstein has found ties to other non-sports entities in industries such as education and finance; he noted that his company has run a school fantasy football game and recently started running financial trading games for banks.

However, it is worth noting that companies such as fantasyleague.com represent just one type of fantasy sport play in Europe; there are over a million more who play US-based fantasy games (Pfanner, 2004). Some of these European participants are transplanted Americans who brought with them their fandom for sports like American football and continued to participate in fantasy sports as a way to remain in contact with their US-based friends and family. Other participants have become fans of American sports through expanded sports television offerings, with sports fandom again being the conduit to ultimately opting for fantasy sport participation.

Uncovering additional information about fantasy sport play and the industry as a whole proved difficult beyond Europe, partly because of language barriers, partly because of lack of response to author queries, and partly because the industry is not as developed in many other parts of the world. However, our research has determined that the market for fantasy sport play is both diverse and expanding.

Consider Australia. Aussies have been playing fantasy sport for decades, and the games have been devoted to athletic competitions from across the globe, ranging from the local to the major international leagues (European Premier League, National Football League). By the mid-1990s, Melbourne-based newspaper *The Age* was offering coupon-based competitions "with dedicated phone lines for game players to call for points updates. What changed everything was, of course, the Internet … number-crunching software … has made the concept more user-friendly" (Law, 2009, p. 14).

By 2006, fantasy sport had become a topic of conversation in Australia. Interestingly, it was represented as having migrated not from North America but from Europe, presumably because of the popularity of soccer in Australia. Australia's *Sunday Herald Sun* (2006) announced that "The fantasy football concept that has swept across Europe has arrived in Australia" (p. 66). Australia's main fantasy games are soccer, rugby, and cricket (Fox Sports Fantasy Game Offerings, 2012) and are offered through media conglomerates familiar in the United States, such as Fox Sports (via www.foxsports.com.au/fantasy). By 2009, more than 700,000 Australians were playing fantasy sport (Law, 2009), a number that has now surpassed 1 million (Virtual Sports.com Homepage, 2012). The demographics of the participants resemble the composite of North American participants (over 90 % are males and the majority are in their 20s; Law, 2009). Given the growth in the overall number of participants, Australian television coverage has embraced the fantasy football participant. As Law (2009) reports:

> Fantasy games have changed mainstream sports coverage [in Australia]. Broadcasters now remind TV audiences to adjust their fantasy teams when a player leaves the field with an injury. Even the vernacular of fantasy sports is bleeding into the general discourse, with terms like 'spuds' (bad players) and 'cash cows' (rookies rising in prices) becoming more common. (p. 14)

In virtually all developed and developing nations, fantasy sport participation is expanding. Scouring myriad databases and websites to research international fantasy sport play yields very little evidence for diminishing popularity of fantasy gaming—although one does encounter the occasional disgruntled fan that laments the lost exclusivity of fantasy sport now that the activity has gone mainstream. Trend lines are up, sometimes startlingly so, and national boundaries are vanishing. For instance, Singapore has hundreds of thousands playing English Premier League (EPL). In 2002, EPL had 72,000 fantasy sport participants; by 2007, that number was 1.28 million (Wee, 2007). Whether we talk about participants in the millions (in Europe, Australia, South American and Asia) or the tens of millions (in North America), the enthusiasm for fantasy sport has never been higher than at the time of this writing.

Conclusion

With the discussion of fantasy sport in international outlets and the conceptions of fantasy sport in the future, the arguments presented in this book have come full circle. From its humble beginnings with the Greater Oakland Professional Pigskin Prognosticators and the Baseball Seminar to the industry as it stands now: global, powerful, and integrated, fantasy sport participation is one of the few industries that has witnessed steady growth over the course of a half century without any major deviations from its upward trend. As with most aspects of society, predicting what will be more or less prominent in the future is difficult to assess, yet the "wisdom of crowds" allows us to offer some critical conclusions. Based on the collective findings of this book, including surveys, interviews, and analyses of existing research and data, the following postulates represent the best educated guesses about the future of fantasy sport:

- *Fantasy sport participation will grow over the course of the next decade.* Given the combination of the fact that the industry is expanding at a 15% annual rate and the general sense that most pitfalls levied at the industry (e.g., ownership of statistics, definitions of online gambling) have largely been alleviated and/or settled, this hypothesis appears fairly easy to advance.
- *Mobile options for fantasy sport participation will increase.* While this prediction certainly involves applications for cellular phones and tablets, it also includes the greater bandwidth at stadiums and other public sports viewing events, so that web access in general becomes expedient enough to enhance fantasy sport participation.
- *Differential skill options for participants will continue to expand.* Both sides of the involvement spectrum appear to be growing in development, ranging from Champions and/or high-stakes leagues, to leagues that involve little to no involvement from the player after the roster is drafted. Such developments will be aimed at advancing the established player to more premium services while offering options to potential participants who may not be traditional sports fans.
- *People in many nations will participate in sports being played outside of their home nations.* As sports media programming continues to expand beyond national borders, interest in these sports traverses these same distances as

well. If interest is amplified surrounding any sport, the fantasy sport ancillary will inevitably follow.

- *Single leagues involving multiple sports and transcending single professional seasons will become mainstream.* Since so many sports have fantasy components and so many players are participating in more than one type of fantasy sport competition, it appears a natural progression to amalgamate these sports into a macro-level league in which, for example, a participant might be able to trade basketball's LeBron James for soccer's Lionel Messi.
- *Daily leagues will become increasingly present and will typically be played in addition to (rather than in place of) more established league formats.* Clearly, there is a rising number of leagues in which a winner is determined on a single day or weekend outcome. However, given the relatively high level of involvement required by consistent play in daily leagues, it is difficult to imagine daily leagues replacing traditional formats that encompass the entirety (or at least the majority) of the season.
- *Mainstream media will find new ways to embrace fantasy sport.* The greatest unknown variable in predicting the rating of any sport is the outcome of a game. A football game that is 28-27 will, without question, garner a higher rating than a contest between the same two teams with a final score of 48-3. However, fantasy players typically have an interest in these games regardless of the margin between the winning and losing team. That makes fantasy participants highly desirable, which, in turn, equates to personalized and specialized media formats for this prime sports media consumer.

Many additional predictions could be articulated beyond these seven macro-level hypotheses. Given the breadth of fantasy sport competition, trends that are invisible at this writing could emerge as prominent in a mere year's time. What is abundantly clear is the validity of our starting thesis: fantasy sport is a game changer. This has been substantiated by the survey responses of 1,201 participants, the interviews of four-dozen industry leaders, the comments from high-stakes players, the results of ESPN data trends, and the predictions of a multitude of constituencies. As a result, the key issue that emerges is not *whether* fantasy sport is growing, but rather the *degree* to which it is permeating society. Questions of whether fantasy sport is a mainstream activity are largely now moot, underscored by a great deal of data reporting that tens of millions of people are devoting an inordinate amount of time to these "games within games." Value judgments pertaining to the impact of fantasy participation on overall fandom will continue to be topics of debate, yet one premise is firmly established: fantasy sport is not a fad. These games represent a powerful force within the powerful industry that is sports media in the twenty-first century.

References

Agyemang, K., and Ballouli, K. (2010, June). "An examination of barriers facing African American membership in fantasy football leagues." Research presentation at 2010 North American Society of Sport management conference. Tampa, FL.

Anderson, C. (2006). *The long tail: Why the future of business is selling less of more*. New York: Hyperion.

——(2009). *Free: The future of a radical price*. New York: Hyperion.

Anderson, J. (2010, Dec. 8). "D.C. slips online, fantasy gaming into bill; 'Games of skill' eyed for lottery." *The Washington Times*, p. 1.

Ariely, D. (2009). *Predictably irrational: The hidden forces that shape our decisions*. New York: Harper Collins.

Askeland, E. (2012, May 6). "FanDuel cashes in on US gaming market." *Scotland on Sunday*, p. 21.

Barmack, E., and Handelman, M. (2006). *Why fantasy football matters (and our lives do not)*. New York: Simon & Schuster.

Bernhard, B.J., and Earle, V.H. (2005). "Gambling in a fantasy world: An exploratory study of *rotisserie* baseball games." *UNLV Gaming Research & Review Journal*, 9(1), 29–42.

Billings, A.C. (2008). *Olympic media: Inside the biggest show on television*. London: Routledge.

——(2010). *Communicating about sports media: Cultures collide*. Barcelona, ESP: Aresta.

Billings, A.C., and Eastman, S. T. (2003). "Framing identities: Gender, ethnic, and national parity in network announcing of the 2002 Winter Olympics." *Journal of Communication*, 53(4), 369–386.

Billings, A.C., and Ruihley, B.J. (2012, March). "The Fantasy Sport Trade Association: An inside look into a billion dollar industry." Paper presented at the Fifth Summit on Communication and Sport, Peoria, IL.

——(2013). "Why we watch, why we play: Fantasy sports, fanship motivations, and the sport fan 2.0." *Mass Communication & Society*.

Bilton, N. (2011). *I live in the future and here's how it works*. New York: Crown.

Biskupic, J. (2008, June 3). "Judges let stand fantasy use of stats." *USA Today*, p. 4C.

Brown, N., Billings, A.C., and Ruihley, B.J. (2012). "Exploring the change in motivations for fantasy sport participation during the life cycle of a sports fan." *Communication Research Reports*, 29(4).

Bryant, J., Brown, D., Comisky, P.W., and Zillmann, D. (1982). "Sports and spectators: Commentary and appreciation." *Journal of Communication*, 32, 109–119.

Bryant, J., and Raney, A.A. (2000). Sports on the screen. In D. Zillmann and P. Vorderer (Eds), *Media entertainment: The psychology of its appeal* (153–174). Mahwah, NJ: LEA.

Carter, A. (2012, January 27). "Bill would allow prizes in fantasy sports; would exempt some competitions from state gambling regulations." *The Capitol* (Annapolis, MD), p. B5.

Chad, N. (2012, October 8). "Couch slouch: NFL's fantasy island is a gambler's paradise." *Charleston Gazette*, p. 5B.

Charland, M. (1987). "Constitutive rhetoric: The case of the 'Peuple vs Quebecois'." *Quarterly Journal of Speech*, 73(2), 133–150.

Chelminski, P., and Coulter, R.A. (2007). "On market mavens and consumer self-confidence: A cross-cultural study." *Psychology & Marketing*, 24(1), 69–91.

Clark, R.A., Goldsmith, R.E., and Goldsmith, E.B. (2008). "Market mavenism and consumer self-confidence." *Journal of Consumer Behavior*, 7(3), 239–248.

Coakley, J. (2007). *Sports in society: Issues and controversies* (9th ed.). Boston, MA: McGraw Hill.

Cockcroft, T.H. (2012). "Fantasy football auction strategy." Retrieved on September 25, 2012 from http://sports.espn.go.com/fantasy/football/ffl/story?page=nfldk2k12auctionstrategy

Coon, L. (2011, November 28). "Breaking down changes in new CBA; New labor deal could mean much heftier luxury taxes for big spenders." Retrieved on December 5, 2012 from http://espn.go.com/nba/story/_/page/CBA-111128/how-new-nba-deal-compares-last-one

Cooper, M. (2011, Apr. 24). The feds fold online poker. *Los Angeles Times*. Retrived on April 12, 2013 from http://articles.latimes.com/2011/apr/24/opinion/la-oe-cooper-online-poker-20110424

Cornell Law Copyright Cases (1997). "NBA vs. Motorola and STATS, Inc." Retrieved on November 30, 2012 from http://www.law.cornell.edu/copyright/cases/105_F3d_841.htm

Criblez, D.J. (2012, October 2). "Fan demonium: High-tech Sunday socials get you ready for some football." *Newsday*, B2.

Crosset, T.W. (1995). *Outsiders in the clubhouse: The world of women's professional golf.* Albany: State University of New York Press.

Davenport, T.H., and Beck, J C. (2002). *The attention economy: Understanding the new currency of business.* Harvard: Cambridge, MA.

Davis, N. (2011, July 25). "NFL, players announce new 10-year labor agreement." Retrieved on December 5, 2012 from http://content.usatoday.com/communities/thehuddle/post/2011/07/reports-nfl-players-agree-to-new-collective-bargaining-agreement/1#.UL-IJaVRlHg

Davis, N.W., and Duncan, M.C. (2006). "Sport knowledge is power: Reinforcing masculine privilege through fantasy sport league participation." *Journal of Sport & Social Issues*, 30(3), 244–264.

Depalma, A., and Raney, A A. (2003, May). "The effect of viewing varying levels of aggressive sports programming on enjoyment, mood, and perceived violence." Paper presented at the annual meeting of the International Communication Association, San Diego, CA.

Di Fino, N. (2011, July 26). "Football's return isn't just a fantasy." *Wall Street Journal Abstracts*, p. D6.

DiIorio, J.A. (1989). "Feminism, gender, and the ethnographic study of sport." *ARENA Review,* 13(1), 49–60.

Docketerman, E. (2012, August 27). "Good Sports: The rise of fantasy everything." *Time*, p. 18.

Doyle, P., and Saunders, J. (1985). "Market segmentation and positioning in specialized industrial markets." *Journal of Marketing*, 49(2), 24–32.

Drayer, J., Shapiro, S., Dwyer, B., Morse, A., and White, J. (2010). "The effects of fantasy football participation on NFL consumption: A qualitative analysis." *Sport Management Review*, 13, 129–141.

Duncan, M.C., and Hasbrook, C.A. (1988). "Denial of power in televised women's sports." *Sociology of Sport Journal*, 5(1), 1–21.

Duncan, M.C., and Messner, M.A. (1998). "The media image of sport and gender." In L.A. Wenner (Ed.) *MediaSport* (170–185). London: Routledge.

——(2000). *Gender in televised sports: 1989, 1993, and 1999.* Los Angeles: Amateur Athletic Foundation of Los Angeles.

Dworkin, S.L, & Messner, M.A. (2002). "Gender relations in sport." *Sociological Perspectives, 45*(4), 347–352.

Dwyer, B., and Drayer, J. (2010). "Fantasy sport consumer segmentation: An investigation into the differing consumption modes of fantasy football participants." *Sport Marketing Quarterly*, 19(4), 207–216.

Dwyer, B., and Kim, Y. (2011). "For love or money: Developing and validating a motivational scale for fantasy sport participation." *Journal of Sport Management*, 25(1), 70–85.

Eagly, A.H., and Chaiken, S. (1993). *The psychology of attitudes.* Fort Worth, TX: Harcourt Brace Jovanovich.

Earnheardt, A.C., Haridakis, P., and Hugenberg, B. (2012). *Sports fans, identity, and socialization: Exploring the fandemonium.* Lanham, MD: Lexington Books.

Eastman, S.T., and Billings, A.C. (2001). "Sportscasting and sports reporting: The power of gender bias." *Journal of Sport and Social Issues*, 24(2), 192–213.

Eastman, S.T., and Land, A.M. (1997). "The best of both worlds: Sports fans find good seats at the bar." *Journal of Sport & Social Issues*, 21, 156–178.

Eastman, S.T., Newton, G.D., and Pack, L. (1996). "Promoting primetime programs in megasporting events." *Journal of Broadcasting & Electronic Media*, 40, 366–388.

"Enjoyment." (2012). In Merriam-Webster.com. Retrieved May 21, 2012, from http://www.merriam-webster.com/dictionary/enjoyment

Enoch, G. (2010, April) "ESPN's top 10 list for sports research." Presentation given to the Broadcast Education Association, Las Vegas.

——(2011, October 3). "Life stages of the sports fan." Lecture conducted from the University of Alabama, Tuscaloosa, AL.

ESPN Department of Integrated Media Research (2010, April 15). "ESPN top ten list for sport research." Broadcast Education Association Research Symposium, Las Vegas, NV.

Fantasy Host Data (2011). "Fantasy basketball 2011 survey. Anonymous location and company. Fantasy sports industry grows to a $800 million industry with 29.9 million players." (2008, July 10). PRWeb.com. Retrieved from http://www.prweb.com/releases/2008/07/prweb1084994.htm

"Fantasy Sports Industry Grows." (2008). "Fantasy sports industry grows to a $800 million industry with 29.9 million players." Retrieved January 3, 2009 from http://www.prweb.com/releases/2008/07/prweb1084994.htm

Fantasy Sport Trade Association (2012a). "Industry demographics." Retrieved on September 24, 2012 from http://www.fsta.org/industry_demographics

——(2012b). "FSTA Code of Ethics." Retrieved on December 21, 2012 from http://www.fsta.org/code_of_ethics

Farquhar, L.K., and Meeds, R. (2007). "Types of fantasy sport users and their motivations." *Journal of Computer-Mediated Communication*, 12(4), article 4. Retrieved from http://jcmc.indiana.edu/vol12/issue4/farquhar.html

Feick, L.F., and Price, L.L. (1987). "The market maven: A diffuser of marketplace information." *The Journal of Marketing*, 51(1), 83–97.

Flanagin, A.J., and Metzger, M.J. (2001). "Internet use in the contemporary media environment." *Human Communication Research*, 27(1), 153–181.

Flynn, L.R., Goldsmith, R.E., and Eastman, J.K. (1996). "Opinion leaders and opinion seekers: Two new measurement scales." *Journal of the Academy of Marketing Science*, 24(2), 137–147.

Fisher, E. (2012). "CBSSports.com eyes bold stroke in fantasy." Retrieved on October 15, 2012 from http://www.sportsbusinessdaily.com/Journal/Issues/2012/01/16/Media/CBS-fantasy.aspx

——(2012). "Upping the ante: High-stakes games put the money on the line as high-rollerplayers try to cash in on their picks." *Sports Business Journal*, p. 14.

Fox Sports Fantasy Game Offerings (2012). Retrieved on Dec. 5, 2012 from http://web.archive.org/web/20080705192920/http://www.foxsports.com.au/fantasy

Fullerton, S. (2010). *Sports marketing* (2nd ed.). Boston: McGraw-Hill Irwin.

Gantz, W. (1981). "An exploration of viewing motives and behaviors associated with television sports." *Journal of Broadcasting*, 25(3), 263–275.

Gantz, W., and Wenner, L.A. (1991). "Men, women, and sports: Audience experiences and effects." *Journal of Broadcasting & Electronic Media*, 25, 233–243.

——(1995). "Fanship and the television sports viewing experience." *Sociology of Sport Journal*, 12, 306–323.

Gladwell, M. (2008). *Outliers: The story of success*. New York: Little, Brown, & Company.

Glaser, B, and Strauss, A. (1967). *The discovery of grounded theory: Strategies for qualitative research*. Chicago: Aldine.

Goldsmith, R.E., Clark, R.A., and Goldsmith, E.B. (2006). "Extending the psychological profile of market mavenism." *Journal of Consumer Behavior*, 5(5), 411–419.

Goodger, K., Gorely, T., Lavallee, D., and Harwood, C. (2007). "Burnout in sport: A systematic review." *The Sport Psychologist*, 21(2), 127–151.

Grantland's Reality TV Fantasy League: The complete rules and draft results (2011). Grantland.com. Retrieved from http://www.grantland.com/blog/hollywood-prospectus/post/_/id/153/grantlands-reality-tv-fantasy-league-the-complete-rules-and-draft-results

Greenhouse, L. (2008, June 3). "No ruling means no change for fantasy baseball leagues." *New York Times*, p. 4.

Gregory, S. (2012, December 17). "Can Roger Goodell save football?" *Time*, Retrieved from http://www.time.com/time/magazine/article/0,9171,2130975,00.html

Gruss, M. (2012, October 13). "I'm totally in control of my (ever-deepening) fantasy sports habit." *The Virginian-Pilot*, p. E1.

Gustin, S. (2012, Mar. 1). "Nearly 50 % of Americans own smartphones; Android, iPhone dominate." *Time*. Retrieved on January 21, 2013 from: http://business.time.com/2012/03/01/nearly-50-of-americans-own-smartphones-android-iphone-dominate/

Hale, M. (2010, April 20). "The few who founded fantasy baseball." *New York Times*, p. 4.

Halone, K.K. and Billings, A.C. (2010). "The temporal nature of racialized sport consumption." *American Behavioral Scientist*, 53(11), 1645–1668.

Hardin, M., and Whiteside, E. (2009). "Token responses to gendered newsrooms: Factors in the career-related decisions of female newspaper sports journalists." *Journalism*, 10(5), 627–646.

Hargreaves, J.A. (1994). *Sporting females: Critical issues in the history and sociology of women's sports*. London: Routledge.

Hartmann, D. (2003). "The sanctity of Sunday football: Why men love sports." *Contexts*, 2(4), 13–21.

Higie, R.A., Feick, L.F., and Price, L.L. (1987). "Types and amount of word-of-mouth communications about retailers." *Journal of Retailing*, 63, 260–278.

Hoffner, C.A., and Levine, K.J. (2007). "Enjoyment of mediated fright and violence: A meta-analysis." In R.W. Preiss, B.M. Gayle, N. Burrell, M. Allen, and J. Bryant (Eds), *Mass media effects research: Advances through meta-analysis*, 215–244. Mahwah, NJ: Lawrence Erlbaum Associates.

Horowitz, B. (2012, November 8). "McDonald's first monthly sales drop in a decade." *USA Today*. Retrieved on November 28, 2012 from http://www.usatoday.com/story/money/business/2012/11/08/mcdonalds-don-thompson-sales-decline/1692631/

Hur, Y., Ko, Y.J., and Valacich, J. (2007). "Motivation and concerns for online sport consumption." *Journal of Sport Management*, 21(4), 521–539.

Ipsos Public Affairs. (2010). Fantasy sports study. Washington, DC: Ipsos.

James, J.D., and Ridinger, L.L. (2002). "Female and male sport fans: A comparison of sport consumption motives." *Journal of Sport Behavior*, 25(3), 260–278.

Jonsson, P. (2012, September 27). "'Inaccurate reception' got NFL and refs back to the labor table—and fast." *The Christian Science Monitor* (Online).

Karg, A.J., and McDonald, H. (2011). "Fantasy sport participating as a complement to traditional sport consumption." *Sport Management Review*, 14(4), 327–346.

Katz, D. (2012, October 3). "New fantasy football law legalizes fantasy league prizes." Retrieved on November 8, 2012 from http://blogs.findlaw.com/tarnished_twenty/2012/10/new-fantasy-football-law-legalizes-fantasy-league-prizes.html

Kaye, B.K. (1998). "Uses and gratifications of the World Wide Web: From couch potato to web potato." *New Jersey Journal of Communication*, 6(1), 21–40.

Kellam, R.K. (2012). "Reading between the numbers: The colonial rhetorics of fantasy football and the illusion of control." Unpublished doctoral dissertation. Wayne State University.

King, C.W., and Summers, J.O. (1970). "Overlap of opinion leadership across consumer product categories." *Journal of Marketing Research*, 7(1), 43–50.

Krohn, F.B., Clarke, M., Preston, E., McDonald, M., and Preston, B. (1998). "Psychological and sociological influences on attendance at small college sporting events." *College Student Journal, 32*, 277–288.

Langford, R. (2012). "Yahoo's fantasy servers down to start NFL 1 pm games." Retrieved on April 12, 2013 from http://bleacherreport.com/articles/1404832-yahoos-fantasy-football-servers-down-to-start-nfl-1pm-games

Lanham, R.A. (2007). *The economics of attention: Style and substance in the age of information*. Chicago: University of Chicago Press.

LaRose, R., and Eastin, M.S. (2004). "A social cognitive theory of Internet uses and gratifications: Toward a new model of media attendance." *Journal of Broadcasting & Electronic Media*, 48(3), 358–377.

Laurent, C. (2013). *A look at the demographic and socio-economic structure of the world in 2030*. Hoboken, NJ: Wiley

Law, B. (2009, May 24). "Dream on sport; Trends." *The Sun Herald* (Sydney, Australia), p. 14.

Lazarsfeld, P.F., Berelson, B., and Gaudet, H. (1948). *The people's choice: How the votes makes Up his mind in a presidential campaign*. New York: Columbia Press.

Leahy, S. (2011, June 6). "Season previews on hold or worse." *USA Today*, p. 3C.

Lee, W.Y., Kwak, D., Lim, C., Pederson, P., and Miloch, K. (2011). "Effects of personality and gender on fantasy sports game participation: The moderating role of perceived knowledge." *Journal of Gambling Studies*, 27(3), 427–441.

Lee, J., Ruihley, B.J., Brown, N., and Billings, A.C. (2013). "The effects of fantasy football participation on team identification, team loyalty, and NFL fandom." *Journal of Sports Media*, 8(1).

Leith, S. (2004, August 25). "The phenomenal rise of fantasy sport—you couldn't make it up." *The Daily Telegraph* (London), p. 20.

Levinson, M. (2006). "Sure bet: Why New Jersey would benefit by legalized sports wagering." *Sports Lawyers Journal*, 13, 143–178.

Levy, D.P. (2009). "Fanship habitus: The consumption of sport in the US." In K. Robson and C. Sanders (Eds), *Quantifying theory: Pierre Bourdieu* (187–199). New York, NY: Springer.

Lewis, N. (2012). "Trait and motivational differences in fantasy football participation." Unpublished Master's Thesis, Indiana University (Telecommunication).

Li, D., Browne, G.J., and Wetherbe, J.C. (2006). "Why do Internet users stick with a specific Web site? A relationship perspective." *International Journal of Electronic Commerce*, 10(4), 105–141.

Longley, R. (2006, August 22). "Fantasy sports not gambling, bill declares." US Government Information (About.com). Retrieved on November 30, 2012 fromhttp://usgovinfo.about.com/b/2006/08/22/fantasy-sports-not-gambling-bill-declares.htm

Lumpkin, A., Stoll, S.K., and Beller, J.M. (2003). *Sport ethics: Applications for fair play* (3rd ed.). Boston; McGraw-Hill.

Mactaggart, G. (2008, September 12). "Fantasy rides again." *Northern Territory News* (Australia), p. 26.

Madrigal, R. (1995). "Cognitive and affective determinants of fan satisfaction with spring events attendance." *Journal of Leisure Research*, 27, 205–227.

Maguire, J.P., Armfield, G.A., and Boone, J. (2012). "Show me the numbers: Fantasy sports and media dependency." In A. C. Earnheardt, P. M. Haridakis, and B. Hugenburg (Eds.) *Sportsfans, identity, and socialization: Exploring the fandemonium* (275–290). Lanham, MD: Lexington Books.

Mahan, J.E., Drayer, J., and Sparvero, E. (2012). "Gambling and fantasy: An examination of the influence of money on fan attitudes and behaviors." *Sport Marketing Quarterly*, 21(3), 159–169.

Martinez, J. (2012, September 9). "Roddy White Twitter apology: Falcons WR apologizes to fantasy football owners for week 1 stats." *Huffington Post Sports*. Retrieved on December 12, 2012 from: http://www.huffingtonpost.com/2012/09/09/roddy-white-twitter-apology-fantasy-football_n_1869356.html

McDorman, T. (2003). "The rhetorical resurgence of Pete Rose: A second-chance apologia." In R.S. Brown and D. O'Roarke (Eds.) *Case Studies in Sports Communication* (1–27). Westport, CT: Preager.

Messner, M., and Cooky, C. (2010). *Gender in televised sports: News and highlight shows*. Center for Feminist Research, University of Southern California.

Miller, J.A., and Shales, T. (2011). *Those guys have all the fun: Inside the world of ESPN*. New York: Back Bay Books.

Montague, J. (2010). "The rise and rise of fantasy sports." Retrieved on November 14, 2012 from http://www.cnn.com/2010/SPORT/football/01/06/fantasy.football.moneyball.sabermetrics/index.html

Moorman, A.M. (2008). "Fantasy sports league challenged as illegal gambling." *Sport Marketing Quarterly*, 17(4), 232–234.

Mullin, B.J., Hardy, S., and Sutton, W.A. (1993). *Sport marketing*. Champaign, IL: Human Kinetics.

——(2007). *Sport marketing* (3rd ed.). Champaign, IL: Human Kinetics.

Nabi, R.L., and Kremar, M. (2004). "Conceptualizing media enjoyment as attitude: Implications of mass media effects research." *Communication Theory*, 14(4), 288–310.

Newman, P. (2012, Sept. 2). "Forget Olympic gold, let's drift off into the realm of fantasy." *The Independent*, p. 12.

NFL.com (2012). "Draft types." Retrieved on October 17, 2012 from http://www.nfl.com/fantasyfootball/help/drafttypes

Norris, P. (2001). *Digital divide: Civic engagement, information poverty, and the Internet worldwide*. Cambridge: Cambridge University Press.

Oliver, M.B. (1993). "Exploring the paradox of the enjoyment of sad films." *Human Communication Research*, 19(3), 315–342.

Pallister, M. (2011, November 11). "Fantasy football: Games are just diversions; perspective matters most." *The Washington Times*, p. 3.

Palmgreen, P., and Rayburn, J.D. (1979). "Uses and gratifications and exposure to public television." *Communication Research*, 6(2), 155–180.

Pedersen, P.M., Miloch, K.S., and Laucella, P.C. (2007). *Strategic sport communication*. Champaign, IL: Human Kinetics.

Perse, E. (1996). "Sensation seeking and the use of television for arousal." *Communication Reports*, 9(1), 37–47.

Pew Internet and the American Life Project. (2005, June). "Online sports fantasy leagues." Washington, DC: L. Rainie. Retrieved on February 19, 2010 from http://www.pewinternet.org/Reports/2005/Online-sports-fantasy-leagues.aspx

——(2007). "Data memo: Findings." Retrieved September 20, 2012 from http://pewinternet.org/Reports/2007/Hobbyists-Online/Data-Memo.aspx

——(2010) "Generations 2010." Retrieved September 20, 2012 from http://pewinternet.org/Reports/2010/Generations-2010.aspx

——(2012a) "Internet use and home broadband connections." Retrieved September 20, 2012 from http://www.pewinternet.org/Infographics/2012/Internet-Use-and-Home-Broadband-Connections.aspx#

——(2012b) "Trend data (adults): What Internet users do online." Retrieved September 20, 2012 from http://pewinternet.org/Trend-Data-%28Adults%29/Online-Activites-Total.aspx

Pfanner, E. (2004, Oct. 30). "Leagues may be fantasy, but revenue isn't; Sports fans worldwide flock to online games." *The International Herald Tribune*, p. 13.

Phan, M. (2005, Aug. 29). "Smaller fantasy football websites prove popular for information." *Newsday*.

Raney, A.A. (2003). "Disposition-based theories of enjoyment." In J. Bryant, D. Roskos Ewoldsen, and J. Cantor (Eds) *Communication and emotion: Essays in honor of Dolf Zillmann* (61–84). Mahwah, NJ: Erlbaum.

Richey, W. (2008, May 30). "High court rejects fantasy baseball challenge." *Christian Science Monitor*, p. 25.

Roberti, J.W. (2004). "A review of behavioral and biological correlates of sensation seeking." *Journal of Research in Personality*, 38(3), 256–279.

Robinson, A. (2010, October 20). "Nerd nation gets own fantasy league." *Dayton Daily News*, p. D4.

Ross, J. (2009, June 4). "Who owns major league stats? Yahoo! sues NFL Players Association to get free access to players' statistics for the fantasy football leagues it runs on the Internet." *Minneapolis Star Tribune*, p. 1B.

Roy, D.P., and Goss, B.D. (2007). "A conceptual framework of influences on fantasy sports consumption." *Marketing Management Journal*, 17(2), 96–108.

Rubin, A.M. (1983). "Television uses and gratifications: The interactions of viewing patterns and motivations." *Journal of Broadcasting*, 27(1), 37–51.

——(1984). "Ritualized and instrumental television viewing." *Journal of Communication*, 34(3), 67–77.

Rubin, A.M., and Step, M.M. (2000). "Impact of motivation, attraction, and parasocial interaction on talk radio listening." *Journal of Broadcasting & Electronic Media*, 44(4), 635–654.

Ruihley, B.J. (2010). "The fantasy sport experience: Motivations, satisfaction, and future intentions." Doctoral dissertation. University of Tennessee libraries. Knoxville,.

Ruihley, B.J., and Billings, A.C. (2013). "Infiltrating the boys club: Motivations for women's fantasy sport participation." *International Review for the Sociology of Sport.*

Ruihley, B.J., and Hardin, R.L. (2011). "Message board use and the fantasy sport experience." *International Journal of Sport Communication,* 4(2), 233–252.

——(2014). "Fantasy sport: More than a game." In A. C. Billings and M. Hardin (Eds) *The Routledge Handbook of Sport and New Media.*

Ruihley, B J., and Runyan, R.C. (2010, April). "Schwabism: An investigation of the sport fan who knows it all." *Research presentation at the Southern Sport Management Conference.* Troy, AL.

Sanchez, J. (2012, November 20). "San Francisco 49ers new stadium to have fantasy football lounge." *Sports Illustrated.* Retrieved from: http://nflspinzone.com/2012/11/20/san-francisco-49ers-new-stadium-to-have-fantasy-football-lounge/

Sandomir, R. (2002, September 13). "Reality of fantasy football: Root, root, root for no Team." *The New York Times.* Retrieved October 27, 2011 from http://query.nytimes.com/gst/fullpage.html?res=9F05E4DE1131F930A2575AC0A9649C8B63.

Schaufeli, W.B., and Buunk, B.P. (2003). "Burnout: An overview of 25 years of research and theorizing." In M.J. Schabracq, J.A.M. Winnubst, and C.L. Cooper (Eds), *The handbook of work and heath psychology* (2nd ed., 383–425). New York: John Wiley & Sons.

Schwartz, A. (2005). The numbers game: Baseball's lifelong fascination with statistics. New York: St. Martins.

Schwarz, E., and Hunter, J. (2012). *Advanced theory and practice in sport marketing.* New York: Routledge.

Sculpher, P. (2011). "An interview with Andrew Wainstein." Retrieved on December 5, 2012 from: http://www.paulsculpher.com/?p=903

Seidman, R. (2011, June 1). "TV ratings broadcast top 25: American Idol, Dancing with the Stars, Glee, Modern Family top season's final week." *TV by the Numbers.* Retrieved on September 15, 2011 from: http://tvbythenumbers.zap2it.com/2011/06/01/tv-ratings-broadcast-top-25-american-idol-dancing-with-the-stars-glee-modern-family-top-seasons-final-week/94311/

Seo, W.J., and Green, B.C. (2008). "Development of the motivation scale for sport online consumption." *Journal of Sport Management,* 22(1), 82–109.

Shank, M.D. (2009). *Sports marketing: A strategic perspective* (4th ed.). Upper Saddle River,NJ: Pearson Prentice Hall.

Sherif, M., and Hovland, C.I. (1961). *Social judgment: Assimilation and contrast effects in communication and attitude change.* New Haven: Yale University Press.

"SI Audience Profile." (2012). Retrieved on October 1, 2012 from: http://web.archive.org/web/20101129133859/http://simediakit.com/property-single.xhtml?property_id=35&propnav=research

Silver, N. (2012). *The signal and the noise: Why so many predictions fail—but some don't.* New York: Penguin Press.

Smith, S.A (2008). "Up front: To heck with fantasy. I'm about what's real." Retrieved on March 9, 2010 from http://sports.espn.go.com/espnmag/story?id=3556641

Smith, W.R. (1956). "Product differentiation and market segmentation as alternative marketing strategies." *Journal of Marketing,* 21(1), 3–8.

Sonderman, J. (2012, May 31). "15 % of online Americans now use Twitter; 8 percent use it daily." *Poynter Institute.* Retrieved on January 21, 2013 from: http://www.poynter.org/latest-news/mediawire/175757/15-of-americans-now-use-twitter-8-use-it-daily/

Spinda, J.S.W., and Haridakis, P.M. (2008). "Exploring the motives of fantasy sports: A Uses and Gratifications approach." In L.W. Hugenberg, P.M. Haridakis, and A.C. Earnheardt (Eds.), *Sports mania: Essays on fandom and the media in the 21st century.* Jefferson, NC: McFarland & Company, Inc.

Starkey, J. (2011, Sept. 1). "Stakes real in fantasy football." *Pittsburgh Tribune Review.*

St. Amant, M. (2005). *Committed: Confessions of a fantasy football junkie.* Scribner: New York.

Stokburger-Sauer, N.E., and Hoyer, W.D. (2009). "Consumer advisors revisited: What drives those with market mavenism and opinion leadership tendencies and why?" *Journal of Consumer Behavior*, 8(2–3), 100–115.

Surowiecki, J. (2005). *The wisdom of crowds.* New York: Anchor Books.

Tajfel, H., and Turner, J.C. (1986). "The social identity theory of inter-group behavior." In S. Worchel, and L.W. Austin (Eds*.), Psychology of intergroup relations.* Chicago: Nelson Hall.

Trail, G. T., and James, J. D. (2001). "The motivation scale for sport consumption: Assessment of the scale's psychometric properties." *Journal of Sport Behavior*, 24(1), 108–127.

Turner, C. (2004, August 8). "Living in a fantasy world; Online football games popular." *El Paso Times* (Texas), p. 1C.

Umbright, E. (2006, May 30). "St. Louis-based fantasy sports firm disputes need for licensing contract." *St. Louis Daily Record.*

Umpire Ejection Fantasy League Portal. (2012). Retrieved from: http://portal. closecallsports.com

VGchartz report (2011). Retrieved on September 15, 2011 from: http://www.vgchartz. com/home.php

Virtual Sports.com Homepage (2012).. Retrieved on December 5, 2012 from: http://www. virtualsports.com.au

Vongsarath, C. (2012, September 20). "Commentary: during football season, fantasizing is a 24/7 job." *San Jose Mercury News.*

Walker, S. (2006). *Fantasyland: A sportswriter's bid to win the world's most ruthless fantasy baseball league.* New York: Penguin.

Walsh, G., Gwinner, K.P., and Swanson, S.R. (2004). "What makes mavens tick? Exploring the motives of market mavens' initiation of information diffusion." *Journal of Consumer Marketing*, 21(2), 109–122.

Wang, G. (2010, October 26). Fantasy football is hardly a game for some high rollers. The Washington Post, p. D4.

——(2011, May 29). "Fantasy football gets benched." *The Washington Post*, p. D3.

Wann, D.L. (1995). "Preliminary validation of the sport fan motivation scale." *Journal of Sport and Social Issues*, 19(4), 377–396.

Wann, D.L., and Branscombe, N.R. (1990). "Die-hard and fair-weather fans; Effects of identification on BIRGing and CORFing tendencies." *Journal of Sport & Social Issues*, 14(2), 103–117.

Wann, D.L., Melnick, M.J., Russell, G.W., and Pease, D.G. (2001). *Sports fans: The psychology and social impact of spectators.* New York: Routledge.

Wann, D.L., Schrader, M.P, & Wilson, A.M (1999). "Sport fan motivation: Questionnaire validation, comparisons by sport, and relationship to athletic motivation." *Journal of Sport Behavior, 22*(1), 114–139.

Wee, T.C. (2007). "Dream soccer boss; Fantasy football allows fanatics to fulfill their ambition to be Alex Ferguson and even to manage their own 'dream team' to victory." *The Straits Times* (Singapore).

"Welcome to Fantasy Congress." (2012). Retrieved on September 15, 2012 from http://www.fantasycongress.net/112/index.php

White, P. (2011). "Done deal: What's in baseball's new labor agreement." *USA Today*. Retrieved on December 5, 2012 from http://usatoday30.usatoday.com/sports/baseball/story/2011-11-22/mlb-collective-bargaining-agreement/51359552/1

Whiteside, E., and Hardin, M. (2011). "Women (not) watching women: Leisure time, television, and implications for televised coverage of women's sports." *Communication, Culture & Critique*, 4, 122–143.

Zillmann, D. (1988). "Mood management: Using entertainment to full advantage." In L. Donohew, H.E. Sypher, and E.T. Higgins (Eds), *Communication, social cognition, and affect* (147–171). Hillsdale, NJ: Erlbaum.

Zillmann, D., and Bryant, J. (1994). "Entertainment as media effect." In J. Bryant and D. Zillmann (Eds), *Media effects: Advances in theory and research* (437–461). Hillsdale, NJ. Erlbaum.

Zillmann, D., and Paulus, P.B. (1993). "Spectators: Reactions to sports events and effects on athletic performance." In R.N. Singer, M. Murphey, and L.K. Tennant (Eds), *Handbook of research on sports psychology* (600–619). New York: Macmillan.

Zuckerman, M. (1979). *Sensation seeking: Beyond the optimal level of arousal*. Hillsdale, NJ: Lawrence Erlbaum Associates.

Index